ARNHEM
A TRAGEDY OF ERRORS

ARNHEM
A TRAGEDY OF ERRORS

PETER HARCLERODE

'Go tell the Spartans, you who read:
We took their orders and are dead.'
– Simonides

CAXTON EDITIONS

This edition published in the United Kingdom in 2000 by
Caxton Editions
20 Bloomsbury Street
London WC1B 3QA
a member of the Caxton Publishing Group

© Peter Harclerode, 1994

Cartography by Cilla Eurich.

Designed and edited by DAG Publications Ltd.
Designed by David Gibbons; Layout by Anthony A. Evans;
edited by Michael Boxall
Cover design by Open Door Limited

Jacket illustration: The Bridge at Arnhem by Alan Fearnley.
Reproduced by kind courtesy of the Military Gallery.

Title: ARNHEM, A Tragedy of Errors
ISBN: 1-84067-146-7

Printed and bound in Great Britain by
Creative Print and Design (Wales)

CONTENTS

FOREWORD

by

General Sir John Hackett

GCB, CBE, DSO, MC, DL

In September 1944 the largest airborne operation of war ever undertaken was launched to open a way for a powerful Allied thrust through Holland into the heart of Germany and the Ruhr. Without the Ruhr the enemy's war effort would probably collapse before the end of the year, with thousands of lives saved and further huge material destruction avoided. 'Market Garden', the codename for the airborne thrust and the follow-up by ground forces, was a costly failure. Why?

In the years since 1944 much has been published in attempts to answer this question, and now that the passage of time brings up the half century, more still can be expected. The number of those who took part in 'Market Garden' continues to dwindle: some important questions will now never be fully answered. Peter Harclerode's timely book looks at the evidence on offer and adds further consideration to one of the more puzzling aspects of events - the failure of XXX Corps to thrust more urgently up to Arnhem from Nijmegen on 20 September, when the single dyke road was still open up to nightfall but was soon to be closed by German defences. These, with heavy anti-tank weaponry deployed in the low-lying wet polderland on either side of the carriageway, prevented armoured movement away from it, and could only be cleared by infantry, of which more was needed. Both German and US commentators expressed surprise that Guards Armoured Division units, instead of using this last chance to charge up a road still open till near midnight and make contact with 1st Airborne Division at the Arnhem bridge, settled down for the night to reorganize, replenish with much needed ammunition and fill up with even more sorely needed fuel, before moving on next morning - when it was too late.

This, though there are many other questions still unanswered, was probably the critical moment of the battle. The Guards Armoured Division has sometimes been accused of taking too little account of the seriousness of the position in 1st Airborne Division's area, referred to by the Germans as 'The Cauldron'. Peter Harclerode, himself a former Irish Guardsman who also served with Airborne Forces, offers in this book a spirited and well informed defence of action forced upon XXX Corps, whose leading troops, by no means affected by 'victory euphoria', had had a hard time fighting their way through the Low Countries. They may well have been near the end of their tether in the late afternoon of 20 September, but how long, some of the defenders at the bridge or those around me in Oosterbeek might have asked, is a tether, and how much more had ours still to run out?

There are other questions to which I shall refer, but I cannot refrain here from a personal interpolation. Commissioned into a family cavalry regiment I was dismayed, like many others, when we were mechanized in Egypt in 1935 for the war with Italy that never happened, and I soon moved off back to horses for a four-year secondment in the cavalry of the Transjordan Frontier Force, which gave me some lively dismounted action against Arab bands and even, on one occasion, some (not very fierce) mounted action with a sword. In reflecting on the suitability of horsed cavalry for modern war I was disturbed watching light RAF bombing of a village to think what it would be like if this happened to my led horses. What concerned me far more was to note that my Arab country-bred troop horses, even when short of forage, could always go on. Anything driven by petrol, if deprived of it, stopped. The Guards Armoured Division certainly had replenishment problems. All the same, the week I spent in the Cauldron before succumbing to a tree-burst did leave me wondering if our friends could have tried a little harder - and sooner. I respect Peter Harclerode's well presented case, however, and am almost persuaded.

There are many other aspects of this operation which deserve comment or clarification, and perhaps defence. Planning for 'Market Garden' was too short. Weeks, even months, of preparation and training preceded 6th Airborne Division's brilliantly successful coup de main in Normandy. 'Market Garden' was mounted in seven days, though able to make use of some of the planning for 'Comet', the plan which, to my own (and Sosabowski's) great relief, was cancelled the week before. Horrocks was no great planner. What was he doing on that single dyke road, against whose use the Dutch had warned us? And why did Montgomery largely ignore the importance of Antwerp, and rather discourteously reject the intelligence Prince Bernhard offered him? And what about the Ultra intelligence - which should have carried a strong health warning - about the presence near Arnhem of German heavy weaponry, including Tiger and Panther tanks? Why had the urgent demands for suitable radio equipment for 1st Airborne Division been so long ignored? Why was the intercommunication between air and ground headquarters in and before the battle so ludicrously inadequate? Why was Browning's cloth-of-gold 1st Airborne Corps advance headquarters, which had no conceivable useful purpose to fulfil or service to offer, put in on the first lift, using 38 gliders which could have carried the anti-tank artillery which my own brigade, put down on 18 September with all surprise totally lost, so badly needed? Why was a US Air Force general, with plenty of experience in air force operations but none of airborne, put in to command the so-called Allied Airborne Army, when there was a brilliantly successful airborne commander in Ridgway who had been put into cold storage in XVIII US Airborne Corps? As for the air plan, a very senior and highly respected RAF commander later made a clean breast of it: it was a bad plan and so the failure of 'Market Garden' must be seen as a failure of the air forces.

The tightness of the time for preparation makes understandable Brereton's adamant refusal to reopen any questions deemed answered - even when they referred to such grave errors as landing 4th Parachute Brigade and much of the rest of 1st Airborne Division on the second day, with surprise gone, five to eight miles from the target area? A well known writer on military matters tells us that after the failure of the German airborne attack on Crete in May 1941 it became the doctrine of Allied airborne forces only to land at a distance from the chosen targets ('The Second World War' by John Keegan, Hutchinson, London 1989, p437): Our own doctrine was in fact the precise opposite: it is set out in the War Office publication 'Airborne Forces' by Terence Otway, compiled on the authority of the Army Council and first published in 1951. Page 387, paragraph 24 begins: 'Dropping and landing zones should be chosen as close as possible to the objectives', and proceeds to give the obvious reasons why. If the whole Division could have been put down (even on the allotted DZs and LZs) on one day, with surprise complete, the outcome to 'Market Garden' would, without any doubt, have been different. A second sortie would have completed deployment in one day. Argument still persists as to where, and by whom and why, the second airborne sortie was vetoed. There were strong arguments against it. Those for it were far stronger. One, perhaps, is stronger than any other. The most powerful fighting brigade in 1st Airborne Division was 1st Airlanding Brigade. It was not put down on 17 September to take its formidable infantry strength straight to the north end of Arnhem bridge but was largely deployed on the LZs and DZs to protect them for the arrival of the second lift which came in on the following afternoon. What could it have done, not guarding a DZ but at the bridge? There is much more to be found in this evocative book which deserves comment. Its author has tried to be objective. The reader must arrive at his own judgements.

In 1945 and 1946, having returned to Britain from my long sojourn in Holland as a convalescent evader hidden, nursed and cherished by Dutch civilians for four and a half months, I wrote down my experiences and published them, virtually unchanged, 30 years later as *'I Was a Stranger'* (Chatto 1978). At the publishers' book launch I was asked: 'At what point in the battle did you realize you were facing disaster?' 'Before it began', I replied, and told of my last conference before we took off, when I briefed everyone down to small sub-units on the task we faced, which was to defend a sector of the perimeter in Arnhem North of the bridge. The conference over, I had dismissed all except my three battalion commanders, brigade staff and other key personnel. 'You can now forget all that,' I said. 'Your hardest fighting, and heaviest casualties, will not be in defending Arnhem from the North, but in trying to get there.' And we never did. Some 2,300 parachutists went in with me; about 200 came out, with the rest killed, wounded or taken prisoner; mostly, I am glad to say, the latter, though over 500 lie in the Oosterbeek war cemetery. But we had to go into this battle - you cannot indefinitely continue to prepare highly trained, highly motivated, superb fighting men and cancel fifteen such operations in a row, some with troops already emplaned and ready to take off, without running a growing risk of cynicism and declining morale. That would have destroyed this unique division, which at Arnhem and Oosterbeek fought splendidly to its very end. The battle planned for two days lasted for nine, with five Victoria Crosses later awarded for gallantry shown during them. Those of us who are still around, recalling the company we shared, would do it again.

PREFACE

Throughout the fifty years which have elapsed since those fateful days of September 1944, the controversy over Operation Market Garden has endured with much discussion, and indeed disagreement, over the reasons for its failure. 1st Airborne Division's epic battle at Arnhem and Oosterbeek has often been referred to as a glorious defeat. It has also been described, in the words of a much respected former senior officer of Airborne Forces, as 'the biggest cock-up of all time'. Regardless of Field Marshal Montgomery's claim that it was ninety per cent successful, Market Garden was in fact a failure of considerable magnitude in that it resulted in the destruction of one of the finest formations ever fielded in war by the British Army and in over 16,000 casualties in the airborne and ground forces which took part in it. The tragedy is that, despite everything that militated against its success, the operation very nearly succeeded because of the heroic stand by 1st Airborne Division and the gallant efforts of the leading elements of XXX Corps to fight their way through to Arnhem.

In certain previous accounts of Market Garden, considerable criticism has been directed at XXX Corps, and in particular at the Guards Armoured Division and 43rd (Wessex) Infantry Division which have stood accused of showing a lack of urgency, of having had a relatively easy time during the advance through Belgium prior to Market Garden and even, in the words of Major General Roy Urquhart, of being 'victory happy'. In this book, I have attempted to show that such criticism is ill-founded and to illustrate the reasons why XXX Corps failed to reach 1st Airborne Division in time. Furthermore, I have drawn attention to the factors which, in my opinion, doomed the operation to failure from the very day of its conception and thus ultimately sealed the fate of 1st Airborne Division at Arnhem and Oosterbeek.

I owe a great debt of gratitude to several individuals who provided me with much valuable assistance and advice during the research for this book. General Sir John Hackett spared me a considerable amount of his very valuable time, providing me with much useful information and devot-

11

ing several hours to checking the book for accuracy, providing constructive criticism and writing the foreword. He and Lady Hackett showed me great kindness and hospitality during my visits to their home and I am very grateful to them both for their great generosity.

Colonel Geoffrey Powell also provided me with much help and also very kindly permitted me to draw on information from *The Devil's Birthday*, his own excellent account and analysis of Operation Market Garden. Much of my information on the enemy order of battle and deployments came from Robert Kershaw's remarkable book *It Never Snows In September*, which tells the story of Market Garden from the German viewpoint, and I am immensely grateful to him for allowing me to use it. Other writers who allowed me to use some of their material were Lewis Golden, author of *Echoes From Arnhem*, which includes a technically accurate account of the signals problems encountered during the operation, and David Irving who wrote *War Amongst The Generals*, which provides a fascinating insight into the disputes and deep antagonism between senior Allied commanders. I would like to extend my grateful thanks to them both. In addition, I would like to express my appreciation to the following publishers who were also kind enough to permit me to draw on information in books published by them: Hutchinson Books (*ULTRA Goes To War* by Ronald Lewin and *The Guards Armoured Division* by Maj Gen G.L. Verney) and Harper Collins (*The Memoirs of Field Marshal Montgomery*).

I would also like to express my thanks to the following for permitting me to quote passages from books written or published by them: Major General Anthony Deane-Drummond (*Return Ticket*), Messrs Cassell (*Arnhem* by Maj Gen R.E. Urquhart and *A Drop Too Many* by Maj Gen John Frost), Colonel Geoffrey Powell (*The Devil's Birthday*), John Baynes (*Urquhart of Arnhem*), B.T. Batsford Ltd. (*The Battle of Arnhem* by Christopher Hibbert), Messrs Harper Collins (*The Memoirs of Field Marshal Montgomery*), Messrs Sidgwick & Jackson (*Corps Commander* by Lt Gen Sir Brian Horrocks), and John Fairley (*Remember Arnhem*).

Colonel Paddy de Burgh provided me with much valuable information on 1st Airlanding Light Regiment's role in the battle and I am most grateful to him and to Major Denis Munford who permitted me to quote from his personal account of the action at the Arnhem bridge.

Finally, I would like to mention the following individuals who provided me with unstinting help during my research for this book: Chris Webb, Diana Andrews, Alan Brown and Stan Ward of the Airborne Forces Museum, Dr Adrian Groeneweg of the Airborne Forces Museum at Hartenstein, and Ms. Jane Carmichael and her staff at the Department of Photographs of the Imperial War Museum. To them all I extend my sincerest thanks.

1
SEEDS OF FAILURE

'I am tired of dealing with a lot of prima donnas. By God, you can tell that bunch that if they can't get together and stop quarrelling like children, I will tell the Prime Minister to get someone else to run this damn war.' — General Dwight D. Eisenhower.

Following the hard-fought campaign in Normandy, and having crossed the River Seine, some 40 British and American divisions forged north-eastwards through France towards Belgium. On the left of the advance was the British 21st Army Group, commanded by Field Marshal Sir Bernard Montgomery, comprising First Canadian and Second British Armies under Lieutenant Generals Henry Crerar and Sir Miles Dempsey respectively. On the right was 12th US Army Group under General Omar Bradley, comprising First and Third US Armies commanded by Lieutenant General Courtney Hodges and General George Patton respectively.

By mid-September Second British Army, comprising VIII, XII and XXX Corps, was drawing up on a line roughly following that of the Meuse–Escaut Canal. To the west, First Canadian Army had advanced to a line stretching from Zeebrugge to Ghent, while to the south-east First US Army had advanced to the German frontier where it had encountered the Siegfried Line. Farther south, Third US Army had established bridgeheads over the River Moselle.

During the advance through France and Belgium, the question of the future conduct of the campaign in north-west Europe had caused considerable discord among the senior commanders of the Allied Expeditionary Forces, each of whom pressed his case with the Supreme Allied Commander. The most vociferous of these had been Montgomery who, alarmed at the apparent lack of any firm plan by Supreme Headquarters Allied Expeditionary Force (SHAEF), had drawn up his own. On 20 August, a conference to discuss ideas had been held at General Dwight Eisenhower's advanced headquarters in Normandy. This was attended by Montgomery's Chief of Staff, Major General Francis de Guingand, who returned to 21st Army Group's Tactical Headquarters to report that Eisenhower had decided that he would assume personal command of the two Army Groups on 1 September. He had also decided that Bradley's 12th US Army Group would advance towards Metz and the Saar where it would link up with General Jacob Devers' 6th US Army Group, comprising Lieutenant General

Alexander Patch's Seventh US Army and General Jean de Lattre de Tassigny's First French Army. Devers' forces, having landed on the Côte d'Azur on 15 August, would have advanced northwards up the Rhône Valley.

Eisenhower's intention was 'to push forward on a broad front with priority on the left', liberating the Channel ports and the port of Antwerp which were vital to the supply of the Allied land forces before swinging eastwards to 'directly threaten the Ruhr'. His ultimate plan was to present the Germans with a long and continuous front which would force them to try to cope simultaneously with more than one threat.

Montgomery was unhappy with both of these decisions. Three days earlier, on 17 August, he had put forward his own alternative plan to Bradley, proposing that both Army Groups advance north-eastwards in a single strong thrust, his own 21st Army Group advancing on the western flank to clear the Channel coast, the Pas de Calais, western Flanders, and subsequently to take Antwerp and southern Holland. Bradley's 12th US Army Group would meanwhile advance on the eastern flank, with the Ardennes on its right, to capture Aachen and Cologne. Thereafter, bridge-heads would be established for a subsequent advance into the German industrial heartland of the Ruhr. Montgomery was aware that an alternative feasible axis of advance existed through Metz and the Saar, but he insisted that a concentrated northern thrust would provide the best results. He was dismissive of the idea of two simultaneous advances, on the grounds that such a course of action would divide the logistical resources that would be required to maintain the momentum of a single strong thrust deep into the heart of Germany.

According to Montgomery, Bradley was entirely in accordance with this plan, and when de Guingand was sent back to Eisenhower's headquarters two days later, the Supreme Allied Commander was advised of this fact. In his memoirs *A Soldier's Story*, Bradley states that he and Montgomery agreed on a plan to be followed after an advance into Belgium and the capture of Brussels. This would consist of a thrust by three corps, one British and two American, eastwards across the plains of Cologne between Düsseldorf and Bonn. Meanwhile, the left-hand corps of Second British Army would advance north-eastwards of this thrust. On its left flank, First Canadian Army would move northwards up the coast, seizing the Channel ports, capturing the V-weapon launch sites and clearing the Scheldt, the area of inland waterway leading to Antwerp.

Despite being told of Bradley's agreement with Montgomery, Eisenhower's attitude towards the plan was somewhat negative. Consequently, Montgomery invited the Supreme Commander to his Tactical Headquarters on 23 August to discuss the matter further. On the morning of the same day, prior to his meeting with Eisenhower, Montgomery flew to the headquarters of 12th US Army Group for further discussions with Bradley. To his surprise, he found that the American had changed his mind and was now supporting Eisenhower's plan for a thrust eastwards on a broad front towards Metz and the Saar. During his meeting with Eisenhower that afternoon, Montgomery urged him to make a firm decision as to the direction of the main thrust, and emphasized the problems concerning logistical support. He then once again put forward his own plan, explaining the advantages of a single bold thrust and the necessity to concentrate all available logistical resources behind it. Turning to Eisenhower's own plan for a broad front, he made his belief clear that such a strategy would result in the Allied advance losing momentum and eventually coming to a halt. This would give the enemy time to recover and regroup, with the result that the war would continue into 1945. Moreover, he pointed out that there were insufficient resources fully to support both Army Groups at full stretch: the only course would be to give priority to either the left- or right-hand Army Group, halting the other in the meantime.

Montgomery then raised the subject of Eisenhower's taking direct command of both Army Groups. He pointed out that the role of the Supreme Allied Commander was to co-ordinate all aspects of the war in Europe – land, sea and air as well as political – and not to become involved in the day-to-day planning and control of land operations which should be delegated to one of his senior commanders. Montgomery would have been aware, however, that the question of command of the land forces was a political problem for Eisenhower and that a decision would not be entirely of his own making. Only five days previously, on 17 August, articles in the American press had revealed that Bradley and his 12th US Army Group were under Montgomery's operational control, which indeed they had been since D-Day on 6 June. This information had incited adverse reaction in the United States, and the Chief of Staff of the US Army, General George C. Marshall, had told Eisenhower that it was no longer acceptable for 12th US Army Group to be under Montgomery's control and that he, Eisenhower, should assume direct command of the land forces.

The subject of command appointments for the invasion of Europe had been discussed at length in August of the previous year at the Quadrant Conference in Quebec, which was attended by Churchill, Roosevelt and their respective Chiefs of Staff. It had been agreed that the Supreme Allied Commander should be an American. President Roosevelt had wished to nominate Marshall, and it had been suggested that his appointment should include responsibility for the whole of the European theatre and that of the Mediterranean. The British had objected on political grounds and, as Marshall was considered by many in Washington to be indispensable as Chief of Staff, Eisenhower was nominated instead.

It was decided that commanders-in-chief of the Allied naval and air forces should be British, but no such equivalent appointment was made in respect of land forces. In view of the fact that American troops would outnumber the British, Canadians and others by a factor of three to one, the US President and his Chiefs of Staff refused to countenance the idea of a British commander for the land forces, despite the fact that there was no American with sufficient experience available to fulfil the role. This problem was compounded by the fact that the Americans disliked Montgomery, resenting his aloof manner and suspecting his methods. In the words of one American war correspondent: 'Montgomery was a general we did not like. We found him arrogant to the point of bumptiousness, bad mannered and ungracious.'

Despite having won the laurels of success as Commander of Eighth Army in North Africa, where he had defeated Generalfeldmarschall Erwin Rommel's Afrika Korps, Montgomery had gained a reputation in American eyes for being slow and methodical in method – a master of the setpiece battle. This stemmed from his insistence on ensuring that all his fighting assets and logistical resources were completely in their allotted place, and that there was a good prospect of success, before launching an offensive.

The only British commander whom the Americans would possibly have accepted as overall commander of the land forces, if the political hurdles had been overcome, was General Sir Harold Alexander who, as Deputy Supreme Commander, had been in command of land operations under Eisenhower in the Mediterranean in 1943. 'Alex' had been universally popular with the Americans, who warmed to his friendly nature and had great respect for him as a commander of outstanding capability. Alexander was Eisenhower's preference as Commander of 21st Army Group, but the Chief of the Imperial General Staff, General Sir Alan Brooke, supported the nomination of Montgomery and enlisted the support of the Prime Minister, Winston Churchill. So it was with no little dismay that the Americans had greeted Montgomery's appointment.

American unease manifested itself when Eisenhower delegated to Montgomery the responsibility for the planning of the invasion of Normandy. At a conference in London on 12 January 1944, Montgomery had implied that he would be in command of all the land forces taking part. This drew a protest from General Omar Bradley, and Montgomery was forced to clarify his position by stating that while he would be commanding the British and Canadian forces, he would make suggestions to Bradley regarding the manoeuvring of US formations. When it came to practicalities during the initial stages of Operation 'Overlord', however, Bradley submitted to Montgomery's authority, but it was understood that this arrangement was only temporary and extended only to tactical matters.

During his meeting with Eisenhower on 23 August, Montgomery was so aware of the political aspects of this thorny problem that he suggested that Bradley take command of the land forces, and offered to serve under him. Eisenhower refused to consider this suggestion, on the grounds that such an arrangement would be unacceptable to the British and because overall control by a single ground forces commander, as advocated by Montgomery, was contrary to American military doctrine. It was Eisenhower's belief and intention that each Army Group commander, of whom there would ultimately be three once the link-up with 6th US Army Group had taken place, should be in control of ground operations within his own area. The discussion returned once again to Montgomery's plan, which centred on the idea of a single thrust across the Rhine into the heart of Germany. This would require formations of sufficient strength to ensure that the momentum of advance be maintained after the Allied troops had crossed the Seine. A vital factor would be the allocation of all available logistical support, to the extent that other areas of the Allied front would have to remain static in the meantime. Of the two possible axes of advance for such a thrust, Montgomery had selected the northern route on the grounds that the plains of Germany in the north would enable better deployment of armoured formations than the heavily forested and mountainous areas in the south.

The major obstacle facing such a thrust was the Rhine. Montgomery was of the opinion that the establishment of bridgeheads over it was of paramount importance, and that it was essential that the enemy be given little or no chance to regroup, but be kept under pressure all the way to the Rhine. Once a bridgehead had been established on the far side, it would provide the launching platform for subsequent operations into the Ruhr and then onwards into the plains of northern Germany. Montgomery believed that the capture of the Ruhr would reduce Germany's capacity to wage war to only six months, so it was likely that the Germans would send all available forces to defend it and thus they would be drawn into an area that favoured the superior mobility of the Allied armoured divisions.

Montgomery's plan was certainly bold and imaginative, but even if Eisenhower had been convinced of the strategic soundness of such a move, which he was not, it contained one ingredient that was politically impossible for him to accept: the halting of Patton's Third US Army on the right flank of 12th US Army Group. American public opinion would not stand for 'Ole Blood 'n Guts', whose charismatic pistol-toting image and reputation as a thrusting commander had endeared him to the nation, being halted in his tracks in favour of the British, particularly in the person of Montgomery.

Nevertheless, Eisenhower fully appreciated the urgent need for the capture of the Channel ports and Antwerp as soon as possible so as to expedite delivery of supplies to the front. Until then his formations would continue to be supplied from the rear maintenance areas established in Normandy during the operations there. As the advance continued through

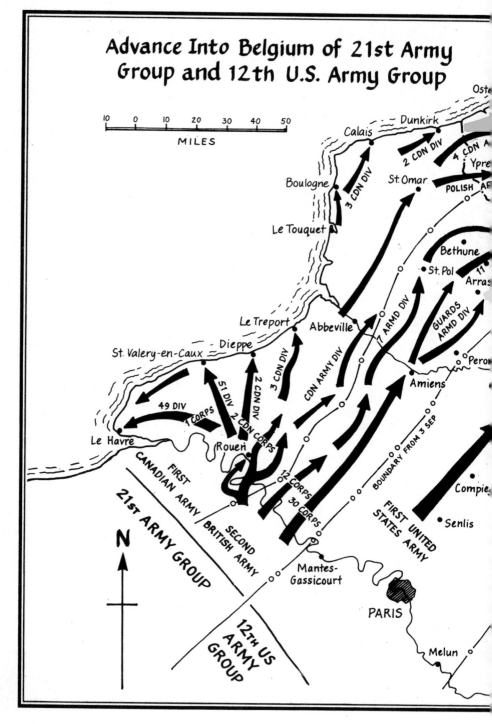

Advance Into Belgium of 21st Army Group and 12th U.S. Army Group

France and Belgium, however, the overstretched lines of supply would pose constant problems for administrative staffs at all levels.

After lengthy discussion, Eisenhower accepted Montgomery's view that 21st Army Group was not sufficiently strong to advance northwards on its own. He agreed that American support would be forthcoming, and that Montgomery should co-ordinate and direct the advance. Montgomery then pressed his case further, requesting that one of 12th US Army Group's two armies should advance on his right flank, but Eisenhower refused, again raising the subject of American public opinion which, he felt sure, would be against the idea of Bradley's retaining only one army under his command. Eventually he compromised, deciding that First US Army would support 21st Army Group's advance to Antwerp, while Third US Army would continue its advance eastwards as far as Rheims and Châlons-sur-Marne. Eisenhower made it clear, however, that as soon as the V-weapon launch sites in the Pas de Calais had been captured and Antwerp seized, Patton's Third US Army would be permitted to continue its advance eastwards to the Saar.

Montgomery was unable to extract any further concessions from Eisenhower, who insisted that a broad front strategy would be adopted. Although Montgomery had been given authority to co-ordinate and direct operations between his own right flank elements and those on the left of 12th US Army Group, when Eisenhower's directive was published the words 'operational direction' had been omitted. Despite this, Eisenhower, after assuming direct command of land forces on 1 September, ordered that the formations on the left of 12th US Army Group were to receive adequate logistic support.

Two days after the meeting between Eisenhower and Montgomery, Second British Army began to cross the Seine during the evening of 25 August. On the morning of the 27th the leading elements of First Canadian Army crossed the river and began expanding the bridgehead. On the 29th Paris was liberated by elements of First US Army which had crossed the Seine between Melun and Mantes–Gassicourt on the 26th and advanced to a line stretching from Péronne to Laon. On 12th US Army Group's right Third US Army, which had crossed the Seine by 21 August, advanced swiftly to Troyes, Châlons-sur-Marne and Rheims.

In 21st Army Group's sector, the advance northwards from the Seine was rapid. On 29 August 11th Armoured Division led the advance out of XXX Corps' bridgehead on two axes. Despite meeting resistance, in the form of small groups of infantry supported by self-propelled and anti-tank guns, it covered some twenty miles and by the end of the day had reached the vicinity of Mainneville. Next day, the Guards Armoured Division took over the right-hand axis while 11th Armoured Division was ordered to press on through the night to Amiens in order to capture intact some bridges over the Somme, both in the town and to the west. This was carried out successfully in the early hours of 31 August.

The Guards Armoured Division carried out a successful crossing of the Somme east of Amiens and by the end of the day had deployed some of its leading formations astride the Albert–Amiens road.

The advance from XII Corps' bridgehead began on 30 August and a distance of 25 miles had been covered by nightfall. At the end of the following day a line between Poix and Aumale, about fifteen miles from the Somme, had been reached by the leading elements of 7th Armoured Division. During the advance, a considerable number of enemy minefields and demolitions were encountered, including blown bridges and cratered roads.

In XXX Corps' sector, the Belgian frontier was crossed on 3 September by the 2nd Household Cavalry Regiment, the divisional reconnaissance regiment of the Guards Armoured Division, and by nightfall the division had liberated Brussels. Meanwhile, 11th Armoured Division was advancing on Antwerp, which it entered on the 4th; the vital docks and installations in the north of the city were captured after opposition that lasted for several days before being overcome. Thereafter, the division reorganized in an area south of Antwerp and prepared for the next stage of the advance.

In the meantime XII Corps had encountered considerable opposition from three enemy divisions in its path: 64th Infantry Division north of Saint-Pol, and 59th and 712th Infantry Divisions in the area between Béthune and La Bassée. These were tackled by 53rd (Welsh) Infantry Division and 4th Armoured Brigade while 7th Armoured Division pressed on to its objective, the city of Ghent, which was captured during the evening of 5 September. Two days later, the city and the area to the south of it having been secured, XII Corps relieved XXX Corps in Alost and Antwerp so that the latter could wheel north-east for the next stage of the advance.

Second British Army had advanced a distance of 250 miles in six days, while on its right flank First US Army had reached a line between Namur and Tirlemont. On its left, First Canadian Army's II Corps, comprising 2nd and 3rd Canadian Divisions and Polish 1st Armoured Division, had crossed the Somme on 3 September and advanced rapidly northwards. By the 6th, Polish 1st Armoured Division had reached Saint-Omer, and by the 9th Nieuport and Ostend had been taken and occupied by 2nd Canadian Division.

In the south-east, meanwhile, General George Patton's Third US Army had reached Commercy and Verdun on the River Meuse, and in the south General Jacob Devers' 6th US Army Group was advancing steadily northwards up the Rhône Valley.

The rapid rate of advance had placed great pressure on logistical resources which were already overstretched. Now that Second British Army had reached Brussels and Antwerp, the lines of communication and supply were some 300 miles long. It had been assumed previously that there would be a pause at the end of the campaign in Normandy prior to the commencement of operations in Belgium, and that this would be used to good effect in establishing forward supply and maintenance areas. There was no such pause, however, and the ample supplies in 21st Army Group's rear maintenance area at Bayeux in Normandy had to be transported by road to XII and XXX Corps, which were advancing at a rate of 40 miles per day. It had been envisaged that 21st Army Group's railhead would be located within 200 miles of its leading formations, but none of the railways in its sector were working and it was not until 30 August that the first train from the Normandy bridgehead arrived in Paris via a lengthy and circuitous route.

Almost total reliance was therefore placed on supply by road, and such was the requirement for trucks that VIII Corps had to be halted and 50 per cent of its first-line transport, together with all of its second-line resources, reassigned to the two leading formations. Furthermore, nearly all of 21st Army Group's heavy, medium and anti-aircraft artillery had been halted west of the Seine because of the shortage of transport. In order that trucks could be used for moving troops forward, the daily rate of importation into Normandy was reduced from 16,000 to 7,000 tons per day. The situation was exacerbated by the fact that 1,400 3-ton trucks had been found to be useless because of faulty pistons in their engines – this quantity of transport could have moved 800 tons per day, sufficient for two divisions. The chronic shortage of transport reduced supplies to First Canadian Army on the left flank, and necessitated the shipping of more trucks from Britain and even the makeshift conversion of tank-transporters to carry supplies.

The formations of 12th US Army Group faced even greater problems: their supply lines extended almost 400 miles back to the Cotentin Peninsula via Paris. Le Havre was still held by the Germans, and the nearest major port available to the Allies was Cherbourg. Although Dieppe was captured by the Canadians on 1 September, the port would not be operational for a further seven days. In an attempt to overcome these problems, 12th US Army Group had established a one-way traffic system between their rear maintenance area and Paris on which only supply transport was permitted to travel. This operated for 24 hours per day and delivered 7,000 tons daily. In accordance with Eisenhower's directive concerning the advance into Belgium, First US Army received 5,000 tons and Second British Army 2,000 tons per day.

On 2 September, Bradley and Patton attended a meeting with Eisenhower at Chartres. Patton in particular was extremely unhappy with the quota of supplies allocated to him, and complained vociferously. His reconnaissance elements had reached Metz, but lack of fuel had forced him to halt his other formations on the line of the Meuse. Indeed, Third US Army's fuel reserves were almost exhausted by 30 August when it received 32,000 instead of the 400,000 gallons it had demanded. Moreover, Bradley had told him that no more would be forthcoming until 3 September.

Supported by Bradley, Patton urged Eisenhower to supply him with more fuel so that he could reach the Rhine as soon as possible. Bradley also took the opportunity to try to persuade the Supreme Allied Commander to allow him to turn First US Army's direction eastwards. Eventually, under such heavy pressure from two of his senior commanders, Eisenhower compromised by agreeing that Third US Army should attack the Siegfried Line as soon as the Calais area had been stabilized, and gave permission for crossings over the Moselle to be established as soon as fuel became available. (Patton had forborne from mentioning that he had captured 110,000 gallons of fuel – sufficient for one of his corps to advance over the Moselle.) Eisenhower also partly acceded to Bradley's request by agreeing that his First US Army's XV Corps should join Third US Army in attacking the Siegfried Line.

By giving in even partly to Bradley and Patton, Eisenhower had committed a major error. Having previously allocated priority to the advance through Belgium, he had now compromised his plan. Any advance eastwards beyond the Moselle would inevitably incur a greater demand for supplies which would have to be diverted from First US Army. It had already been reported that fresh enemy formations – 3rd and 15th Panzer Divisions and two SS brigades – had recently moved up to the far side of the Moselle to confront Patton, so it was important that any move against them should be made rapidly before they could establish themselves firmly. The quantity of additional fuel allocated to Third US Army was sufficient for it to engage the enemy but not enough for it to win the battle.

Despite having won concessions from Eisenhower, Patton was extremely unhappy with his commander's decision, which he later referred to as being 'the most momentous error of the war'. On returning to his headquarters, he found that his XII US Corps had halted at Saint-Dizier because its tanks were very short of fuel. Patton responded by ordering its commander, Major General Manton Eddy, to continue his advance until the fuel ran out. Although he was disregarding Bradley's orders, Patton was no doubt fully aware that if the situation became sufficiently dire and his tanks were literally immobilized, Bradley would be forced to supply him with fuel that would have been diverted from First US Army.

Montgomery, meanwhile, was becoming increasingly unhappy with the situation. He had received reports from his liaison officer at HQ 12th US Army Group that First US Army formations on the right flank of 21st Army Group were no longer receiving priority for resupply. He complained to Bradley who refuted the charge, saying that he was allotting the tonnage according to Eisenhower's orders: while doing so, however, Bradley had succeeded in keeping Patton's tanks mobile by allocating the major part of Third US Army's tonnage allocation to fuel, and only a small part of it to ammunition.

Montgomery decided to try once more to persuade Eisenhower to adopt his own plan for a single thrust northwards with the Ruhr as its objective. On 4 September, the day on which Antwerp was captured, he sent a signal to Eisenhower at the latter's advanced headquarters on the Cherbourg Peninsula, some 400 miles away from the front and, in Montgomery's eyes, too far away for the Supreme Allied Commander to be able to keep in touch with the land operations aspect of the campaign. Moreover, the headquarters was inadequately equipped for communications with either Army Group's headquarters, having no form of radio communications or telephone links.

Once again Montgomery strongly put the case for a thrust to the north, reiterating that there were only two possible axes of advance, via the Ruhr or via Metz and the Saar, and again recommending the Ruhr option. He went on to point out that whichever route was selected, it had to receive the fullest possible logistical support, at the expense of other areas of the front, and that any compromise would only divide resources and lead to a prolongation of the war. He also emphasized the urgency of the situation, stating that the time factor was vital.

Eisenhower replied to Montgomery's signal next day, 5 September. While agreeing with the idea of a strong thrust for Berlin, he could not accept that this should be carried out at the expense of all other operations. He stated that it was his belief that the major part of the German forces in the west had been destroyed and that this factor should be exploited by an Allied attack on the Siegfried Line, followed by a crossing of the Rhine over a wide front and a subsequent advance to capture the Saar and the Ruhr. This would secure two of Germany's main industrial areas and destroy much of its capability to continue waging war, and would give the Allies freedom to deploy in any direction and thus force the Germans to disperse any of their forces still in the west. Eisenhower continued by saying that, during the advance, the ports of Antwerp and Le Havre would be opened as quickly as possible, they being essential for the support of any thrust into Germany. However, he expressed the belief that reallocation of available resources would be insufficient to support a thrust to Berlin. He concluded his signal by stating that it was his intention to capture the Saar and Ruhr, by which time Antwerp and Le Havre would be able to support either or both of the thrusts advocated by Montgomery. He reminded Montgomery that he had always given priority to the northern axis of advance and the Ruhr as an objective. He informed him that rail transport resources were in the process of being allocated on the basis of such priority, so as to support both army groups.

On the same day, Eisenhower issued a new directive which ordered 21st Army Group and 12th US Army Group to secure Antwerp, advance across the Rhine and ultimately seize the Ruhr. Meanwhile, Third US Army was to take and hold the sector of the Siegfried Line covering the Saar and then capture Frankfurt. The directive stated that Patton was to launch his offensive as soon as possible, but added the clear and important proviso that those elements of 12th US Army Group tasked with taking the Ruhr 'must first be adequately supported'.

The inference was that priority of resupply within 12th US Army Group was to be given to First US Army, but next day Eisenhower issued a memorandum in which he referred to his broad front policy and stated that he saw no reason to change it. He added that Third US Army's operation should commence as soon as possible. This gave Bradley the signal to unleash Patton and to increase Third US Army's share of the daily available supply tonnage from 2,000 to 3,500 tons per day. Patton's forces had already been reinforced by the transfer of V US Corps from the centre of First US Army to its right so as to cover Third US Army's northern flank during its advance eastwards; they would now be strengthened further on their southern flank by XV US Corps.

Inevitably, these transfers of resources resulted in First US Army being unable to advance alongside 21st Army Group at the same rate. It required a minimum daily supply of 4,500 tons but its allocation had been reduced to 3,500 tons. Moreover, its strength had been reduced by the transfer of 79th US Infantry Division from its left flank, alongside 21st Army Group, to XV US Corps on the right of Patton's Third Army. This division had been operating as part of XIX US Corps which was immobilized on the Belgian border for lack of fuel.

It was under such circumstances that Montgomery replied to Eisenhower by signal on 7 September, stating that his logistical resources were strained to the limit. His requirement was 1,000, tons per day but he had received only 375 tons per day during the previous two days. He pointed out that his transport was operating over a distance of 300 miles from his ports, his rear maintenance area still being at Bayeux. Under such circumstances, he did not have the resources to capture the Ruhr. With the opening of a port in the Pas de Calais, he would require 2,500 trucks in addition to sufficient air lift allocation to ensure a minimum daily delivery of 1,000 tons. He restated his conviction that a re-allotment of available resources would be sufficient to support a single strong thrust to Berlin, and ended by asking Eisenhower to visit him to discuss matters further. Eisenhower agreed to do so and a meeting was arranged for the afternoon of 10 September.

Montgomery's estimate of his supply requirements had been disputed on more than one occasion by Bradley, who was convinced that a single strong thrust northwards could be accomplished with less tonnage than that stipulated by Montgomery. He resented what he saw as Eisenhower's support of 21st Army Group at his own forces' expense, maintaining that deficiencies in British transport had been rectified with the use of vehicles from First US Army, and arguing his own case strenuously with Eisenhower. Moreover, he was under constant pressure from Patton, who was interested only in obtaining sufficient resources to enable Third US Army to continue its advance. On one occasion Patton said to Bradley, 'To hell with Hodges and Monty ... We'll win your goddam war if you'll keep Third Army going.'

On the morning of 10 September, prior to his appointment with Eisenhower, Montgomery had a meeting with Lieutenant General Sir Miles Dempsey, commander of Second British Army, at the latter's headquarters. The purpose of this was to discuss plans for the use of airborne forces in an operation to be carried out as the spearhead of 21st Army Group's northward thrust. Also present, but not in attendance at the meeting, was Lieutenant General Frederick 'Boy' Browning, commander of 1st British Airborne Corps, who had received a summons but was unaware of the reason for it.

The Allied airborne forces in Britain had recently been grouped together under the newly formed First Allied Airborne Army commanded by Lieutenant General Lewis S. Brereton, a USAAF officer. This formation comprised XVIII US Airborne Corps, consisting of 17th, 82nd and 101st US Airborne Divisions, and the British 1st Airborne Corps, which consisted of 1st and 6th Airborne Divisions, 1st Special Air Service Brigade and 1st Polish Independent Parachute Brigade Group. 6th Airborne Division had only just returned from the campaign in Normandy and the advance to the Seine, during which it had been in constant action since D-Day, and was resting and refitting. Brereton's command also embraced 38 and 46 Groups RAF, 9th US Troop Carrier Command USAAF and The Glider Pilot Regiment, these providing the transport aircraft and gliders in which the airborne formations were flown into battle.

First Allied Airborne Army formed Eisenhower's only strategic reserve and on 4 September he allocated it to 21st Army Group for use in its northward thrust. Plans were drawn up for an operation, code-named 'Comet', to be carried out by 1st Airborne Division and 1st Polish Independent Parachute Brigade Group. This involved night landings with the use of gliderborne coup de main forces to capture bridges over the rivers Maas, Waal and Lower Rhine at Grave, Nijmegen and Arnhem respectively, to coincide with an advance by Second British Army from Brussels and Antwerp. The operation had been planned to take place on 8 September, but had been postponed subsequently for 72 hours.

During his meeting with Dempsey, Montgomery revealed that he proposed to use three airborne divisions and 1st Polish Independent Parachute Brigade Group in an enlarged version of Operation 'Comet' which had been renamed 'Market Garden'–'Market' for the airborne phase of the operation and 'Garden' for the advance by Second British Army to Arnhem. The four airborne formations, under the command of Browning's 1st Airborne Corps, would seize the bridges over the three rivers and two canals, the Wilhelmina and the Zuid Willems Vaart, to establish a 'corridor' along which Second British Army would advance rapidly with the ultimate task of crossing into Germany and subsequently advancing south-eastwards into the Ruhr. The plan, however, had yet to be approved by Eisenhower. That afternoon the Supreme Allied Commander arrived in his personal aircraft, accompanied by his deputy, Air Chief Marshal Sir Arthur Tedder. The meeting took place in the aircraft because Eisenhower had suffered an injury to his knee and was unable to walk. Montgomery began by asking that Eisenhower's Chief Administrative Officer, Lieutenant General Sir Humphrey Gale, should not be present but that his own, Major General Miles Graham, should remain. This was impolite, to say the least, but Montgomery's request may have been prompted by the fact that he was aware that Gale was among a number of senior officers at SHAEF who were strongly opposed to his plan. Gale himself had gained considerable experience in administrative matters while serving at Allied HQ during the North Africa campaign, and he had told Eisenhower that the supply situation was such that it ruled out Montgomery's proposal. In his opinion, even if Bradley's forces were halted and all supplies given to 21st Army Group, the operation was still not administratively feasible so long as there was a possibility of German resistance and the port of Antwerp was unavailable for the landing of supplies.

Eisenhower, always the diplomat, agreed to Montgomery's request and Lieutenant General Gale left the aircraft. Montgomery then launched into violent criticism of Eisenhower's broad front policy, which resulted in the latter's now famous gentle rebuke, 'Steady Monty. You can't speak to me like that. I'm your boss.'

Having apologized but remaining unabashed, Montgomery explained his own situation and advanced his plan for a single thrust, which was yet again rejected by Eisenhower. At this point he presented Eisenhower with information, received from London the previous day, concerning V-2 missile attacks on England which were being launched from sites in Holland, and emphasized the importance of the early capture of the V-weapon launch sites in western Holland.

Eisenhower responded by saying that he had allotted priority to the northern advance and that this had been observed. Montgomery argued that this was not the case and eventually Eisenhower admitted that he had not given it 'absolute priority', but insisted that he could not reduce support for the advance to the Saar. Montgomery then spoke of stiffening enemy resistance along the Albert Canal and emphasized that because he would not be able to launch a strong thrust northwards as soon as he had hoped, the enemy would be given more time to regroup.

Montgomery then unveiled details of Operation 'Market Garden'. Despite his annoyance at his subordinate's high-handed manner, Eisenhower was impressed by the plan. Although he appreciated that it would mean the diversion of supplies from Third US Army and a delay in the opening up of Antwerp, he realized that Montgomery's proposal would inject renewed momentum into the slowing Allied advance and would carry the pursuit of the enemy into Germany itself. He was also aware, however, of Montgomery's ambitions for an advance into the Ruhr and ultimately on to Berlin. So he placed certain limitations on the operation and emphasized that it was 'merely an extension of the northern advance to the Rhine and the Ruhr'. Montgomery attempted to argue his case further but Eisenhower was adamant and Montgomery was forced to accept the situation.

Immediately after the meeting Montgomery notified Dempsey that approval had been given for 'Market Garden'. Dempsey in turn briefed Browning. In addition to seizing and holding five major bridges and a series of crossings, 1st Airborne Corps would also have to hold the 'corridor' which would stretch for 64 miles from the Dutch border to Arnhem. While this was the type of operation for which airborne forces had been designed, huge task that faced Browning's force. Browning returned to England immediately, having been told by Dempsey that planning and preparations for the operation were to be carried out with the utmost speed and that it was to be mounted within a matter of days. On being pressed for a date by which his corps could be ready, he proposed 15 or 16 September.

The problems of inadequate levels of resupply still dogged Montgomery, who had not been able to extract a satisfactory response from Eisenhower. On the following day, 11 September, he sent another signal to Eisenhower, the essence of which was that Operation 'Market Garden' could not be mounted before 23 September because of the decision not to accord the northern advance priority over other operations. He emphasized that such a delay would give the enemy the opportunity to reorganize, thereby increasing resistance and slowing the Allied advance.

The response to this signal was, in Montgomery's own word, 'electric'. Eisenhower's Chief of Staff, Major General Walter Bedell Smith, arrived at HQ 21st Army Group next day, 12 September, to announce that Eisenhower had reversed his previous decision and that Patton's advance eastwards would be halted and complete priority given to 21st Army Group and 12th US Army Group's northern thrust. First US Army would be allotted priority of support within Bradley's command, and Montgomery was given permission to liaise direct with its commander, Lieutenant General Courtney Hodges. Furthermore, three more American divisions would be halted and their transport resources directed to move supplies for 21st Army Group. On this basis, Montgomery agreed that 'Market Garden' would be launched on 17 September.

On 13 September, however, four days before the scheduled start of 'Market Garden', Montgomery received a signal from SHAEF which indicated that the logistical support allocated to him would not be of the level agreed with Bedell Smith. It revealed that the Americans would transport 500 tons daily by road to Brussels and that a further 500 tons would be flown in daily except during the airborne phase of the operation. As the requirement for a division engaged on operations was 450 tons per day, this extra tonnage would only permit Montgomery to retain two extra divisions in action. Furthermore, the signal stated that First US Army would only receive a level of supply deemed 'adequate' to enable it to carry out its tasks.

When, a few days later, Bradley learned from his liaison officer at 21st Army Group of Eisenhower's decision to support Montgomery's plan, he made his objections known very strongly. His opposition to 'Market Garden' stemmed not only from the fact that 21st Army Group would be veering off on a tangent, opening up a gap which his own troops would have to fill, but also because he feared that Montgomery, in his enthusiasm to outflank the enemy, had underestimated the strength and capability of the German forces along the line of the Lower Rhine. Furthermore, he believed that 21st Army Group had insufficient assets and resources at its disposal to carry out such an operation successfully. Eisenhower refused to listen to Bradley's objections, maintaining that Montgomery's plan might enable the Siegfried Line to be outflanked and a bridgehead to be established over the Rhine.

Bradley decided to ignore this change in strategy and to permit Patton and his Third US Army to become so heavily engaged beyond the Moselle that Eisenhower would be unable to reduce support or to halt the advance to the Saar. Patton's reaction, when told of Eisenhower's decision, was typical. He wrote in his diary: 'To hell with Monty, I must get so involved with my own operations that they can't stop me'. To Bradley he said, 'Don't call me till after dark on the 19th'.

2
INTELLIGENCE IGNORED

'We had made the cardinal mistake of underestimating our enemy – a very dangerous thing to do when fighting the Germans, who are among the best soldiers in the world. Their recovery after the disaster in Normandy was little short of miraculous.'
— Lieutenant General Sir Brian Horrocks.

It was on 4 September 1944 that Adolf Hitler turned for help to Generalfeldmarschall Gerd von Runstedt, whom he had dismissed only two months previously as Commander-in-Chief West. The latter's outburst 'Make peace you fools ... What else can you do?' on the night of 1 July, when asked for advice by Hitler's despairing Chief of Staff, Generalfeldmarschall Wilhelm Keitel, had resulted in his replacement by one of the Führer's favourites, Generalfeldmarschall Günther von Kluge. On 17 August von Kluge was in turn replaced by Generalfeldmarschall Walther Model, another of Hitler's favoured commanders.

The situation looked extremely grim for Germany. During the last week of August, shattered German divisions had retreated in disorder before Montgomery and Bradley's formations which had advanced relentlessly through France, across the Somme and the Marne and on into Belgium. On the day that von Runstedt re-assumed his old command, the leading element of Montgomery's 21st Army Group, 11th Armoured Division, had reached the vital port of Antwerp.

Hitler was pinning his hopes on checking any Allied thrust eastwards into Germany on the Siegfried Line, a static defensive belt of fortifications which stretched from the border with Holland in the north to Switzerland in the south. Comprised of layers of minefields, concrete 'dragon's teeth', barbed wire fences, concrete casemates, and underground bunkers, it had however lain neglected since the early days of 1940. Many of the guns had been removed, fences dismantled and mines lifted. Much work was needed to restore it to a state of proper defence, but this would require time, a commodity of which Germany was in short supply.

Tasked by Hitler with stemming the Allied advance, von Runstedt faced an almost impossible task. In the west, from Calais to just south of the Scheldt estuary in the low-lying areas of Flanders, was Fifteenth Army, commanded by General der Infanterie Gustav von Zangen, facing First Canadian Army to the south and in danger of being trapped between the sea and Lieutenant General Sir Miles Dempsey's Second British Army to the east. The only possible route of escape was northwards by sea across the estuary to the island of Walcheren, and then by road eastwards on to the mainland. In the east, the surviving remnants of SS-Oberstgruppen-führer und General der Waffen-SS Paul Hausser's Seventh Army, which had suffered greatly in Normandy, were retreating in disorder northwards and north-eastwards in the direction of Maastricht, Aachen, the Meuse and the Ardennes, harried everywhere by General Omar Bradley's 12th US Army Group. Between the two armies was a 50-mile-wide gap which stretched from Antwerp to Maastricht.

Having relinquished his post of Commander-in-Chief West, to von Runstedt, Generalfeldmarschall Model was able to concentrate his atten-tion on his other command, that of Army Group B, which he had taken over from Generalfeldmarschall Erwin Rommel after the latter had been wounded in France during July, and which was the northernmost of the two German army groups in the west – the other being Generaloberst Johannes Blaskowitz's Army Group G in the south.

Army Group B was little more than a formation in name only, having already been split in half by Montgomery and Bradley's forces. It mainly comprised 719th Division under Generalleutnant Karl Sievers which, as part of 88th Corps, had been deployed on the Dutch coast for the previous four years and had seen no action. On 4 September Model ordered 88th Corps' commander, Generalleutnant Hans Reinhard, to send 719th Divi-sion southwards to the line of the Albert Canal as his first move in attempting to block the gap which lay in the path of the advancing Second British Army. At the same time, Model requested reinforcements from Ger-many, stating that if he was to hold a line that would stretch from Antwerp via Maastricht to south of Metz, along the line of the Albert Canal, the Meuse and the Siegfried Line, he would require twenty-five infantry divi-sions supported by half a dozen panzer divisions.

Model had no hope of receiving such reinforcement. Any available divisions had already been sent in late August to the area west of the Saar in an attempt to stem the armoured thrusts of General George Patton's Third US Army. Within Germany itself there were new units and forma-tions being formed, but these comprised men and equipment from training regiments, depots, officer cadet schools, logistics units and convalescent depots. Luftwaffe and naval personnel, and even members of the Todt labour organization, also found themselves being pressed into service. All these men, totalling some 135,000, were sent to the Siegfried Line and to Metz to rebuild the defences and to man them.

On the afternoon of 4 September, Generaloberst Kurt Student, founder of the Luftwaffe's airborne forces, received orders by telephone from Hitler's headquarters to form immediately '1st Parachute Army'. Since the campaign in Crete in 1941, when Student's 11th Fliegerkorps had suf-fered more than 6,000 casualties, Hitler had forbidden any further large-scale airborne operations, and Student had found himself commanding an airborne training establishment while his crack parachute regiments were being used as infantry in different theatres.

Student's abrupt return to active service was the result of a revelation made to the German High Command by the head of the Luftwaffe, Reichsmarschall Hermann Göring, that there were six Luftwaffe parachute regiments under training and that two more could be raised from paratroopers convalescing in depots. These numbered some 20,000 in total and could be augmented by a further 10,000 Luftwaffe air and ground crew personnel who were redundant because of shortage of aviation fuel.

Student was informed that the task of 1st Parachute Army, which at this stage did not even exist on paper, was to plug the gap from Antwerp to Maastricht, along the line of the north bank of the Albert Canal. In addition to his parachute units, he had been allocated two divisions: 719th, which had already been ordered by Generalfeldmarschall Model to move to the Canal from the Dutch coast, and 176th, which comprised units formed from men from convalescent units. The latter, commanded by Oberst Christian Landau, was at that time located on the Siegfried Line near Aachen, but had been ordered to move with all haste to the Albert Canal. In addition, there were a number of units composed of Luftwaffe and naval personnel. Neither of the two divisions possessed any supporting artillery or armour. When querying the availability of the latter, Student was informed that he had initially been allotted 25 tanks.

On the afternoon of 5 September, SS-Obergruppenführer and Generalleutnant der Waffen-SS Willi Bittrich, commander of 2nd SS Panzer Corps, arrived at Headquarters Army Group B near Liège. His corps, comprising 9th 'Hohenstaufen' and 10th 'Frundsberg' SS Panzer Divisions, had been badly mauled during and since the operations in Normandy, suffering heavy losses in tanks and personnel. Having been out of contact with Model for three days, Bittrich had come to obtain orders from the commander of Army Group B in person. These proved to be brief and to the point, as is illustrated by the text of a German radio signal intercepted and recorded by the Government Code and Cipher School's Station X, at Bletchley Park in Buckinghamshire, where all enemy communications were monitored, deciphered and passed to the relevant Allied departments and formations under the code-name 'ULTRA'. Model's orders were reproduced in ULTRA Intercept No. XL9245 of 6 September:

'Army Group B Order quoted by FLIVO [Luftwaffe liaison officer] 1730 hrs 5th. (1) Stab Panzer Army Five with subordinated headquarters 58th Panzer Corps to transfer beginning 6th to area Koblenz for rest and refit by C-in-C West. (2) Headquarters 2nd SS Panzer Corps subordinated Army Group B, to transfer to Eindhoven to rest and refit in co-operation with General of Panzer Troops West and direct rest and refit of 2nd and 116th Panzer Divisions, 9th SS Panzer Division and 217th Heavy Assault Gun Abteilung. (COMMENT: Elements these divisions and 10th SS Panzer Division ordered 4th to area Venlo–Arnhem–Hertogenbosch for refit in XL9188).'

The scene on the northern bank of the Albert Canal on the afternoon of 5 September was one of frenetic activity. The first of the German parachute units had arrived and were digging in while engineers placed demolition charges on the bridges over the Canal. At the same time, 719th Division was arriving in its allotted area north of Antwerp where it was to take up positions.

Meanwhile, orders had gone out for 3rd, 5th and 6th Fallschirmjäger Regiments to be brought up to strength with personnel from the Luftwaffe's 1st Air Force and its Training Division. In addition to 719th Division, 347th Division was to join 1st Parachute Army's order of battle, together with SS training units and garrison troops from Holland, the Hermann Göring Training Regiment, and ten battalions of Luftwaffe infantry and flak troops from the 6th Military District, which were to be equipped with heavy anti-tank guns and close-range anti-tank weapons. Finally, orders were given for heavy weapons, especially artillery, to be dispatched to 1st Parachute Army as soon as possible. More armour had been promised: Hitler had allotted 200 new Panther tanks to Army Group B, and a few days previously had ordered all available Tiger tanks, Jagdpanther self-propelled anti-tank guns and 88mm anti-tank guns in Germany to be sent to the west.

While the units of 1st Parachute Army were hastily establishing their line of defence along the Albert Canal, other German formations and units were streaming northwards in retreat. Amongst these were elements of 84th, 85th and 89th Infantry Divisions which had suffered heavily during the Normandy campaign and thereafter. The commander of 85th Infantry Division was Generalleutnant Kurt Chill who, on arriving in the north of Belgium on 4 September, was instrumental in slowing down, if not halting, the retreat. Disregarding orders from HQ Seventh Army to move his troops to the Rhineland to rest and reorganize, he deployed them along the north bank of the Albert Canal, between Massenhoven and Kwaadmechelen, and established roadblocks on the bridges over the Canal in his area to halt and gather together all German personnel trying to cross.

By the end of the following day, Chill had collected several thousand men whom he organized into units which were then dispersed throughout his command. On discovering the presence of Chill and his men, Generalleutnant Hans Rheinhard, the commander of 88th Corps, allocated him responsibility for the area of the front between Antwerp and Herenthals. He also reinforced Chill with a regiment from 719th Division. Two days later, on 7 September, Oberst Landau's 176th Division arrived and took up positions along the front between Hasselt and Maastricht.

Meanwhile, in the west, General der Infanterie Gustav von Zangen was evacuating half of his Fifteenth Army across the Scheldt estuary via Walcheren. On the 5th, having heard of the capture of Antwerp the day before, he had ordered his forces to assemble in the area of Audenarde with a view to attacking eastwards in the direction of Brussels. Before this operation was under way, however, von Zangen received orders from Generalfeldmarschall von Runstedt to abandon it and prepare to evacuate part of his forces across the Scheldt estuary to the island of Walcheren and the South Beveland isthmus. Designated elements of Fifteenth Army were to remain behind and man the fortresses at Le Havre, Boulogne, Calais and Dunkirk, as well as positions on the northern and southern shores of the Scheldt estuary. Their task would be to deny the four Channel ports and Antwerp to the Allies. The rest of Fifteenth Army would be evacuated and would then march eastwards to join 1st Parachute Army.

While designated formations and units were sent to the ports and the shores of the Scheldt, the rest of Fifteenth Army busied itself with constructing defensive positions along the line of the canal between Bruges and Ghent to protect the evacuation operation. At the same time, two large Dutch freighters, three large rafts and sixteen small craft were assembled. The hour-long crossings to Walcheren and South Beveland were carried out at night and, despite attacks by Allied aircraft which scored a number of direct hits, the entire force was evacuated in sixteen days. By 21 September this numbered 65,000 men, 225 artillery pieces, 750 trucks and other vehicles, and 1,000 horses, which represented the remnants of nine infantry formations: 59th, 70th, 245th, 331st, 344th, 346th, 711th and 712th Infantry Divisions and 17th Luftwaffe Field Division.

On 16 and 17 September, two of von Zangen's divisions arrived to help bolster Generaloberst Kurt Student's 1st Parachute Army: 59th Infantry Division under Generalleutnant Walter Poppe and 245th Infantry Division commanded by Oberst Gerhard Kegler. Badly equipped and understrength, they took up positions in depth, the 245th west of Eindhoven and the 59th south-west of s'Hertogenbosch near HQ 1st Parachute Army.

Hitler had ordered von Runstedt to check the Allied advance along the line of the Albert Canal, the Meuse and the Moselle, in an endeavour to gain time for the Siegfried Line to be prepared for defence. But he was also ordered '... regardless of losses, to advance deep into the American east flank, attacking in a north-westerly direction from the Epinal area'. Von Runstedt's formations had little or no mobility, however, several thousand trucks and much horse-drawn transport having been destroyed during the campaign in Normandy. Moreover, they certainly did not possess sufficient armour to mount any serious threat against the highly mobile armoured divisions of Third US Army; the total number of operational tanks in Army Group B at that time was approximately 100 (compared with an Allied total of some 2,000), consisting mainly of heavy Tiger and Panther tanks which, armed with 88mm and high-velocity 75mm guns which could knock out any Allied tank, did not possess the mobility and speed of the Sherman medium tanks with which the British and American armoured divisions were equipped. This was because Hitler had allocated all available production of the faster and more agile Mk IV to the Eastern Front. Indeed, the only course of action open to von Runstedt, given the state of the German forces in the west, was one of static defence until such time as the Siegfried Line was ready.

Despite these efforts on the part of the Germans, Dempsey's Second British Army succeeded in established a bridgehead across the Albert Canal at Beeringen and pushed on northwards. However, the leading element, Lieutenant General Brian Horrocks' XXX Corps, encountered stiff resistance and it took four days of hard fighting to reach its next objective: the Meuse–Escaut Canal. On 10 September bridgeheads were established at Neerpelt and Gheel and by mid-September the area north of the Albert Canal had been cleared of all enemy and the front had stabilized along the line of the Meuse–Escaut Canal.

By the end of the first week of September, the German analysis of Allied intentions had pointed to a thrust northwards to cut off German forces in western Holland, as is illustrated by the text of ULTRA Intercept No. HP242 of 15 September:

'Allies in German reports: (A) addressed to unspecified on evening 9th. 30 British Corps (2nd Br Army) between Antwerp and Hasselt. Bringing up further corps possible. Eleven to fourteen divisions with eight to nine hundred tanks. Photo recce tasks (COMMENT: presumably known from intercepts) indicate probable intention is thrust mainly from Wilhelmina Canal on both sides Eindhoven into Arnhem (COMMENT: further specification of area incomplete but includes "west of Nijmegen"and "Wesel") to cut off and surround German forces western Netherlands.'

It also appears, however, that the Germans firmly believed that the Allies' ultimate objective was the Ruhr and that the latter's airborne forces would be dropped and landed in an area to the rear of the Siegfried Line, between Duisburg and Düsseldorf, in a two-pronged operation to seize it. Evidence of this is an intelligence report from HQ Army Group B which states:

'2nd British Army will assemble its units at the Maas–Scheldt [Meuse–Escaut] and Albert Canals. On its right wing it will concentrate an attack force mainly of armoured units, and, after forcing a Maas crossing, will launch operations to break through to the Rhenish–Westphalian Industrial Area [Ruhr] with the main effort via Roermond. To cover the northern flank of this drive the left wing of the 2nd British Army will close the Waal at Nijmegen and thus create the basic conditions necessary to cut off the German forces committed in the Dutch coastal areas. In conjunction with these operations a large-scale airborne landing by 1st Allied Airborne Army north of the Lippe River in the area south of Münster is planned for an as yet indefinite date.'

So the Germans were expecting an advance northwards to Nijmegen, although they incorrectly anticipated airborne landings to the east, and therefore made their dispositions accordingly. Among these, however, was the allocation of responsibility for the area north of Arnhem to SS-Obergruppenführer Willi Bittrich's 2nd SS Panzer Corps with its 9th and 10th SS Panzer Divisions. The 9th was commanded by SS-Obersturmbannführer Walter Harzer, who had taken over from SS-Brigadeführer Sylvester Stadler after the latter had been wounded. Located in the area between Arnhem and Apeldoorn, where it had arrived on 7 September, its headquarters were at Beekbergen. The 10th, under SS-Brigadeführer Heinz Harmel, was located in the area extending eastwards from Zutphen to the area of Ruurloi on the border between Holland and Germany.

Both divisions had been badly mauled during the fighting in Normandy and throughout the withdrawal through northern France to Belgium, suffering heavy losses of men, vehicles and equipment. By the time it reached its rest and refit area around Apeldoorn, 9th SS Panzer Division's strength stood at one armoured infantry regiment, its divisional armoured reconnaissance battalion, a company of armour equipped with Panther tanks, an artillery battalion, two batteries of self-propelled guns, and remnants of an anti-aircraft battalion and an engineer battalion.

10th SS Panzer Division had suffered more heavily, having lost most of its divisional signals regiment and its equipment in Normandy. It was reduced to less than 3,000 men comprising an armoured infantry regiment, its divisional reconnaissance battalion, two artillery battalions and an engineer battalion. All of these units were only partially motorized because of heavy losses of vehicles in Normandy.

On 10 September HQ 2nd SS Panzer Corps, which by now was located at Doetinchem, received further orders from HQ Army Group B. In addition to overseeing the resting and refitting of its two divisions and maintaining responsibility for the area north of Arnhem, the Corps had also been given the priority task of forming two mobile battle groups which had already been dispatched to the front: one to reinforce German SeventhArmy in the area of Aachen, to the east of Maastricht, the other to join 1st Parachute Army. Now its strength was to be reduced further: to Bittrich's great displeasure, he was ordered to send one of his divisions back to Germany. After a discussion with his two divisional commanders and his staff, decided to send 9th SS Panzer Division to Germany – where it would be deployed near Siegen, north-east of Koblenz, and retain 10th SS Panzer Division which had been reinforced by 1st SS Panzer Regiment and 1st SS Panzerjäger Regiment, both equipped with Panther tanks.

SS-Obersturmbannführer Harzer was ordered to hand over immediately to 10th SS Panzer Division all his formation's serviceable armoured vehicles, plus certain of his units including a battalion of 20th SS Panzer Grenadier Regiment, two self-propelled howitzer batteries of 9th SS Panzer Artillery Regiment, two other panzer grenadier battalions and two artillery batteries.

Of the two formations, 9th SS Panzer Division was marginally the stronger. Numbering less than 3,500 men, as opposed to its full establishment of 18,000, and with only about twenty Panther Mk V tanks as opposed to its full complement of 170, it did however possess a number of armoured vehicles including armoured cars, armoured troop carriers and self-propelled guns. Despite having been told that his division would be refitted on its return to Germany, Harzer decided to ignore Bittrich's orders and retain as many of his vehicles as possible; by ordering his units to remove wheels, tracks and weapons, he was able to list a number of his vehicles as 'unserviceable'.

Bittrich, aware that even the reinforcements from 9th SS Panzer Division would not bring Harmel's 10th Division sufficiently up to strength, decided, without informing Model, to send Harmel to the Waffen-SS headquarters in Berlin to explain the situation and, he hoped, obtain the sorely needed reinforcements and replacement equipment.

While the handing over of units and equipment was taking place, Bittrich ordered 9th SS Panzer Division to form small mobile combat teams, known as 'Alarmeinheiten', to be deployed as listed below:

Beekbergen	Divisional HQ staff, Divisional HQ defence company, Military police company, One company divisional signals battalion
Apeldoorn	One infantry company plus a composite company of infantry and support unit personnel
Wormen	One company of anti-tank troops without their guns
Hoenderloo	An armoured reconnaissance unit of three companies; 500 men with their vehicles
Zutphen	Two companies of 19th SS Panzer Grenadier Regiment
Brummen	One company of 9th SS Panzer Engineer Battalion
Dieren	Two companies 9th SS Panzer Artillery Regiment without

	their guns. One AA company, four 20mm guns
Rheden	Two companies of 20th SS Panzer Grenadier Regiment
Velp	Two companies of 9th SS Panzer Medical Battalion
Arnhem	Two companies of 9th SS Panzer Regiment, in barracks north-east of the town
Oosterbeek	16th SS Panzer Grenadier Depot & Reserve Battalion; this unit was not under command of 9th SS Panzer Division at the time.

The relative ease with which the Allies had advanced through northern France into Belgium had resulted in a dangerous and misplaced sense of euphoria which permeated their forces at all levels. There was a feeling of certainty that the war would be over by Christmas. This in turn had led to a genuine belief that the German forces in the west were shattered and that there were few if any resources by which they could be reinforced from Germany or other theatres. This is summed up by a SHAEF intelligence summary of 9 September:

'The whole wreck of the Balkans and Finland may yield up perhaps half a dozen divisions. These will go no way to meet the crying need for more divisions to man the West Wall; moreover, a line in Transylvania will need to be manned. Where then are more divisions to be found?

Not in Norway, withdrawal would take too long ... Denmark might still supply one division, and a dozen or more may yet be formed in Germany, given time, from training units,   remnants and so forth. The Italian and Russian fronts risk collapse if anything more is   withdrawn   from them ... In short, C-in-C West may expect not more than a dozen divisions within the next two months to come from outside to the rescue.'

During this period, a steady stream of information on enemy dispositions and movements was being provided by Station X at Bletchley Park. Information was passed down as far as army headquarters level only and no further. From examination of the ULTRA intercepts during the period 1 to 17 September, it can be seen that very detailed information was available to senior Allied commanders, and it included the movement of 2nd SS Panzer Corps as it withdrew towards Eindhoven and Arnhem, having been ordered to do so on the afternoon of 4 September.

It appears, however, that intelligence officers at Eisenhower's headquarters were paying little heed to ULTRA. It was not until 16 September that SHAEF reported the presence in the Arnhem area of elements of 2nd SS Panzer Corps. Intelligence Summary No. 26, published on that date, states: '9th SS Panzer Division, and presumably the 10th, has been reported withdrawing to the Arnhem area in Holland; there they will probably collect new tanks from a depot reported in the area of Cleves'.

21st Army Group was one of the formations that received ULTRA intelligence. The Chief of Intelligence, Brigadier Bill Williams, was suffi- ciently concerned about the presence of 2nd SS Panzer Corps, and more particularly that of 9th SS Panzer Division north of Arnhem, that he drew it to the attention of Montgomery on 10 September, after the latter's meet- ings with Dempsey and Eisenhower on that day. He failed, however, to per- suade Montgomery to alter his plans for the airborne landings at Arnhem. Undaunted, Williams tried again two days later with the support of Brigadier David Belchem, the Brigadier General Staff (Operations) in Mont- gomery's headquarters, who was standing in as Chief of Staff in the absence of Major General Francis de Guingand who was on sick leave. Unfortunately, their warnings fell on deaf ears.

Three days later a further attempt was made to warn Montgomery. Eisenhower's Chief of Staff, Major General Walter Bedell Smith, received a report from SHAEF's Chief of Intelligence, Major General Kenneth Strong, concerning the presence of 9th and 10th SS Panzer Divisions in the area to the north and east of Arnhem. Bedell Smith immediately brought this information to the attention of Eisenhower and advised him that a second airborne division should be landed in the Arnhem area. Eisenhower gave the matter urgent consideration but was wary of ordering any changes to the operational plan at the risk of incurring Montgomery's wrath. He decided that any alteration could only be decided upon by Montgomery himself and accordingly sent Bedell Smith and Strong to HQ 21st Army Group at Brussels. At his meeting alone with Montgomery, Bedell Smith voiced his fears about the presence of German armour in the Arnhem area, but these were waved aside; indeed, Montgomery belittled the information and dismissed the idea of any alteration to his plan.

Another visitor to HQ 21st Army Group was His Royal Highness Prince Bernhard of The Netherlands. He arrived on 6 September with a briefcase containing copious details of enemy deployments around Arnhem and elsewhere in Holland. But he received a cold welcome from Mont- gomery who was dismissive of this intelligence offered to him. While Mont- gomery was obviously not prepared to brook any interference with 'Market Garden', his attitude towards the information would have been coloured by the fact that its source was the Dutch Resistance. Towards the end of 1941, elements of the Resistance had been penetrated by the Abwehr, the military intelligence department of the Oberkommando der Wehrmacht headed by Admiral Wilhelm Canaris, in an operation code-named 'North Pole'. Masterminded by Major, later Oberstleutnant, Hermann Giskes of the Abwehr and SS-Sturmbannführer Josef Schreieder of the Sicherheit- spolizei, 'North Pole' had been extremely successful in penetrating the Resistance through a collaborator who betrayed a radio operator named Hubertus Lauwers, who had been dropped by parachute into Holland on 7 November. Lauwers was arrested and, after interrogation, coerced into continuing to communicate (under German supervision) with the Dutch Section of the Special Operations Executive (SOE) in London. He continually attempted to warn SOE of his predicament by deliberately omitting a pre-arranged security check in each message.

Unbelievably, his warnings were ignored and more and more agents and radio operators were dropped into Holland to German reception committees. With very few exceptions, they were forced to reveal their codes and security checks and to work their sets back to London. The result of 'North Pole' was that, from early 1942 until early 1944, a total of sixty agents, fifteen tons of supplies, 500,000 guilders in cash, more than fifty radio sets, 2,000 pistols and revolvers, 900 automatic weapons, 8,000 grenades, 50,000 rounds of ammunition and large quantities of explosives were dropped into German hands. In addition, twelve bombers and eighty-three aircrew of the RAF special duties squadrons were shot down by Luftwaffe night-fighters after they had carried out their drops.

'North Pole' was not 'blown' until 31 August 1943 when two agents, Ben Ubbink and Pieter Dourlein, succeeded in escaping from a Catholic theological college at Haaren, in southern Holland, where all sixty SOE agents were imprisoned under guard by Dutch SS troops. It took them three months to make their way through occupied Europe to Switzerland, where they headed for Bern and the Dutch Legation where they told their story. In late November 1943, the two men wrote a lengthy report for SOE which gave full details of 'North Pole' and exposed the extent of the penetration of the Dutch Resistance. Thereafter SOE continued to communicate with the German-controlled radios, giving the impression that it suspected nothing. The Abwehr, however, was not deceived and on 1 April 1944 'North Pole' was terminated.

Once details of the débâcle became known, steps were taken to repair the damage to the movement throughout Holland, but suspicion lingered among the British towards the Resistance and its information. Unfortunately, this was to have adverse effects on 'Market Garden'.

At HQ Second British Army there were also misgivings about the plan for 'Market Garden' because it was becoming evident that the enemy would do everything possible to impede any further Allied advance. Intelligence reports stated that there was considerable railway activity at Arnhem and Nijmegen and that flak defences around both towns were being reinforced. Moreover, reports from the Dutch Resistance indicated that enemy armoured formations had arrived in the areas of Eindhoven and Nijmegen for refitting. This information caused serious doubts in the mind of Lieutenant General Sir Miles Dempsey who committed them to paper when making an entry in his diary on 9 September, in which he not only refers to the stiffening German resistance but also expresses his misgivings about the wisdom of a thrust northwards:

'It is clear that the enemy is bringing up all the reinforcements he can lay hands on for the defence of the Albert Canal, and that he appreciates the importance of the area of Arnhem–Nijmegen. It looks as though he is going to do all he can to hold it. This being the case, any question of a rapid advance to the north-east seems unlikely. Owing to our maintenance situation, we will not be in a position to fight a real battle for perhaps ten days to a fortnight. Are we right to direct Second Army to Arnhem, or would it be better to hold a left flank along the Albert Canal, and strike due east towards Cologne in conjunction with First Army?'

These doubts were sufficiently strong for Dempsey to decide on proposing an alternative direction of attack further eastwards, parallel to the path of Bradley's 12th US Army Group, towards the town of Wesel on the Rhine, and he intended to do so at his meeting with Montgomery at the latter's headquarters on 10 September. However, he was forestalled on his arrival by Montgomery, who showed him the signal from London, received two days earlier, announcing the first attack by V-2 missiles on the city. This was undoubtedly a key factor in reinforcing Montgomery's case for continuing the thrust north and Dempsey apparently obviously decided not to reveal his misgivings to him.

Second British Army's intelligence summaries covering the period from 8 to 17 September provide plentiful evidence of the build-up of enemy forces during that period and their ability to impede the Allied advance. In Summary No. 97 of 9 September there are references to the identification of 2nd and 6th Fallschirmjäger Regiments, and to 'stiff rearguard actions by enemy troops who were reported to include numbers of SS troops amongst them'. The doggedness of the enemy resistance is borne out by reports of counter-attacks mounted with determination and vigour, as remarked in Summary No. 100 of 12 September:

'Nearly all reports received so far emphasize two features of the enemy's resistance, namely its fanatical spirit ... the general impression is that we are up against a different type of opponent from that which was driven back, almost without a pause, from the Seine to Antwerp.'

Among the British element of the airborne forces due to take part in the landings, there was an overriding desire to see action before the war ended. This was mixed with mounting frustration within 1st Airborne Division which, as strategic reserve during the campaign in Normandy, had seen fifteen planned airborne operations cancelled at the last minute during the period June to September. This had resulted from the speed of the Allied advance or other reasons which either negated the requirement for them or prevented their taking place.

The first of these cancelled operations had been Operation 'Tuxedo' which would have involved 4th Parachute Brigade being dropped into Normandy in the event of difficulties arising during the landings. Next came 'Wastage', a larger version of 'Tuxedo' in which 1st Airborne Division would have been landed in Normandy in the event of the seaborne landings being delayed through bad weather. A third, unnamed, operation would have seen the division being dropped between 7 and 10 June in support of 82nd US Airborne Division. The fourth, 'Wild Oats', called for 1st Airborne Division to be landed in Normandy west of Caen to block an enemy withdrawal to the south west. The fifth, 'Beneficiary', would have taken place at the end of June, the division being landed, together with 1st Polish Independent Parachute Brigade, a squadron of 1st Special Air Service Regiment and a number of American airborne units, in Brittany with the task of taking the port of Saint-Malo in conjunction with XX US Corps. In a sixth, unnamed, operation 1st Airborne Division would have been landed to the south of Caen to assist in the breakout from the bridgehead.

In the seventh, 'Swordhilt', at the end of July, 1st Airborne Division was to have destroyed a viaduct at Morlaix, east of Brest, in order to cut off the enemy line of communication with the city. In the first half of August the eighth operation, 'Hands Up', involved the capture of an airfield at Vannes on the Brittany coast, south-east of Brest by 1st Airborne Division, 1st Polish Independent Parachute Brigade and 52nd (Lowland) Division in support of Third US Army. Next was 'Transfigure' in mid-August, designed to cut off the enemy's withdrawal route by landing 1st Airborne Division, 101st US Airborne Division, other American airborne units and 52nd (Lowland) Division between Paris and Orléans.

The tenth cancelled operation was 'Boxer', using the same force as for 'Transfigure' and planned for the second half of August, involving an assault on the town of Boulogne near which were V-1 launching sites. Following this in late August was 'Axehead', involving 1st Airborne Division and 1st Polish Independent Parachute Brigade in the capture of bridgeheads along the Seine to assist 21st Army Group to cross the river in its advance northwards through France. This was followed by 'Linnet I' which was planned for late August and involved 1st Airborne Corps, comprising 1st Airborne Division, 82nd US Airborne Divison, 101st US Airborne Division, 52nd (Lowland) Division, 1st Polish Independent Parachute Brigade, 878th Airborne Aviation Engineer Battalion and 2nd Airlanding Light Anti-Aircraft Battery RA. The corps' task would have been to seize and secure a bridgehead over the River Escaut near Tournai, in Belgium, cutting the roads to the north and west and thus severing the enemy's line of withdrawal.

'Linnet II', the thirteenth operation to be cancelled, involved the same force as for 'Linnet I'. 1st Airborne Corps would have been dropped and landed to block the gap between the Dutch town of Maastricht and that of Aachen, in Germany, to the east. This was followed by Operation 'Infatuate' which was designed to put pressure on the German 15th Army in the west of Holland and to expedite its retreat northwards over the Scheldt estuary.

The fifteenth, and final, cancelled operation was 'Comet', planned for 10 September. This called for 1st Airborne Division, with 1st Polish Independent Parachute Brigade under command, to seize bridges over the Maas, Waal and Lower Rhine at Grave, Nijmegen and Arnhem respectively. This was part of a thrust northwards by 21st Army Group through Holland, followed by a crossing of the Rhine and then an advance into Germany towards the Ruhr.

After so many cancellations, there was an understandable mood of cynicism within 1st Airborne Division by the time 'Market Garden' was announced. This is summed up best by the words of its commander, Major General Roy Urquhart:

> 'By September 1944 my division was battle-hungry to a degree which only those who have commanded large forces of trained soldiers can fully comprehend. In fact, there were already signs of that dangerous mixture of boredom and cynicism creeping into our daily lives. We were ready for anything
> ...'

This same enthusiasm to see action was felt at 1st Airborne Corps. Its commander, Lieutenant General 'Boy' Browning, had overseen the formation of Britain's airborne forces and had briefly commanded 1st Airborne Division before taking up the appointment of Major General Airborne Troops, a mainly administrative appointment. Although a gallant soldier who had seen action with his regiment, the Grenadier Guards, during the First World War, when he had been awarded the Distinguished Service Order at the age of 23, Browning had not led his airborne troops in action. Appointed to command 1st Airborne Corps when it was formed in June, he was understandably keen to lead his formation in battle and thus viewed the forthcoming operation with a degree of enthusiasm coupled with a sense of unease that his corps was perhaps being over-committed.

One person in Browning's headquarters who did not share the same degree of enthusiasm for the forthcoming operation was Major Brian Urquhart, the GSO 2 (Intelligence), who was receiving his intelligence for the forthcoming operation from HQ 21st Army Group as opposed to 1st Airborne Corps' parent formation headquarters at First Allied Airborne Army. Although he was ignorant of the existence of ULTRA, as a result of the severe limitations placed on the dissemination of its information, Urquhart did have access to the information from the Dutch Resistance and was worried by its reports of enemy armour in the area of Arnhem.

While he took them very seriously, others dismissed them on the grounds that the Resistance was known to have been penetrated by the Abwehr so their reports could not be relied upon as being genuine.

Urquhart's concern was such that he requested a low-level photographic reconnaissance mission to be flown over the Arnhem area by the RAF on 12 September. Three days later he received the results: the photographs clearly showed the presence of armoured vehicles in areas close to the locations of the planned dropping and landing zones. Urquhart immediately brought this information to the attention of Browning who made light of it. Urquhart was not deterred, however, and persisted in warning about this potential threat to the operation. He was rewarded by being removed from the headquarters and sent on sick leave. In a letter to the author, he commented nearly fifty years later:

'The photographs would already also have been sent to the higher headquarters, so I merely showed them to General Browning. As I recall it, General Browning's response was to show interest but generally to downplay the importance of the information. He would probably have had to do this anyway, as he had his orders and obviously did not wish to spread alarm and despondency. As far as I remember, the other people who would have received the evidence would be Colonel Gordon Walch, the GSO1, and my own intelligence staff, particularly Captain David Ballingall. Our contact with the intelligence staff of 1st Airborne Division would have been quite limited at this time, since they were packing up for the operation. I would not have communicated any doubts and fears I might have had to Major Hugh Maguire [GSO2 Intelligence, 1st Airborne Division] but would have merely passed on firm intelligence. My main job was to provide intelligence for my own commander, General Browning, whose responsibility it would be to pass on conclusions and any change in orders to 1st Airborne Division.'

Urquhart's was not the only warning voice raised within the airborne forces. At HQ First Allied Airborne Army, which received only a certain amount of ULTRA information, an RAF air intelligence officer, Wing Commander Asher Lee, was alarmed at what he discovered when studying evidence of enemy activity in the area of Arnhem. Lee had previously worked in Section AI3b of the Air Staff, a department which received a large volume of ULTRA material as part of its work in assembling and updating the Luftwaffe's order of battle. Subsequently posted to First Allied Airborne Army, Lee nevertheless had managed to retain access to another ULTRA source and a visit to it produced material which confirmed the presence of enemy armour in the vicinity of Arnhem. On informing Lieutenant General

Lewis Brereton, the American commander of First Allied Airborne Army, Lee was ordered to raise the matter with 21st Army Group. He visited Montgomery's headquarters but could find no one who would listen to him.

So it was against this background of disregard for detailed intelligence about enemy movements and dispositions in northern Holland, provided by ULTRA, RAF photographic reconnaissance and the Dutch Resistance, that the planning and preparations for Operation 'Market Garden' went ahead.

3
BEST LAID PLANS

'The Germans are very good soldiers and will recover quickly if allowed to do so. All risks are justified – I intend to get a bridgehead over the Rhine before they have time to recover.' — Field Marshal Bernard Montgomery.

On his return to his headquarters at Moor Park after his meeting with Dempsey on the afternoon of 10 September, Lieutenant General 'Boy' Browning travelled to HQ First Allied Airborne Army near Ascot, Berkshire, where he met its commander, Lieutenant General Lewis Brereton. That evening he held a conference at which he gave an outline briefing on Operation 'Market Garden' to the commanders and key staff officers of all the airborne formations involved in it.

The forces allotted to 1st Airborne Corps for the operation were 1st Airborne Division, 82nd US Airborne Division, 101st US Airborne Division, 52nd (Lowland) Division and 1st Polish Independent Parachute Brigade Group. In outline, these were allocated tasks in order of sequence as follows.

101st US Airborne Division would seize the bridges and crossings between Eindhoven and Grave.

82nd US Airborne Division would capture the two major bridges at Nijmegen and Grave, and would take and hold the high ground between Nijmegen and Groesbeek.

1st Airborne Division, with 1st Polish Independent Parachute Brigade under command, would capture the bridges at Arnhem and establish a bridgehead in preparation for a further advance northwards by Second British Army.

52nd (Lowland) Division, an airportable formation, would be in reserve and would be flown by transport aircraft to landing strips established north of Arnhem, when the situation permitted. These strips would be constructed by 878th Aviation Engineer Battalion which would be flown in by glider with 2nd Airlanding Light Anti-Aircraft Battery RA, the latter being charged with their defence. Operation of the strips would be the responsibility of the Airborne Forward Delivery Airfield Group, a joint Army-RAF unit.

While the airborne formations were carrying out their tasks, Second British Army, spearheaded by XXX Corps with VIII and XII Corps on its flanks in echelon, would break out of its bridgehead on the Meuse–Escaut

Canal and advance as rapidly as possible along the road through Valkenswaard to Eindhoven and thereafter through Zon, St. Oedenrode, Veghel, Uden, Grave, Nijmegen and Elst to Arnhem, linking up with the airborne forces along the way. Thereafter, it was to secure and dominate the country northwards to the Zuider Zee, cutting off the line of communications between Germany and its forces in the Low Countries. XXX Corps' flanks would be protected on the right by VIII Corps, which would capture the towns of Weert and Soerondonk, and secure as far north as Helmond, and on the left by XII Corps which would take Rethy, Arendonck and Turnhout before advancing to the River Maas. Responsibility for protection of the line of communication along the corridor was allotted to VIII Corps.

Montgomery's intention was that once all of this had been achieved, Second British Army would subsequently establish a line facing eastwards from Arnhem through Deventer to Zwolle with bridgeheads established over the River Ijssel. Thereafter, an advance would take place eastwards to the area of Rheine–Osnabruck–Hamm–Münster. From Hamm a strong thrust would thereafter be made along the eastern face of the Ruhr.

Montgomery's plan for a thrust into Germany via Arnhem was based on three factors: first, an advance from the north towards the Ruhr would outflank the northern end of the Siegfried Line; secondly, any thrust via Wesel, as favoured by Dempsey and others, would have meant that any airborne landings would have been exposed to a strong Luftwaffe presence and to the flak defences in the area of the Ruhr; thirdly, the information from London that England had just been subjected to the first attacks by V-2 missiles, far more devastating than the V-1, together with a request that the launching sites in Holland be captured and put out of action as soon as possible. This recent development had finally settled in Montgomery's mind the decision to advance towards Arnhem; his forces would be better placed to neutralize this latest threat more quickly than would have been the case if they had been advancing north-eastwards towards Wesel.

Those officers listening to Browning at his conference on the afternoon of 10 September were highly experienced in the planning and execution of airborne operations, but even they were taken aback, not only by the boldness of the plan and the size of the operation but also by the very limited time available to plan and prepare for it. Whereas the planning for the airborne operations in Normandy had taken months, the time allowed for 'Market Garden', which was on a far larger scale, was just seven days. The problems attendant on such hasty preparation were immense, and the consequent shortcomings in planning would later make themselves felt during the operation. The magnitude of the problems facing the staffs at all levels is best summed up by Geoffrey Powell in his book *The Devil's Birthday*:

'Although the British and the Poles had done a certain amount of groundwork when making their preparations for "Comet", decisions would now have to be taken, in a very short time, on such involved questions as the allotment of tasks to divisions, the allocation of transport aircraft, the choice of dropping zones for the paratroops and landing zones for the gliders, the choice of flight paths and the planning of air resupply. At the same time, arrangements had to be made with the various air forces, based both in Britain and on the Continent, for the preliminary bombing of targets, for photographic reconnaissance, for fighter protection for the long and vulnerable columns of troop-carrying aircraft and glider tugs, for flak suppression, and for fighter-bombers to give close support to the airborne troops once they were on the ground. Formation and unit commanders, from divisional generals to the lowliest squad or section corporals, had in turn to plan their part in the coming battle, a sequence that would culminate in every individual soldier knowing just what he had to do from the moment he touched down on mother earth.

'Some details, such as equipment loads and battle drills, were standardized, the former the subject of detailed loading-tables, but for all that the interlocking work at a multiplicity of levels was vast in scope and complicated in detail. Nor did it make matters any simpler that three allies and two fighting services were involved, and that the staff of 1st Allied Airborne Army had worked together for little more than a month. With some 35,000 troops to be briefed and then moved to the twenty-four take-off airfields scattered between Lincolnshire and Dorset, Brereton was justified in making it clear to his senior commanders at the initial conference on 10th September that any decisions arrived at must stand.'

On the following day, 11 September, a conference was held at HQ 9th US Troop Carrier Command to commence the planning of the air side of the operation. The first question, to be resolved by Brereton himself, was whether the landings should take place by night or in daylight. The absence of a moon during the week beginning 17 September meant that large-scale landings at night could be discounted – moreover, previous large-scale airborne operations carried out at night, for example in Normandy, had resulted in navigational errors and dispersal of units over wide areas. Brereton decided that the landings would be made in daylight.

The next most pressing problem was the allocation of aircraft. A total of 35,000 men would have to be dropped or landed in the three areas covered by the operation. However, there were only sufficient aircraft to carry 16,500 men. The total aircraft requirement for 1st Airborne Corps, comprising three and a half divisions, was 3,790: 2,495 aircraft to carry paratroops and 1,295 to tow gliders. Unfortunately, the combined resources of 9th US Troop Carrier Command together with those of 38 and 46 Groups RAF were insufficient to meet this requirement. Moreover, in order to ensure that the southernmost objectives were seized successfully, the greater number of aircraft had to be allotted on the first day to 101st and 82nd US Airborne Divisions which were both larger than 1st Airborne Division and whose landings would take place in the areas covering Eindhoven–Grave and Grave–Nijmegen respectively. The allocation of aircraft was made as follows:

HQ 1st Airborne Corps	38 glider tugs (RAF)
101st US Airborne Division	424 para a/c, 70 glider tugs (USAAF)
82nd US Airborne Division	482 para a/c, 50 glider tugs (USAAF)
1st Airborne Division	161 para a/c (USAAF), 320 glider tugs (RAF)

In order that the greater part of 1st Airborne Corps could be dropped or landed on the first day, it was suggested that two lifts would have to be made. Air Vice Marshal Leslie Hollingshurst, who commanded 38 Group RAF and was responsible for co-ordinating its operations with those of its sister formation 46 Group RAF, was prepared to allow his aircraft to make two sorties on the first day, the first taking off before dawn. But Major General Paul Williams, the commander of 9th US Troop Carrier Command, would not agree on the grounds of aircrew fatigue and aircraft maintenance. He was supported by Brereton who was himself an airman, having previously commanded 9th US Air Force, but who had no experience of airborne operations. Williams's reasoning was also partly based on the fact that his command had recently been doubled in number of aircraft but had not received any reinforcements in ground crew. Furthermore, the USAAF crews were not as experienced in night flying as their RAF counterparts. Williams, who would be co-ordinating the air transport aspects of the operation, was popular with the British and American airborne forces for his normally very co-operative attitude in supporting them. Unfortunately, their high regard for him prevented them on this occasion from taking issue with him over what was a totally wrong decision on his part, and one which would prove fatal.

The one person who should have objected strongly was Browning because Williams's decision meant that, like the two American airborne formations, 1st Airborne Division would have to be flown in three lifts over three consecutive days – this should have been regarded as unacceptable, given that the division was to be dropped and landed at the furthermost point from Second British Army and the vital element of surprise would be lost on the first day. But Browning had recently been at loggerheads with

Brereton, whom he disliked and regarded as weak, over one of the recently cancelled airborne operations, 'Linnett II', in which airborne forces were to be landed between Aachen and Maastricht. Browning had objected to the fact that insufficient time had been allowed for maps of an adequate scale to be issued down to sub-unit level so that all personnel could be properly briefed. Brereton responded by telling Browning that he intended to replace him and ordered Major General Matthew Ridgway, commander of XVIII US Airborne Corps, to prepare to take over command of the operation from Browning.

Browning had riposted immediately by submitting his resignation as Deputy Commander of First Allied Airborne Army. The dispute had been resolved, however, the operation was cancelled, and Browning had withdrawn his resignation. Nevertheless, his already fragile relationship with Brereton had deteriorated further and he obviously felt that he was in no position to become involved in another confrontation with his superior and thus did not object to Williams's decision.

Objection was raised at higher level. When Montgomery read the copy of the 1st Airborne Corps operational plan sent to him, he immediately dispatched Brigadier David Belchem, his Acting Chief of Staff, to HQ First Allied Airborne Army to take up the matter with Brereton and to persuade him to permit modifications to the air transport plan so that 1st Airborne Division could be carried in two lifts at the most. But Brereton was adhering rigidly to his previous edict of no changes once decisions had been made. While his insistence on abiding by Williams decision is understandable, given the late stage at which Montgomery voiced his objection and that the time factor was crucial, it does not alter the fact that the decision was wrong and would have disastrous consequences. Another person who was far from happy was the commander of 1st Airborne Division, Major General Roy Urquhart. He was dissatisfied with the number of aircraft allocated to him and approached Browning with a request for 40 more, pointing out that the two American divisions had been allocated more than his own. Browning explained that the allocation had been made on the basis that priority on the first day had to be given primarily to 101st US Airborne Division and then to the 82nd: it was essential that the southernmost objectives be secured to ensure that XXX Corps could begin its advance to Arnhem after breaking out of the bridgehead.

The major risks of flying 1st Airborne Division into the Arnhem area in three lifts were obvious: not only would those troops landed on the first day have to take and hold the division's main objective, the road bridge at Arnhem, but they would also have to secure and protect the dropping and landing zones until the arrival of the remainder of the division over the next two days. This would prevent the use of a large proportion of them in taking and securing the division's objectives on the first day. Furthermore, surprise, the need for which was emphasized very heavily by Brereton, would be lost after the first day and the enemy would be prepared for further landings: any strong counter-attack on the leading elements of the division could spell disaster for the operation.

Next day, 11 September, Urquhart's problems were yet further compounded. During a second conference, the locations of the dropping and landing zones were discussed. Urquhart, correctly following the principle that airborne troops should be dropped or landed as near as possible to their objectives, wished to land his forces on both sides of the Lower Rhine and as near as possible to the Arnhem bridge. However, he encountered strong opposition from the commander of 38 Group RAF, Air Vice Marshal Leslie Hollingshurst, on the grounds that there were heavy anti-aircraft defences in the area of Arnhem and around the bridge – these had apparently been encountered previously by RAF bombers en route to the Ruhr on night bombing missions. In addition, Hollingshurst maintained that RAF tug aircraft, turning north after casting off their gliders, would encounter heavy flak over the Luftwaffe base at Deelen, seven miles north of Arnhem; if they turned south there was a danger of their becoming mixed up with aircraft dropping 82nd US Airborne Division over the Nijmegen area.

It now appears that Hollingshurst was incorrect with regard to the flak defences at Deelen. On 3 September, RAF bombers had carried out a raid on the base and had rendered it temporarily unusable; all aircraft had been evacuated and the anti-aircraft guns had been removed shortly afterwards. This was confirmed by air photographic reconnaissance carried out by No. 541 Squadron RAF on 6 September. For some reason, this information apparently was not known either to 38 Group RAF or to Hollingshurst.

Urquhart had also considered landing a glider-borne coup de main force near the bridge, with the intention of emulating 6th Airborne Division's successful capture of Pegasus Bridge over the River Orne at Benouville, in Normandy, on the night of 5/6 June. His idea had the support of Colonel George Chatterton, Commander Glider Pilots, but Browning rejected it, as Chatterton related forty years later:

> 'I went to see General Browning and suggested to him that we were landing too far away but he said that it was out of our hands. It was an RAF decision because they said that the bridge was so well defended by anti-aircraft guns that they wished to keep their tugs away from it. I nevertheless suggested that my pilots could land their gliders near the bridge and although there would be more casualties on landing due to the size and unevenness of the enclosures, it would surely be preferable to landing miles away.

'When General Browning said that no doubt there would be more tugs shot down this way, I suggested that this could be avoided by a remote release, so allowing the tugs to turn back for home well before the bridge. He replied, "George, it's too late. It has all been decided."'

Chatterton's reference to the 'size and unevenness of the enclosures' was based on RAF intelligence reports which stated that the terrain to the south of the bridge was unsuitable for either parachutists or gliders, consisting of low-lying swampy polderland interlaced with dikes. This view was supported by the Dutch Resistance which had supplied detailed descriptions of the area. The idea of a glider-borne coup de main force was discarded.

The RAF did agree to the dropping of elements of the third lift south of the river near the bridge because it was assumed that all flak defences would have been neutralized by then. So it seems that their refusal to drop elements of the division there beforehand was based entirely on the intelligence concerning the flak defences and that the reports of unsuitable terrain counted for little.

Initially, Urquhart was inclined to reject the RAF's refusal to accept the areas around the bridge and to the south of the river as dropping and landing zones, and in the event their fears about the flak defences and the unsuitability of the terrain south of the river proved to be unfounded, but unfortunately the RAF could not be overruled because they were responsible for the air aspects of the operation.

Having been denied the opportunity of dropping and landing his division near its objectives, and bearing in mind the experiences of 6th Airborne Division in Normandy when its units found themselves scattered over wide areas, Urquhart accepted the next best alternative, which was to land his forces together so that they could form up as quickly as possible. For this reason he chose the area to the west and north-west of Arnhem where the terrain was flat with open areas screened by woodland.

Urquhart eventually selected five dropping and landing zones: two (LZs 'L' and 'S') to the north of the railway line running between Arnhem and Utrecht; one (DZ 'Y') on Ginkels Heath; and two (DZ and LZ 'X' and LZ 'Z') on Renkum Heath, south of the railway line. The area chosen was far from ideal, being some eight miles from the Arnhem bridge. There was nothing now to be gained from surprise and there was the danger that the second lift would by then be prevented from linking up with the leading elements of the division holding the objective. Moreover, as already mentioned, some of the units of 1st Airlanding Brigade in the first lift would have to remain on the dropping and landing zones to hold them until the remainder of the division had landed, leaving fewer to take and secure the bridge and other objectives. But the terrain was favourable for use by para-troops and gliders.

In addition to the five main dropping and landing zones, a sixth (DZ 'K') was selected south of the town for use by 1st Polish Independent Parachute Brigade Group which would be dropped by USAAF aircraft on the morning of the third day, flak defences presumably having been silenced by then. Finally, a supply dropping point (SDP 'V') was located on the north-western outskirts of Arnhem, east of LZ 'L', which would be within the planned divisional perimeter.

One of Urquhart's major concerns was the lack of information concerning enemy forces in the area. His intelligence staff were, in his own words, 'scratching around for morsels of information'. The small amount available filtered down from HQ Second British Army and HQ 1st Airborne Corps. In the light of the intelligence now known to have been available to HQ 21st Army Group, First Allied Airborne Army and 1st Airborne Corps from ULTRA, the Dutch Resistance and RAF photographic reconnaissance, the lack of information passed on to HQ 1st Airborne Division seems scarcely credible. In the opinion of Urquhart, and others in his division, there seemed to be an increasing disregard of the enemy on the part of those responsible for the planning of operations. In his book *Arnhem*, Urquhart states:

'Then came "Comet". In this operation we were to seize the three river crossings in The Netherlands along the projected axis of 2nd Army – the Maas, the Waal and the Neder Rhine. It was certainly taking a chance because of the wide dispersal involved and also because of our ignorance of German movements on the ground in the area. We were all becoming increasingly aware of a certain naïvety in upper level planning of airborne operations, particularly at the HQ of 1st Allied Airborne Army. I recall one conference during the preparations for "Comet", when both Shan Hackett and General Sosabowski, commanding the Polish brigade which was under my command for the operation, reacted strongly. Sosabowski, who had been a professor at Warsaw War Academy, interrupted several times as I explained the plan which had come down to us. "But the Germans, General ... the Germans!"More and more we saw that German reactions had not been taken into account at all.

'Sosabowski visualised them clearly enough, and so determined was he to come to grips on a footing at least equal to that held by an enemy which had overrun and ravaged his own country, that his protestations were not born of despair so much as rage that a victory might be denied us because of a lack of foresight in planning.'

Brigadier John Hackett also had very firm views on those responsible for planning these operations, as he later made clear:

'I have never forgotten the conference on Cottesmore Airfield when Roy Urquhart gave my very good friend Sosabowski and me our orders for "Comet". We had both fought Germans and knew all about that. Apparently the airborne planners did not. Their plans to put down an airborne division were impeccable. What would happen after that was beyond them. They were to me like cooks who prepare a superb dish and then add salt and pepper to taste. They prepared a superb deployment and then added a few Germans. I shall always recall the deep disbelief in Sosabowski's voice: "But the Germans, General, the Germans ...". Happily this ghastly plan was, like the earlier ones, cancelled at the last moment.'

Urquhart himself, who had seen a considerable amount of action in North Africa and Sicily as GSO1 51st Highland Division and as Commander 231st Independent Infantry Brigade Group during 1942-3, had a healthy respect for the enemy:

'I had no illusions about the enemy folding up at the first blow. I counted on the likelihood that his retaliation would get fiercer by the hour. He would be steadily reinforced whereas we would not be at full strength until well into the third day. He would also have whatever advantages were going in the way of heavy weapons ...'

Urquhart decided to land 1st Parachute Brigade, the major part of 1st Airlanding Brigade, some divisional troops and his own tactical headquarters on the first day. 4th Parachute Brigade, together with the remainder of 1st Airlanding Brigade, the glider-borne element of 1st Polish Independent Parachute Brigade Group and remaining divisional troops would be dropped and landed on the second day. The main element of 1st Polish Independent Parachute Brigade Group would complete the division's order of battle on the ground when it was dropped south of the river on the third day.

Urquhart gave his orders for the operation on the afternoon of 12 September. Those present included his four brigade commanders, accompanied by their brigade majors, the commanding officers of the division's artillery and engineer units, and the respective heads of its medical, transport and ordnance services.

In outline, his plan was as follows:

On the morning of 17 September, pathfinders of 21st Independent Parachute Company, commanded by Major B. A. 'Boy' Wilson, would land and mark out the three dropping and landing zones to be used in the first lift. They would be followed by the major part of 1st Airlanding Brigade, commanded by Brigadier Philip 'Pip' Hicks, which would secure and hold the dropping and landing zones, and Brigadier Gerald Lathbury's 1st Parachute Brigade which was to make its way with all speed to Arnhem where it would capture the railway bridge south of Oosterbeek, the road bridge in Arnhem itself and a pontoon bridge half a mile to the west. Accompanying the two brigades in the first lift would be 1st Airborne Reconnaissance Squadron, commanded by Major Freddie Gough, which would make a dash in its armed jeeps for the road bridge which it would seize and hold until the arrival of 1st Parachute Brigade.

In addition to the two brigades and the reconnaissance squadron, the first lift would also include Tactical HQ 1st Airborne Division, 1st Airlanding Light Regiment RA (less one battery), 1st Airlanding Anti-Tank Battery RA, 1st Parachute Squadron RE, 9th Field Company RE, 16th Parachute Field Ambulance and 181st Parachute Field Ambulance.

2nd Parachute Battalion, under Lieutenant Colonel Johnny Frost, would move into Arnhem via Heelsum and the southern edge of Oosterbeek, making its way along the northern bank of the lower Rhine. On reaching the bridge, where it would relieve 1st Airborne Reconnaissance Squadron, the battalion would take up positions on both banks. 3rd Parachute Battalion, commanded by Lieutenant Colonel Tony Fitch, would move through Arnhem via Heelsum and Oosterbeek and approach the bridge from the north, taking up positions on its north-eastern approach. Lieutenant Colonel David Dobie's 1st Parachute Battalion would initially be in reserve, but thereafter would move to the high ground immediately north of the town.

On the morning of the second day, 18 September, 4th Parachute Brigade would land together with a battery of 1st Airlanding Light Regiment RA, 4th Parachute Squadron RE, 133rd Parachute Field Ambulance, the rest of 1st Airlanding Brigade, 2nd Airlanding Anti-Tank Battery RA and those divisional troops that had not landed with the first lift on the first day. Its task would be to establish a northern defensive sector around the bridgehead, linking up with 1st Parachute Battalion. 1st Airlanding Brigade, meanwhile, would move into the town and establish the western sector of the bridgehead.

On its arrival on the morning of the third day, 1st Polish Independent Parachute Brigade, after landing on DZ 'K' just south of the road bridge, would cross over and deploy into the eastern suburbs of the town. This would result in the complete establishment of the bridgehead on the northern side of the river, awaiting arrival of Second British from the south.

The commander of the Polish brigade, Major General Stanislaw Sosabowski, had severe misgivings about Urquhart's plan. Not only was he unhappy about the apparent underestimation of the enemy, but he was also very disturbed about the distance between the dropping zones and the division's objectives. Nor was he enthusiastic about his glider-borne element landing north of the river on the second day when the rest of the brigade would be dropped south of the river on the third day. If the bridge had not been taken by 1st Parachute Brigade by that time, he would be separated from all his heavy weapons, first line ammunition resupply and vehicles. While Urquhart gave his orders, however, Sosabowski kept his fears and doubts to himself as he felt little would be accomplished by giving vent to them.

Meanwhile, Major General Maxwell Taylor's 101st US Airborne Division would land and capture the bridges and crossings between Eindhoven and Veghel. Its objectives consisted of two canal crossing points and nine road and railway bridges along the 15-mile stretch of road in its sector. Taylor's plan called for 502nd and 506th Parachute Infantry Regiments to land in the centre between Eindhoven and Veghel while 501st Parachute Infantry Regiment would be dropped on two DZs a few hundred yards north and west of Veghel. Its task would be to capture four of the bridges and one of the canal crossings, at Veghel itself, which spanned the River Aa and the Zuid Willems Vaart Canal.

Brigadier General James Gavin's 82nd US Airborne Division had an equally onerous task. In addition to being dropped and landed four miles from its objectives and taking the bridge over the Maas at Grave, as well as at least one of the railway bridges over the Maas–Waal Canal, the division was to seize the bridge which crossed the River Waal at Nijmegen, and secure and hold the Groesbeek Heights – the high ground between Nijmegen and Groesbeek which dominated the area. 505th and 508th Parachute Infantry Regiments, accompanied by General Gavin's headquarters, would land in two drops a mile and a half from the Groesbeek Heights and about four miles south-west of Nijmegen. 504th Parachute Infantry Regiment would be dropped on the western side of the heights between the Maas and the Maas–Waal Canal, a mile from the eastern end of the bridge at Grave and two miles from the canal bridges. A company of the 504th would also be dropped a mile from the western end of the Grave bridge, enabling the regiment to attack it from both sides of the river.

Given the number of objectives that had to be seized and held, both American commanders had decided that all their parachute infantry would be dropped or landed on the first day, which limited the support elements that could accompany them in the first lift. In the case of 82nd US Airborne Division, these would comprise 376th Parachute Field Artillery Battalion, Battery 'A' 80th Airborne Anti-Aircraft Battalion and three companies of 307th Airborne Engineer Battalion. In order to provide maximum mobility by bringing in as many jeeps and trailers as possible by glider, Major General Maxwell Taylor had decided that the support elements accompanying the three parachute infantry regiments of 101st US Airborne Division would be limited to two companies of 326th Airborne Engineer Battalion. Both divisions' glider-borne infantry regiments would arrive with the artillery, anti-tank units, engineers and transport on the second and third days of the operation.

The success of 'Market Garden' depended on the ability of Lieutenant General Brian Horrocks' XXX Corps to punch its way through the German defences and thrust its way up the main road to Arnhem to link up with 1st Airborne Division before the enemy had time to react and launch a strong counter-attack. Speed was absolutely essential, as was emphasized more than once to Horrocks by Montgomery when the latter summoned him for a briefing on 12 September.

The main problem facing XXX Corps was the flat, low-lying terrain over which it would have to advance. To the north and on the flanks of its bridgehead over the Meuse–Escaut Canal the land was heavily wooded and very marshy, being intersected by dikes, canals and large rivers which made it almost impossible for armour to move off the few roads which traversed the area. It was assumed that any intact bridges would have been prepared for demolition. Moreover, the bridgehead itself was small and served only by two bridges. The combination of adverse terrain and the daily arrival of German reinforcements strengthening the enemy presence meant that the breakout itself would not be an easy task. Horrocks realized that a successful breakout would be heavily reliant on a very heavy artillery concentration and effective close air support.

The route for the advance was the main road which stretched from the canal via Valkenswaard to Eindhoven and then on to Zon, St. Oedenrode, Uden, Grave, Nijmegen and Arnhem. The road varied in width between 20 and 30 feet, increasing to 40 near Arnhem, and was of tarmac or concrete construction except on stretches between Nijmegen and Arnhem where it was composed of rolled cinders. Between Eindhoven and Grave it was in very bad condition, but the final stretch leading to Arnhem was new, as was the bridge over which it crossed the Lower Rhine, and part of it was still under construction. It was considered to be capable of taking tracked vehicles, although those would somehow have to bypass two fly-over bridges.

In several areas, including the initial stage to be covered in the breakout, the road was embanked between four and six feet above the level of the surrounding terrain and was flanked by deep ditches which would make make deployment off it impossible: vehicles travelling along it would be clearly silhouetted to make easy targets for anti-tank guns. Furthermore, almost the entire stretch of the road between Grave and Nijmegen was dominated by the high ground of the Groesbeek Heights south and east of Nijmegen.

57

BEST LAID PLANS
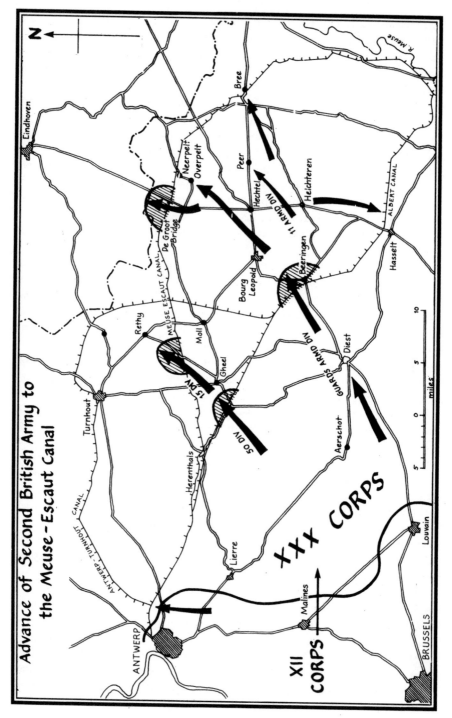
Advance of Second British Army to the Meuse-Escaut Canal

Restriction to the road meant that the breakout and subsequent advance would be confined to a very narrow front. Along this route, which would be very vulnerable to blocking or cutting by the enemy, would have to travel the 20,000 armoured and soft-skinned vehicles of XXX Corps. Certain sections were recognized as being potential bottlenecks, such as the bridge over the Wilhelmina Canal which could take single-line traffic only; efficient traffic control and march discipline would be essential if the speed of advance were to be maintained. Moreover, Horrocks had to be able to call forward units that might be required from an operational viewpoint once the breakthrough had taken place, but the very nature of the operation militated against a fixed order of march so a meticulous order of assembly in the corps concentration area and an efficient organization to get units forward was necessary. With only five days to go before the start of 'Market Garden', the time available for concentration of the corps was very short.

The number of water obstacles in the path of the advance meant that likely engineer tasks had to be accorded a high priority in XXX Corps' planning. In addition to the four major obstacles of the Maas, the Maas–Waal Canal, the Waal and the Lower Rhine, there were two others: the Wilhelmina Canal and the Zuid Willems Vaart Canal. The Maas and the Waal were between 800 and 850 feet in width; the Lower Rhine normally measured 300 feet, although this could increase to about 1,640 feet in winter. The approaches to the Maas were via flat fields and heaths offering little cover; such woods as there were seldom reached to within 550 yards of the river. The banks of the Waal – the most important shipping channel of the Rhine via which ships could reach the estuary ports of Holland – and those of the Lower Rhine were dyked on each side. In the case of the latter, there was little cover on either bank east or west of Arnhem.

Despite the fact that the airborne forces were tasked with capturing the bridges intact, XXX Corps' engineer planning had to be based on assuming the worst case for each obstacle: that it would have to be bridged. Moreover, in the event of bridges having been destroyed, it was possible that bridging would have to be carried out simultaneously on more than one obstacle, in which case bridging equipment would have to be ferried forward on rafts.

To cope with such a commitment, a large force of some 9,000 engineers was assembled at Bourg Leopold under the Corps Commander Royal Engineers of XXX Corps. In addition to XXX Corps' own sappers and those of its three divisions, these included nine formations of Army Troop and GHQ Troop engineers. Bridging equipment mounted on vehicles included virtually the whole of 21st Army Group's Bridge Column under the command of Montgomery's Commander Royal Army Service Corps: this was sufficient to provide bridging over the initial obstacles, bridges and rafts

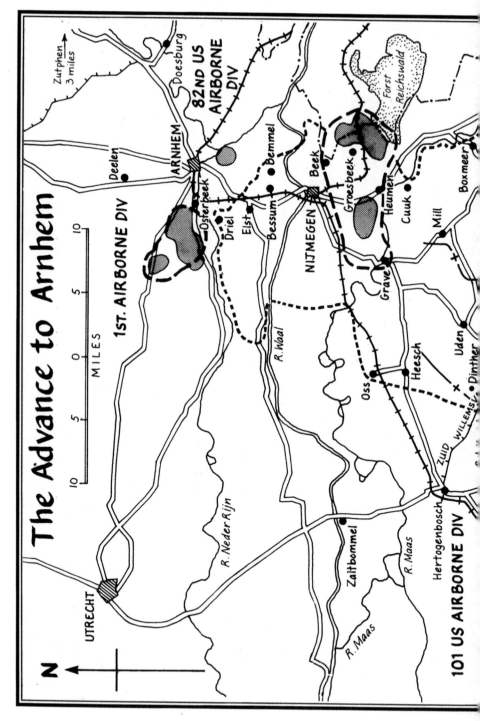

The Advance to Arnhem

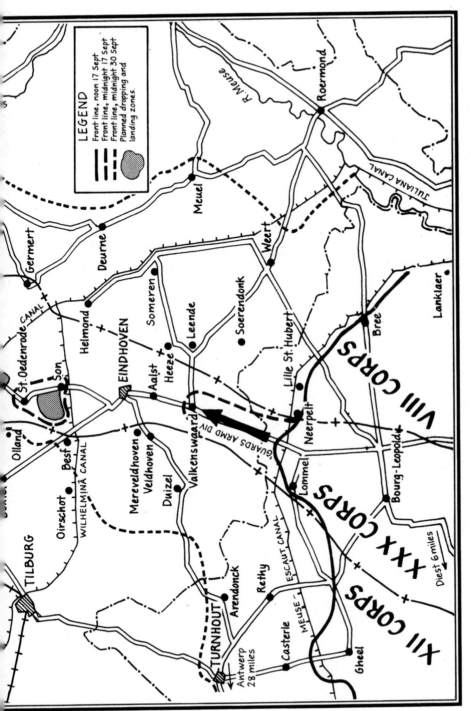

over the Maas–Waal Canal, close support rafts over the Waal and Lower Rhine, and a Class 9 bridge over the latter. A further 2,000 truckloads of bridging equipment were dumped in the concentration area at Bourg Leopold, sufficient for the provision of three pontoon bridges over each major obstacle and to refill all bridging vehicles.

Horrocks' outline plan was for the Guards Armoured Division, commanded by Major General Allan Adair, to lead the breakout, advancing behind a rolling artillery barrage laid down by six field and three medium regiments. Further artillery support would be forthcoming from three more field regiments, a heavy battery, a heavy anti-aircraft regiment firing airburst shells, and from Dutch and Belgian artillery, which would fire concentrations at specified times during the breakout.

Close air support would be provided by RAF rocket-firing Typhoon fighter-bombers of 83 Group RAF. One squadron of aircraft would strafe and rocket areas of likely enemy locations on either side of the road in the path of the advance every five minutes for a period of thirty-five minutes. These would be followed by a 'cab rank' of Typhoons which would fly above the leading squadrons of tanks, to engage targets on the ground. All the aircraft would be controlled from the ground by an RAF forward controller, travelling in a vehicle equipped with VHF radios, who would be in contact with the pilots. This meant that close air support was expected to be rapidly available when required by the leading troops on the ground.

Another RAF vehicle would travel alongside that of the corps commander, to supply information from RAF tactical reconnaissance aircraft, advising on the progress of the airborne landings. This vehicle would also be in radio contact with other reconnaissance aircraft covering the area. More air support would come from 83 Group RAF in the form of fighter cover tasked with engaging any enemy aircraft that might make an appearance.

The Guards Armoured Division was to advance to Eindhoven where it would link up with units of 101st US Airborne Division which would be responsible for establishing, securing and protecting a 'corridor' stretching to Grave. At that point the Guards would meet up with 82nd US Airborne Division and advance down its 'corridor', pushing on to Nijmegen and then on to Arnhem where they would link up with 1st Airborne Division. In the event of the bridges at Grave, Nijmegen or Arnhem being destroyed, the division's task was to deploy to the flanks on the south bank of the river concerned and support subsequent assault crossing and bridging operations. This latter task included clearing the area on either side of the bridge site and, if possible, securing a small bridgehead. On reaching Arnhem, the division would advance through the town and bypass Apeldoorn which lay to the north, thereafter securing and dominating the area stretching from east of Apeldoorn to Nunspeet.

Behind the Guards Armoured Division would be 43rd (Wessex) Infantry Division, commanded by Major General Ivo Thomas, which had undergone extensive training in assault crossing and bridging operations in England prior to the invasion of Normandy. If the bridges over any of the three major water obstacles were found to have been blown, the division would be required to put its expertise to good effect. On reaching Arnhem, it was to secure the area from Apeldoorn due south along high ground to a point where it would link up with the northernmost elements of 1st Airborne Division. Thereafter it would send troops to secure crossing points over the River Ijssel at Deventer and Zutphen.

The reserve formation in XXX Corps, 50th (Northumbrian) Infantry Division under Major General D. A. H. Graham, was holding the bridgehead over the Meuse–Escaut Canal and would continue to do so while sending units to secure a crossing over the River Ijssel at Doesburg. Thereafter, when ordered forward, it would advance to Arnhem and pass through to secure the high ground to the north of the town where it would relieve 43rd Infantry Division of part of its area of responsibility and maintain contact with 1st Airborne Division.

So the stage was set for the largest airborne operation yet to be carried out by the Allies. There were mixed feelings among those in 1st Airborne Division, many of whom fully expected 'Market Garden' to become the sixteenth operation to be cancelled: boredom, but also an overwhelming desire to get into action before the war ended, as summed up by Major General Roy Urquhart:

'By the time we went on Market Garden we couldn't have cared less. I mean I really shouldn't admit that, but we really couldn't ... we became callous. Every operation was planned to the best of our ability in every way. But we got so bored, and the troops were more bored than we were ... We had approached the state of mind when we weren't thinking as hard about the risks as we possibly had done earlier.'

Some of those with previous experience of fighting the Germans elsewhere, however, had few illusions about the difficulties that would face them after landing at Arnhem. Brigadier John 'Shan' Hackett, the commander of 4th Parachute Brigade, who had seen a considerable amount of action in the Middle East and Italy, having given his final orders to his staff and the COs of his three battalions, and other key personnel, told them:

'You can now forget all that. Your hardest and worst casualties will not be in defending the northern sector of the Arnhem perimeter, but in trying to get there!'

4
INTO BATTLE

'Intelligence told us we had nothing to worry about. There was no armour in the area and only second-rate line-of- communications troops and Luftwaffe personnel – a piece of cake in fact.' — Private James Sims, 2nd Para Bn.

There was fog over southern England at dawn on Sunday 17 September, but it had lifted by 0900 hours. Three-quarters of an hour later the first aircraft, carrying the leading elements of all three airborne divisions, took off from eight RAF and fourteen USAAF airfields in Oxfordshire, Gloucestershire, Dorsetshire and Lincolnshire, en route for Holland.

The flight plan was based on two large groups of aircraft following separate routes via rendezvous and turning-points marked by Eureka radio beacons and signalling lamps flashing coded signals. Those aircraft carrying 1st Airborne Division, 82nd US Airborne Division and HQ 1st Airborne Corps flew to initial rendezvous points over the towns of March in Cambridgeshire and Hatfield in Hertfordshire, before flying to a second rendezvous point over Aldeburgh on the coast of Suffolk. Thereafter, they flew across the North Sea, guided by Eureka beacons installed on ships at sea, via the Dutch island of Schouwen and then on to an interception point over the town of Boxtel. From there the aircraft carrying 82nd US Airborne Division turned in the direction of the dropping and landing zones near Nijmegen, while those transporting 1st Airborne Division headed for Arnhem.

The aircraft carrying 101st US Airborne Division flew via a more southern route. The initial rendezvous point was over Hatfield, followed by two more over North Fenland and North Foreland, after which the route took the aircraft eastwards over the Channel to Gheel, in Belgium, before they turned north-east towards Eindhoven.

Protection for the vast armada of transport aircraft, tugs and gliders was provided by squadrons of Spitfires, Tempests and Mosquitoes of the RAF's Air Defence of Great Britain, and by Thunderbolts, Lightnings and Mustangs of the 9th US Air Force. At the same time, aircraft of the RAF's 2nd Tactical Air Force carried out armed reconnaissance tasks in the areas of the dropping and landing zones.

During the night of 16/17 September, some 1,400 Allied bombers had carried out raids on flak defences, troop positions and barracks in all

Above: General Dwight Eisenhower with General Montgomery at the latter's headquarters on 28 August 1944, just before Montgomery's promotion to Field Marshal. Eisenhower's vacillation and attempts at compromise led to Operation 'Market Garden' being launched too late. (Photo: Imperial War Museum)

Above: General Bernard Montgomery with Generals George Patton and Omar Bradley. The poor relationship and strong rivalry between these three senior Allied commanders was to have an adverse effect on Operation 'Market Garden'. (Photo: Imperial War Museum)

Top right: Field Marshal Montgomery with some of his senior commanders. Left to right: Maj Gen Allan Adair (GOC Gds Armd Div), FM Montgomery, Lt Gen Sir Brian Horrocks (Comd XXX Corps) and Maj Gen 'Pip' Roberts (GOC 11th Armd Div). (Photo: Imperial War Museum)

Right: General Eisenhower with Lt Gen Sir Miles Dempsey, Commander Second British Army, and Lt Gen Neil Ritchie, Commander XII Corps. (Photo: Imperial War Museum)

Above: Lt Gen 'Boy' Browning, Commander 1st Airborne Corps. The deployment of his headquarters on the first day resulted in the use of thirty-eight Horsa gliders which could otherwise have flown in more of 1st Airborne Division's infantry or an anti-tank unit on the first day. (Photo: Imperial War Museum)

Top right: A 'stick' of 101st US Airborne Division waiting to board its C-47. Unlike their British counterparts, American paratroops were equipped with a reserve parachute. (Photo: US Army)

Right: Men of 82nd US Airborne Division emplaning aboard a C-47 prior to take-off on 17 September. (Photo: Imperial War Museum)

Top left: Elements of 1st Parachute Brigade land among the gliders on 17 September. (Photo: Imperial War Museum)

Bottom left: C-47s of 9th US Troop Carrier command dropping elements of 82nd US Airborne Division in the area of Grave. Waco gliders lie abandoned on the landing zone. (Photo: Imperial War Museum)

Above: An aerial view of the Nijmegen road and railway bridges, two of the objectives of 82nd US Airborne Division. (Photo: Imperial War Museum)

Above and opposite page: Two aerial photographs of Deelen airfield taken by a reconnaissance aircraft of 541 Squadron RAF on 6 September, showing the absence of anti-aircraft guns, which were withdrawn after the bombing of the airfield by the RAF three days previously. (Photo: Crown copyright)

Right: The bridge over the Maas at Grave, one of 82nd US Airborne Division's objectives, which was captured on 18 September. (Photo: Imperial War Museum)

Left: A group of prisoners captured shortly after the landings by 1st Airborne Division west of Arnhem on 17 September. (Photo: Imperial War Museum)

Bottom left: Local people providing refreshment to members of 1st Parachute Brigade shortly after the landings on DZ 'X' on Renkum Heath on the first day. Those seen here are believed to be, left to right: Pte Kinsey (21 Indep Para Coy), Sgt Tennuci (16 Para Fd Amb) and Sgt Travis (21 Indep Para Coy). The Dutch couple are Mijnheer and Mevrouw Pfennengs. (Photo: Imperial War Museum)

Below: Members of 'C' Troop 1st Airborne Reconnaissance Squadron take up positions on the crossroads at Wolfheze on 17 September. (Photo: Imperial War Museum)

Above: Infantry and 6-pounder anti-tank guns of 2nd Battalion The South Staffordshire Regiment head towards Arnhem along the Urechtseweg. (Photo: Imperial War Museum)

Opposite page, top: A group of glider pilots moving through Oosterbeek on 17 September. (Photo: Airborne Forces Museum)

Right: The road bridge at Arnhem after the attempt by the reconnaissance unit of 9th SS Panzer Division to cross it on the morning of 18 September. (Photo: Imperial War Museum)

Opposite page, top: Sturmgeschutz III self-propelled guns of 9th SS Panzer Division at the intersection of the Utrechtseweg and Oranjestraat in Arnhem on 19 September. (Photo: Airborne Forces Museum)

Above: A 6-pounder anti-tank gun of 1st Battalion The Border Regiment in action, engaging an enemy self-propelled gun at a range of eighty yards. (Photo: Imperial War Museum)

Left: Members of 1st Parachute Battalion in a fire trench. (Photo: Imperial War Museum)

Above: A Vickers machine-gun crew engages enemy snipers in a house seen in the background. (Photo: Imperial War Museum)

Below: A patrol moving through a ruined house in Oosterbeek. (Photo: Imperial War Museum)

three objective areas. In one sortie alone, 282 Lancasters and Mosquitoes attacked a major flak position and four Luftwaffe airfields, one of which was a base for the recently introduced Messerschmitt Me 262 jet fighter, and rendered them unusable. Meanwhile, USAAF B-17 bombers attacked another airfield, also causing extensive damage. Early on the morning of 17 September, further raids were carried out by bombers of the 8th US Air Force: 821 heavily escorted B-17s attacked a total of 117 flak positions, dropping 3,139 tons of bombs, while RAF Lancasters and Mosquitoes attacked three coastal flak positions in the area of Walcheren Island and the Scheldt estuary. Meanwhile, RAF aircraft of 2nd Tactical Air Force attacked barracks at Nijmegen, Arnhem, Cleve and Ede. Further attacks on flak positions were carried out by a large number of fighters of the 9th US Air Force.

As the two groups of transport aircraft and glider combinations formed up over their rendezvous points, the pathfinders of the three airborne divisions were already en route for Holland and their respective dropping and landing zones. Twelve Stirling bombers carried six officers and 180 men of 1st Airborne Division's pathfinder unit, 21st Independent Parachute Company, while six C-47s of 9th US Troop Carrier Command bore the pathfinders of 82nd and 101st US Airborne Divisions. These would jump twenty minutes before the arrival of their respective formations and would set up Eureka radio beacons, lay out dropping zone marker panels and set off smoke signals to guide in the transport aircraft and gliders.

The flight over England and the North Sea on both routes was uneventful, with good visibility and only a light wind. Of the total of 320 gliders in 1st Airborne Division, only two failed to take off. Before the English coast had been reached, however, a further twenty-four were adrift, at least half of them because of problems caused by cloud: one crashed and twenty-three force-landed. The loads of twenty-two of the latter were recovered and transferred to the second lift. Four gliders were forced to ditch in the Channel: two because of broken tow-ropes and two because of tug engine trouble.

As they crossed the Dutch coast, the leading aircraft encountered light flak and a certain amount of heavy flak in the coastal area. One tug and glider combination, carrying men of 82nd US Airborne Division, was shot down over Schouwen Island; the glider broke up in mid-air and the tug crashed, all members of its crew being killed. A C-47 transport, also carrying men of the 82nd, was also hit and set ablaze; the entire stick of paratroopers and jumpmaster managed to jump clear, but the remainder of the crew perished when the aircraft crashed.

Thereafter there was little or no flak until the aircraft were nearing their target areas. On the approach to Nijmegen, light and medium flak was encountered from the areas of the towns of Groesbeek and Cuijk but only slight damage was caused to aircraft. One glider suffered a broken tow-rope and was forced to land in enemy territory, a few miles from its designated landing zone. On the Arnhem route, a further eight gliders were lost as a result of problems caused by the wakes of aircraft in front of them. Heavy, medium and light flak was met near the target areas but only one pathfinder aircraft and six tugs were hit and damaged.

The Luftwaffe was notable by its apparent absence, undoubtedly because of the very heavy fighter cover for the two groups of transport aircraft. The only enemy aircraft encountered were a few at high altitude and these were engaged by Allied fighters.

As the two great fleets of aircraft flew over the peaceful Dutch countryside, the roar of the engines caused people below to come out of their houses and gaze in awe at the spectacle of a seemingly endless stream of transport aircraft and gliders overhead. One of those watching was the commander of 1st Parachute Army, Generaloberst Kurt Student, who was working at his headquarters at Vught:

'At about noon I was disturbed at my desk by a roaring in the air which increased in intensity so that I finally left my desk and went on to the balcony. Wherever I looked I could see aircraft, troop transports and large aircraft towing gliders. They flew both in formation and singly. It was an immense stream which passed quite low over the house. I was greatly impressed by the spectacle and I must confess that during these minutes the danger of the situation never occurred to me. I merely recalled with some regret my own earlier airborne operations, and when my Chief of Staff joined me on the balcony I could only remark, "Oh, how I wish that I had ever had such a powerful force at my disposal."'

Equally as surprised as Student, who later admitted that the possibility of an Allied airborne operation in his area had never occurred to him, was Generalfeldmarschall Model, the commander of Army Group B, whose headquarters by now were located in two hotels, the Tafelberg and the Hartenstein, at Oosterbeek. Only three days previously, he and his staff had considered likely Allied moves and had agreed that any thrust by Second British Army, after crossing the Maas, would probably be towards the Ruhr via Roermond, with Dempsey's left-hand formations moving up to the Waal at Nijmegen to provide protection for the northern flank and to cut off German forces in western Holland. Model's staff had also predicted that Allied airborne forces would be deployed in an operation south of the German town of Münster, north of the River Lippe. It was for this reason, therefore, despite fears of airborne landings in the area expressed to him by Hoherer SS und Polizeiführer und General der Waffen-SS Hans Rauter,

Commander-in-Chief of the SS and the German police in Holland, who had visited him on 15 September, that Model considered that he and his headquarters were safe and secure in Oosterbeek.

News of the imminent landings resulted in a hasty exodus by Model and his staff who made off towards Arnhem and the headquarters of the German garrison which was still recovering from an air raid that morning. After a brief halt, during which he succeeded in restoring a degree of order, Model travelled on with all speed to Doetinchem and HQ 2nd SS Panzer Corps.

At approximately 1300 hours, the pathfinders of 21st Independent Parachute Company, commanded by Major 'Boy' Wilson, dropped on to Dutch soil. As they did so, they came under fire from a small group of German troops in a position on the DZ and two of them were hit just before they landed. As Wilson freed himself from his parachute harness, he encountered a young German soldier who made plain his wish to surrender and led him to the position where his comrades indicated likewise. While keeping a weather eye on his captives, Wilson quickly gave final orders to his three platoon commanders by radio. Meanwhile, his men busied themselves with laying out the coloured cloth drop zone markers and setting up their Eureka radio beacons to guide in the approaching transport aircraft.

At 1330 hours, the 147 Horsa gliders carrying 1st Airlanding Brigade, less two companies of the 2nd Battalion The South Staffordshire Regiment, arrived on LZ 'S'. Ten minutes later another 150 gliders, including eighteen Hamilcars, carrying Tactical HQ 1st Airborne Division, 1st Airborne Reconnaissance Squadron, 1st Airlanding Light Regiment RA (less one battery), two airlanding anti-tank batteries and half of 1st Parachute Brigade's transport, landed safely on LZ 'Z'. These were followed at 1400 hours by 161 transport aircraft carrying 1st Parachute Brigade Group and the advance party of 4th Parachute Brigade which landed intact.

The landings were unopposed, the small groups of enemy troops in the area of the DZs and LZs putting up no resistance. The majority of casualties were among the gliders, some of which, landing downwind and overshooting the landing zones, crash-landed in the woods nearby. Two Hamilcars, carrying 17pdr anti-tank guns of 1st Airlanding Anti-Tank Battery RA, overturned when landing on soft ground. Unfortunately, the two pilots and both their co-pilots were killed and the two anti-tank guns lost. Elsewhere, only a few loads were lost and casualties were minimal.

Soon after 1500 hours, 2nd and 3rd Parachute Battalions, having rallied and joined up with their transport, were on the move towards Arnhem. 1st Parachute Battalion, which was in reserve, moved off at 1530 hours.

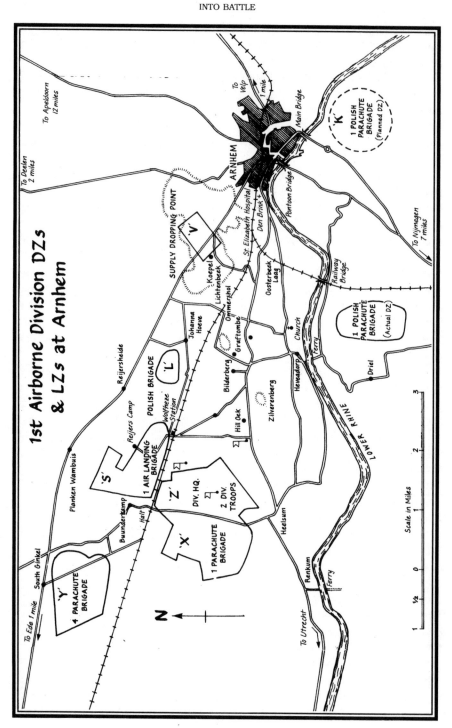

1st Airborne Division DZs & LZs at Arnhem

The spearhead of the division was 1st Airborne Reconnaissance Squadron, commanded by Major Freddie Gough, whose task was to get to the Arnhem road bridge as rapidly as possible and seize and hold it until the arrival of 1st Parachute Brigade. After landing, the parachute element of the squadron had assembled at the squadron's rallying point where it awaited the arrival of their armed jeeps which had just landed by glider. It was at this point that the difficulties arose that subsequently gave rise to the myth that the squadron had lost the majority of its vehicles during the landings.

In fact, the situation was that the squadron's HQ Troop was missing one vehicle, its glider having been forced to turn back after take-off, and 'A' Troop's jeeps were either missing or were trapped inside their gliders: two gliders carrying No. 2 Section's two jeeps had not arrived and the four vehicles of Nos. 1 and 3 Sections could not be extricated, as was the case with one of the troop headquarters' jeeps. In addition, two of 'D' Troop's vehicles were trapped inside their gliders and it would take some time to get them out. Other than these losses, the squadron was nearly complete and still capable of performing its coup de main task of seizing the bridge. In any case, 'A' Troop had been designated squadron reserve, its role being to remain on the DZ until required, so the loss of its vehicles was not too great a blow initially. Far more serious, however, was the absence of a detachment of 9th Field Company RE whose sappers and four jeeps were to have accompanied the squadron during its task. It later transpired that their gliders had not been dispatched immediately after those of the squadron, as had been intended, and they had subsequently landed on a different LZ.

At 1540 hours the Squadron, less 'A' Troop and numbering twenty-eight jeeps, moved off towards the level crossing at Wolfheze. From there it would travel down a track running parallel to the railway line to Wolfheze station, through the northern edge of Oosterbeek towards Arnhem, and thereafter head straight for the bridge.

Having reached the level crossing and headed down the track, the Squadron had covered about 600 yards when No. 8 Section of 'C' Troop, which was in the lead, came under fire from troops of 16th SS Panzer Grenadier Depot & Reserve Battalion who were in positions on the railway embankment and on a wooded ridge to the north. The battalion was a reserve unit in an ad hoc formation of Wehrmacht, Luftwaffe and Kriegsmarine personnel, organized into seven battalion-sized units. Under the overall command of Generalleutnant Hans Von Tettau, hitherto Inspector of Military Training on the staff of the Commander-in-Chief of German Armed Forces in Holland, General der Luftwaffe Friedrich Christiansen, these forces were deployed as a screen along the banks of the Waal.

Under the command of SS-Sturmbannführer Sepp Krafft and totalling twelve officers and 294 other ranks, 16th SS Panzer Grenadier

Reserve & Depot Battalion comprised a headquarters with its defence platoon, a support company consisting of trench mortar, anti-tank, anti-aircraft, flame-thrower and heavy mortar platoons, and two rifle companies: Nos. 2 and 4. At the time of the first landings, its tasks as 'divisional reserve' were to reconnoitre its own sector along the River Waal, to prepare for and counter any airborne landings and to defend (and prepare for demolition) the bridges and ferries over the Rhine in the area of Arnhem.

On learning of the landings, Krafft had taken immediate measures to deploy his battalion. Before doing so, he carried out a rapid appreciation of the British forces' intentions, considering these as being the capture of Model's headquarters at Oosterbeek, the seizure of the airfield at Deelen or the capture of the bridges over the Lower Rhine at Arnhem and the establishment of a bridgehead. He considered the last to be the most likely and made his dispositions accordingly, realizing that his best choice lay in blocking or delaying any British advance until the arrival of reinforcements.

Knowing that the most effective response to an airborne landing is an immediate counter-attack while the enemy troops are still on their landing zones, Krafft gave orders at 1345 hours to his No. 2 Company and a section of his heavy machine-gun platoon to mount an attack as soon as possible. He then ordered his battalion headquarters and No. 4 Company to make their way to the Hotel Wolfheze and summon No. 9 Company, one of the independent quick-reaction units garrisoned in Arnhem, to move up as quickly as possible to join the battalion.

In his appreciation of British intentions, Krafft had given due consideration to the likely approaches by the airborne troops. These included the railway cutting between Oosterbeek and Arnhem, which he saw as providing a rapid entry into the centre of the town, as well as the wooded terrain between the railway and the main Utrecht–Arnhem road, called the Utrechtseweg, farther to the south. His conclusions were proved correct when a British dispatch-rider was later captured and found to have maps in his possession on which these two lines of advance were marked.

Krafft decided to establish a defensive line west of Oosterbeek facing westwards, in an endeavour to block any advance by the British into Oosterbeek and Arnhem. Accordingly, he deployed his battalion in positions stretching northwards from the junction of the Utrechtseweg with the Wolfhezeweg, along the eastern side of the latter and then along the southern side of the railway cutting before crossing the railway and the Johannahoeveweg which ran parallel to the railway on its northern side. No. 2 Company would be on the left with No. 4 Company on its right, and a reserve platoon would be deployed north of the railway line to protect the battalion's right flank and to block the railway line. Krafft deployed two anti-tank guns on the Wolfhezeweg, in the vicinity of the Hotel Wolfheze where he established his battalion headquarters and his anti-aircraft platoon. His trench and heavy mortar baselines were located 300 yards south of the hotel on the line of the Wolfhezeweg. At the same time, he sent patrols to reconnoitre the railway westwards in the direction of Wolfheze and the area north of the Ede–Arnhem road respectively.

Obeying Krafft's orders to move against the DZs and LZs as quickly as possible, the commander of No. 2 Company had begun his attack at 1400 hours without carrying out any form of reconnaissance and thus had not pinpointed beforehand the exact location of the drop and landing zones which had been concealed from him by the wooded terrain. Accordingly, during its advance through the woods, the company inadvertently betrayed its presence by emerging unexpectedly on to LZ 'Z'. After a brief engagement, it withdrew. Meanwhile, its heavy machine-gun section, which had deployed to the north to protect the company's right flank, was in a good position to bring fire to bear, engaging four gliders and killing all those in them. However, it was forced to withdraw from its position after about twenty minutes, to avoid being outflanked and cut off, and to rejoin No. 2 Company as it withdrew to take up positions along the eastern side of the Wolfhezeweg.

It was Krafft's No. 4 Company which engaged the leading elements of 1st Airborne Reconnaissance Squadron as they headed eastwards along the track. 'C' Troop suffered casualties as the panzer grenadiers opened fire on No. 8 Section with machine-guns, mortars and snipers. Heavy machine-gun fire raked the vehicles and pinned down their crews who were shortly afterwards forced to surrender. The rest of the troop, Nos. 7 and 9 Sections, together with the troop commander, Captain John Hay, tried to work their way forward to assist No. 8 Section but came under fire from the railway embankment to their right. The survivors of No. 8 Section, all of them wounded, were taken prisoner.

Meanwhile the squadron commander, Major Freddie Gough, had received a summons from Major General Urquhart who, on visiting HQ 1st Airlanding Brigade soon after landing, had been informed of the report that the squadron had lost the majority of its vehicles and was thus incapable of carrying out its coup de main task. As Urqhuart later stated in his memoirs:

'Hicks was away visiting his battalions when I reached his HQ. The brigade had arrived in good order, but I was given some disturbing news about the Recce Squadron. This mixed force of glider troops and parachutists which was to effect the coup de main against the Bridge had not even started, for the simple reason that among the gliders which had failed to arrive were those containing most of the squadron's vehicles. This part of the plan – the race for the Bridge – had gone com-

71

pletely awry. It was important now that I should make an alternative plan with Freddie Gough, commander of the Reconnaissance Squadron, and that Lathbury should be told that his 2nd Battalion, under John Frost, was now going hell-bent for the bridge alone. There was the added snag that one troop of Gough's men was designed to work with my HQ, and that I now needed Gough to drive ahead of me towards the town. Nobody knew of his whereabouts. I left orders that he should contact me immediately, and returned to my own HQ. Not only was there no news of Gough when I got back but the communications were a complete failure. Some short-range inter-unit exchanges were going on, but the 1st Parachute Brigade, and the outside world, had not been contacted.'

Having summoned Gough, Urquhart decided not to wait for the latter's arrival but moved off in his jeep to catch up with HQ 1st Parachute Brigade in order to determine the progress of 2nd Parachute Battalion and to inform Brigadier Gerald Lathbury that Lieutenant Colonel Johnny Frost and his men would not find the bridge held by the Reconnaissance Squadron on their arrival.

Gough, whose headquarters was a few hundred yards to the rear of 'C' Troop, was obviously loath to leave his men while they were pinned down by the enemy, but he reckoned that he would be absent from the scene for only a few minutes. He headed back in the direction of Urquhart's headquarters, accompanied by elements of his squadron headquarters and one of 'D' Troop's vehicles. On his arrival back at the drop zone and learning of Urquhart's departure, he set off after the divisional commander, while becoming increasingly anxious about the situation of his squadron which was still pinned down by elements of No. 4 Company of 16th SS Panzer Grenadier Depot & Reserve Battalion on the railway embankment.

Urquhart was meanwhile trying to contact Gough via the radio mounted in the back of his jeep. There has been much criticism of the inadequacy of radio communications at Arnhem, and indeed, as will be explained more fully in a later chapter, it was well known that the radios with which the British airborne formations were equipped were insufficiently powered to be reliable under the conditions and distances characterized by airborne operations.

In this instance, however, the fault lay not in the equipment itself but in the misuse of radio communications. In trying to contact Gough, Urquhart's operator had to switch from the divisional frequency, thus breaking communications with divisional tactical headquarters, and try to locate him on 1st Airborne Reconnaissance Squadron's frequency. This was a very difficult exercise and it proved unsuccessful because Urquhart and Gough's jeeps were both moving. In the event, contact between the two men was never established.

During his search for Urquhart, Gough was forced on more than one occasion to turn back or make a detour; at one point he was saved from inadvertently driving into an enemy-held area by the commander of 3rd Airlanding Light Battery RA, Major Dennis Munford. Finally, as dusk was approaching, Gough headed east along the southernmost road following the river and caught up with the rear element of HQ 1st Parachute Brigade from whom he learned that Urquhart and Brigadier Lathbury were with 3rd Parachute Battalion.

Gough also discovered the reason for Urquhart's summons: he was to bring the rest of his squadron forward and follow up behind 2nd Parachute Battalion. By now, however, he was out of contact with the squadron and was not even sure of its whereabouts. At this point, the brigade signallers succeeded in establishing contact with Brigadier Lathbury. Gough asked them to try to make contact with divisional headquarters so that his squadron could be instructed to make its way to join him. But the signallers were unsuccessful and Gough had no option but to press on with his small group of men and vehicles towards the bridge and 2nd Parachute Battalion. Meanwhile, the three battalions of 1st Parachute Brigade were advancing towards Arnhem along three routes: 2nd Parachute Battalion moved towards the village of Heelsum, taking the southern route into Arnhem along the river; 3rd Parachute Battalion moved in a south-easterly direction to the Utrechtseweg, the main road to Arnhem, to support 2nd Parachute Battalion at the bridge. 1st Parachute Battalion's route took it towards the main Arnhem–Ede road to the north-east and subsequently into Arnhem itself from the north.

2nd Parachute Battalion pushed on with all speed, 'A' Company, commanded by Major Digby Tatham-Warter, in the lead. On the way, the company ambushed a number of enemy vehicles and took a number of prisoners. As it entered the village, the local inhabitants came pouring out of their homes to welcome the battalion with open arms and it was with difficulty that Frost and his men continued on their way through the throngs of excited men, women and children. On nearing the next village, called Heveadorp, 'A' Company came under fire and suffered light casualties, but pressed on towards Oosterbeek.

On leaving Oosterbeek, Major Victor Dover and 'C' Company headed towards the river and the railway bridge. No sooner had the company reached the bridge and started to cross under cover of smoke and covering fire from some of its Bren guns, than the enemy blew the bridge, leaving the southernmost span lying half-immersed in the river. Lieutenant Peter Barry, the leading platoon commander, and two of his men were wounded in the blast. As the bridge had been rendered useless, 'C' Company was ordered to move on to its secondary objective, a building reported to house an enemy headquarters.

'A' Company, meanwhile, had reached a point on the western outskirts of Arnhem near the railway line and had encountered armoured cars which were preventing any further movement along the roads. At the same time, any attempt to cross the railway line itself resulted in heavy machine-gun fire and sniping from a feature known as Den Brink. Major Douglas Crawley's 'B' Company, which was the battalion's reserve, was sent by Lieutenant Colonel Frost to deal with the enemy on Den Brink, and Major Tatham-Warter called up a 6pdr anti-tank gun to deal with the armoured cars. It was at this point that Lieutenant Peter Cane, one of 'A' Company's platoon commanders, was killed.

Dusk was falling as Major Tatham-Warter led his company through the back gardens of houses and on into Arnhem where they had another encounter with the enemy. He was followed shortly afterwards by Battalion HQ and elements of HQ Company which pushed on quickly through the town to the pontoon bridge, the centre section of which was found to be missing – it was thought at the time that it had been dismantled but it was later discovered lying alongside the rest of the bridge. Shortly afterwards, Lieutenant Colonel Johnny Frost and his group caught up with 'A' Company which by 2100 hours had stealthily taken up positions on an embankment near the northern end of the bridge and was watching the traffic crossing to and fro.

While 'A' Company prepared to send a platoon forward to take the southern end of the bridge, Battalion HQ commandeered a house overlooking the bridge while HQ Company moved into the next building. As they did so, Lieutenant A. J. McDermont and fifteen of his men ran up the embankment and started to cross the bridge to secure the southern end of it, but they had not advanced very far before they came under fire from a machine-gun in a pillbox. At the same time, armoured cars approached the southern end of the bridge and, having been engaged by 'A' Company, opened fire on the battalion's positions. McDermont and his men were forced to withdraw. A second attempt was made shortly afterwards by Lieutenant Jack Grayburn and his platoon but this was also unsuccessful. Grayburn was wounded in the shoulder but continued to press forward until forced to withdraw after suffering heavy casualties.

Almost immediately afterwards, an enemy battalion, later identified as being part of 10th SS Panzer Division en route for Nijmegen, approached the northern end of the bridge and came under fire from 2nd Parachute Battalion. Just before dusk, a company of 21st SS Panzer Grenadier Regiment also arrived from north-west of Arnhem and joined the fray.

Soon after this, part of HQ 1st Parachute Brigade, accompanied by its defence platoon, arrived under Major Tony Hibbert, the Brigade Major. It was followed by a troop of 1st Parachute Squadron RE under Captain Eric Mackay, Major Freddie Gough and the small element of his squadron, a platoon of divisional RASC troops with a captured truck loaded with ammunition collected from the dropping zone, and a troop of 6pdr anti-tank guns accompanied by some glider pilots. Later, a platoon of 9th Field Company RE also arrived. During the night, further welcome reinforcements arrived in the form of 'C' Company 3rd Parachute Battalion whose headquarters and one platoon took up positions on the eastern side of the bridge. However, there was no sign of Brigadier Lathbury.

At 2000 hours, the commander of 3rd Airlanding Light Battery RA, Major Denis Munford, arrived at HQ 1st Parachute Brigade's location with one of his troop commanders, Captain Tony Harrison, Captain 'Buck' Buchanan of 1st Forward Observation Unit RA and his signallers. He discovered that all efforts to contact divisional headquarters had failed, as he recounted later:

'Major Tony Hibbert, the Brigade Major, told me that communications within the division were practically non-existent. I decided to establish an observation post on the roof at the south-east corner of brigade headquarters and another with Tony Harrison in 2nd Parachute Battalion's headquarters. "Buck" Buchanan, from the forward observation unit, would find another east of the road by the river with "A"Company. Returning to my jeep to collect my chaps, I was informed that none had adequate radio contact; this was most embarrassing to say the least – all those vehicles and radios and no joy. Freddie Gough was also out of touch. I told Tony Hibbert, who was also a gunner and understood our problem, that I intended to return to the gun area, leaving the forward observation unit chaps but taking Tony Harrison in an effort to rectify the radio problems.

'We set off at high speed, taking the Germans completely by surprise; it was dusk and they were brewing up and parking vehicles, and by the time they had got around to shouting and shooting we had gone. Lance Bombardier Crook, my driver/signaller enjoyed himself as we raced westward at illegal speed. Eventually, somewhere south-east of Wolfheze, I spotted the CRA's tent and Major Philip Tower, the Brigade Major RA, to whom I gave a report on the situation at the bridge. Meanwhile, my crew were changing a shot-up wheel; afterwards I told them to follow Tony Harrison to the gun area, off-load the extra gun ammunition (under our seats), re-net the 22 sets, check the batteries and return to pick me up. My driver returned with a message from Tony Harrison, telling me not to wait as he had been ordered by the Commanding Officer, Lieutenant Colonel "Sheriff" Thompson, to help bring up the guns. He had the foresight, however, to put his signaller, Lance Bombardier Hall, into my jeep and he became indispensable during the next three days.

'Once again Lance Bombardier Crook took us back through the town with his foot on the floor. This time it was almost dark and it was a quieter journey apart from the complaining jeep engine and the signallers' tuning calls. I had been expecting a roadblock but surprisingly the Germans had not thought of it; however, they did seal the road shortly afterwards and thus prevented Tony Harrison from rejoining us at the bridge. On arrival I reported to the brigade headquarters, reoccupied the O.P. and got some sleep, once more in radio contact.'

Meanwhile in 2nd Parachute Battalion, 'A' Company was still attempting to dislodge the enemy from the bridge. A platoon under Lieutenant Robin Vlasto, accompanied by a small group of sappers equipped with a flame-thrower, moved off to carry out an attack from the flank. While they were doing so, the enemy put in a counter-attack supported by mortar fire. This was repulsed and shortly afterwards the pillbox on the bridge was engaged by Vlasto's platoon with PIATs and the flame-thrower. This resulted in a number of large explosions and the sound of ammunition exploding. 'A' Company was preparing to attempt to cross the bridge again when a convoy of four enemy trucks carrying infantry approached over the bridge from the south. A hail of fire greeted them and they were soon set ablaze, their few surviving occupants surrendering quickly.

A major problem faced Lieutenant Colonel Frost in that he was out of radio contact with both 'B' and 'C' Companies. The latter company was pinned down by fire near its objective, the enemy headquarters building, and was unable to break out to rejoin the battalion. Frost planned to send 'B' Company, which had been detached to take the Den Brink feature, and the brigade headquarters defence platoon across the river using small craft, seen earlier near the pontoons, to attack the southern end of the bridge. 'C' Company would leave its positions at the enemy headquarters and take over 'B' Company's task on Den Brink. A message was taken to 'B' Company, ordering it to move to the area of the pontoon bridge, but it was unable to do so because of heavy enemy activity. A patrol attempted to make its way through to 'C' Company but was unsuccessful. The rest of the battalion spent a quiet night, its signallers continually trying to establish radio contact but without success.

3rd Parachute Battalion had set off shortly after 2nd Parachute Battalion, following the middle road to Arnhem. It had rallied with 95 per cent of its strength and just before dusk met up with its glider-borne element with the vehicles and anti-tank guns. At 1600 hours Lieutenant James Cleminson's No. 3 Platoon, which was in the lead, reached a crossroads a mile west of Oosterbeek when an enemy staff car suddenly approached at high speed. This was ambushed from both sides of the road and its occupants all killed. Among them was Generalmajor Kussin, the Commandant of Arnhem, who had been paying a visit to 16th SS Panzer Grenadier Depot & Reserve Battalion.

As the battalion started to push on again, the enemy brought down mortar fire on the crossroads. As the bombs burst in the trees overhead, the battalion started to suffer casualties among those who had taken cover in the undergrowth – others who had taken shelter in some old German trenches nearby were more fortunate. Shortly afterwards, Brigadier Lathbury ordered Lieutenant Colonel Tony Fitch to resume his advance. Radio communications were such that Lathbury could not make contact with 1st Parachute Battalion and only occasionally with 2nd Parachute Battalion, so he was becoming increasingly concerned at the lack of information as to his brigade's progress.

At this point a mortar bomb hit the jeep of Major General Urquhart, who had arrived while 3rd Parachute Battalion was being mortared, wounding his signaller and rendering the radio inoperable, thus severing the divisional commander's sole link with his tactical headquarters. Deciding to remain with Lathbury, Urquhart followed 3rd Parachute Battalion as it resumed its cautious advance towards Arnhem.

As dusk was falling 'B' Company, under Major Peter Waddy, came under fire at close range from a self-propelled gun. Having decided how to deal with it, Waddy led a patrol off to the left flank while Lieutenant Cleminson and a group deployed to the right. As both groups were about to engage the gun, a 6pdr anti-tank detachment appeared and proceeded to bring their weapon to bear, but they were too slow and the German self-propelled gun quickly put the 6pdr out of action. Its crew then draped one of the wounded anti-tank gunners across the front of their vehicle, using him as a human shield as it reversed towards the German lines. No sooner had it disappeared and 3rd Parachute Battalion resumed its march, than other self-propelled guns and some armoured cars appeared and prevented any further advance.

While the battalion were dealing with this problem, 'C' Company, commanded by Major Peter Lewis, was sent in a flanking move to the north. Advancing along a road leading to the railway, it encountered a number of enemy vehicles near Oosterbeek Station. These were destroyed before the company resumed its advance along the railway line to Arnhem

Station. Moving through the town via side-streets, Lewis and his men succeeded in reaching 2nd Parachute Battalion's positions later that night. This brought the total of Frost's force to between six and seven hundred men.

Meanwhile the remainder of 3rd Parachute Battalion had encountered enemy units supported by patrols from a battle group of 9th SS Panzer Division, and was being held up by them on the outskirts of Oosterbeek, near the Park Hotel at Hartenstein. By then dusk was falling and Brigadier Lathbury suggested that the battalion halt for a few hours. While he and Major General Urquhart, together with other members of their group, took shelter in a large house, a patrol from 'B' Company, led by Major Peter Waddy, entered the Park Hotel where they discovered the remains of a hastily abandoned meal. Waddy then sent a party ahead to find a safe route into Arnhem, but no sooner had it reached the edge of the nearby woods than it came under fire and was forced to withdraw to the hotel.

1st Parachute Battalion had made a perfect drop, and moved off virtually intact from the dropping zone. As it headed towards the high ground north of Arnhem, it had also been met by crowds of jubilant Dutch people waving and cheering. However, as 'R' Company, which was in the lead, approached a crossroads north of the village of Wolfheze at about 1630 hours, it came under heavy fire from armoured vehicles, mortars and machine-guns. The failing light and heavy rain compounded the difficulties of engaging the enemy as the company moved into the woods. Armoured vehicles were moving about in the area of the crossroads, and enemy infantry attacked the company. The air was filled with the rattle of small arms and the explosions of grenades and mortar bombs as a bitter close-quarter battle was fought. Heavy casualties were suffered on both sides and by the time 'R' Company managed to extricate itself from the woods and fight its way to the northern outskirts of Arnhem, its strength had been reduced by 50 per cent.

Lieutenant Colonel David Dobie had meanwhile decided to bypass the opposition and, leaving 'R' Company heavily engaged, move eastwards along a track by the edge of the woods before striking north once more to the main road. On reaching it, however, 1st Parachute Battalion encountered tanks and other armour advancing from the south-east and at the same time observed enemy troops digging-in in the woods farther to the east. At midnight, having waited for some time for 'R' Company to rejoin it, the battalion headed south once more, leaving behind a guide for 'R' Company.

Hearing over the radio that 2nd Parachute Battalion was in dire straits at the bridge, Dobie decided that he must go to Frost's aid. His attempts to contact Brigadier Lathbury were unsuccessful and so, taking responsibility for departing from the plan, Dobie issued orders for the battalion to head for the bridge later that night.

News of the landings near Nijmegen and Arnhem had reached HQ 2nd SS Panzer Corps via a report from the Luftwaffe. Bittrich reacted immediately by ordering 9th SS Panzer Division to seize the Arnhem bridge and occupy the town. 10th SS Panzer Division was to head south, cross the Lower Rhine by ferry at Pannerden, and take part in the defence of Nijmegen. At the same time, Bittrich sent 9th SS Panzer Division's reconnaissance battalion southwards across the Lower Rhine, via the bridge at Arnhem, as part of the effort to stem any advance by 82nd US Airborne Division from Nijmegen and thus cut off any link-up between Second British Army and the airborne forces in the Arnhem area. His analysis of the Allied plan would soon be confirmed by the complete set of orders, including marked maps, discovered shortly after the landings on the body of an American officer in a glider which had been shot down near Vught, the location of Generaloberst Kurt Student's HQ 1st Parachute Army.

SS-Brigadeführer Heinz Harmel, commander of 10th SS Panzer Division, returned late that afternoon from his mission to Berlin where he had been lobbying on behalf of Bittrich for more men and equipment. On arrival at his headquarters he found that part of his division was already moving southwards, via the ferry at Pannerden, towards Nijmegen where it was to hold the bridges over the Waal. One of his units, a panzer grenadier battalion with an attached company of engineers, had already crossed and was heading for Nijmegen where it relieved 9th SS Panzer Division's reconnaissance battalion.

It soon became apparent to Harmel, however, that a heavy ferry would have to be constructed to take his heavy Tiger and Panther tanks across. This would take his engineers some time to complete because the work would have to be done at night for fear of Allied air attack. The alternative would be the removal of the British paratroop holding the northern end of the Arnhem bridge, and the containment and destruction of the remaining British airborne forces heading towards it. Bittrich had concurred and given the task to SS-Obersturmbannführer Walter Harzer, commander of 9th SS Panzer Division.

Harzer divided his forces into two battle groups. The first of these, commanded by SS-Sturmbannführer Brinkmann, commander of 10th SS Panzer Division's reconnaissance battalion which had replaced 9th Division's own unit now sent to Nijmegen, would clear the British from the area of the bridge. It would be reinforced by a panzer grenadier battalion and a small number of tanks.

The second battle group, consisting of the mobilized units of 9th SS Panzer Division under command of SS-Obersturmbannführer Ludwig Spindler, commander of 9th SS Panzer Division's self-propelled artillery regiment, would advance westwards along the main routes leading from Arnhem to Oosterbeek. Thereafter it would establish a line from the Ede–Arnhem road in the north, southwards to the lower Rhine, to prevent any British forces from reinforcing those at the bridge, and to form the eastern side of a 'box' which would eventually be formed to hem in those elements of 1st Airborne Division in Oosterbeek. 16th SS Panzer Grenadier Depot & Reserve Battalion, which would be under command of 9th SS Panzer Division, would assist in forming the northern 'lid' of the box. Advancing from the west towards the dropping and landing zones would be the forces under Generalleutnant von Tettau that would ultimately form the western 'side' of the box whose base would be the Lower Rhine.

Throughout its area, elements of 9th SS Panzer Division were hastily mobilized. Men of 20th SS Panzer Grenadier Regiment, located on a training area at Harskamp, east of Arnhem, were awaiting their move to Siegen in Germany that night, having handed in all their weapons and equipment. They suddenly received news of the landings and orders to move to Arnhem. Weapons were re-issued and they set off towards the town. At the same time, a company group of 9th SS Panzerjäger Battalion, with two of its self-propelled anti-tank guns and some 7.5mm Pak towed anti-tank pieces, received orders to make its way to Arnhem. Similarly, the divisional anti-aircraft battery, under command of SS-Obersturmführer Gropp, was interrupted during training and instructed to move with its two 88mm and 20mm flak guns to Arnhem. SS-Hauptsturmführer Hans Moeller, commander of 9th SS Pionier Battalion, was also ordered to move his unit to Arnhem, but as if drove through the town on the Arnhem–Utrecht road, heading towards the sounds of battle coming from the direction of Oosterbeek, it was ambushed and pinned down west of St. Elizabeth's Hospital.

That night, at 2130 hours, SS-Sturmbannführer Sepp Krafft received orders for his battalion to move. Earlier that evening he had received a signal from his divisional commander, Generalleutnant von Tettau, saying that another battalion would attack the airborne troops from the north, but this had not materialized. Having just suffered casualties from an attack by 3rd Parachute Battalion which was repulsed with difficulty, Krafft was becoming increasingly worried in the mistaken belief that his unit was almost surrounded and that it would soon be cut off entirely. His fears were prompted by the fact that his companies were making contact with British troops to their front and on both flanks: in front they encountered patrols from the 1st Battalion The Border Regiment which, together with the rest of 1st Airlanding Brigade, was holding the DZs and LZs; to the north and south, on their right and left flanks, they were engaging 1st and 3rd Parachute Battalions respectively.

Krafft had therefore sent a radio message to Generalleutnant von Tettau, advising him that he intended to fight his way out to the north-east over the railway line, and at 2100 hours the first of his platoons had begun to withdraw. An hour and a half later, he and his men met elements of SS-Obersturmbannführer Spindler's battle group of 9th SS Panzer Division on the Arnhem–Ede road.

While the three parachute battalions were fighting their way into Arnhem, 1st Airlanding Brigade had been holding the dropping and landing zones ready for 4th Parachute Brigade's arrival on the morning of 18 September. The brigade itself would drop on DZs 'X' and 'Y', with its glider-borne element and remaining divisional troops landing on LZs 'S' and 'Z'. The glider-borne element of 1st Polish Independent Parachute Brigade would land on LZ 'L'. The 7th Battalion The King's Own Scottish Borderers was positioned in the woods bordering the edge of Ginkels Heath covering DZ 'Y', while the 2nd Battalion South Staffordshire Regiment protected LZ 'S' at Reyerscamp. LZs 'X' and 'Z', which lay immediately to the north of the villages of Heelsum and Renkum, were held by the 1st Battalion The Border Regiment. Brigadier 'Pip' Hicks's headquarters was located just to the east of DZ 'Y'.

To the east of LZs 'X' and 'Z', and to the south of Wolfheze, were the gun lines of the two batteries of 1st Airlanding Light Regiment RA which was commanded by Lieutenant Colonel W. F. K. 'Sheriff' Thompson; 1st Airlanding Light Battery RA, commanded by Major Arthur Norman-Walker, which was tasked with supporting 1st Airlanding Brigade in the defence of the dropping and landing zones; and 3rd Airlanding Light Battery RA, under Major Denis Munford, which was in support of 1st Parachute Brigade. 2nd Airlanding Light Battery RA, commanded by Major Jeffrey Linton, would arrive with 4th Parachute Brigade.

1st Airlanding Anti-Tank Battery RA, under Major Bill Arnold, had arrived in the first lift and a troop of its 6pdr anti-tank guns had accompanied 2nd Parachute Battalion to the bridge while the rest of the battery remained with 1st Airlanding Brigade. Some of the Hamilcar gliders, carrying the battery's 17pdr anti-tank guns and their tractors, had come to grief when landing on unexpectedly soft ground, but although two of them had turned over on their backs, some of the guns and tractors were removed intact and in working order. The division's other anti-tank unit, 2nd Airlanding Anti-Tank Battery RA, commanded by Major A. F. Haynes, would also arrive in the second lift.

The afternoon of 17 September was relatively uneventful for 1st Airlanding Brigade and those divisional troops in the vicinity of the DZs and LZs, until the arrival of a detachment of 3rd Dutch SS Landsturm Niederland Battalion, comprising bandsmen under the command of their drum-major. At 1700 hours, the Dutchmen appeared in trucks on the road bordering Ginkels Heath and began to reconnoitre the woods on the western edge of DZ 'Y', but they were ambushed by a platoon of the 7th Battal-

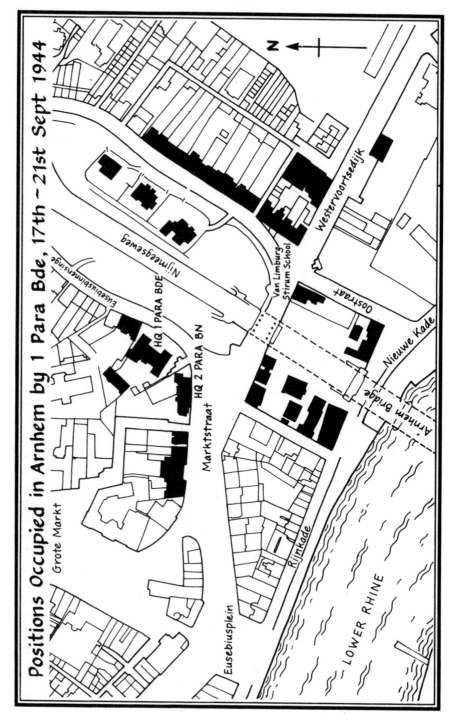

Positions Occupied in Arnhem by 1 Para Bde, 17th – 21st Sept 1944

ion The King's Own Scottish Borderers who opened fire at close range. The detachment commander was killed and the remainder fled.

Nothing further transpired until after 2100 hours when the Dutch SS battalion's No. 4 Company appeared, having been ordered to make its way eastwards along the Ede–Arnhem road and subsequently through the woods on the eastern side of Ginkels Heath to probe the British positions. It soon suffered the same fate as the battalion band, the Borderers opening fire at close range and causing heavy casualties.

Another engagement took place between the 2nd Battalion The South Staffordshire Regiment and a force of some ninety men from a Luftwaffe signals unit based at Deelen airfield. Under the command of Hauptmann Willi Weber, the signallers attacked the positions covering LZ 'S' at Reyerskamp and then withdrew to take up defensive positions in the vicinity of the airfield.

The Dutch SS battalion, commanded by SS-Hauptsturmführer Paul Helle and based at Amersfoort to the north-west of Arnhem, where it performed guard duties at a concentration camp, was the leading element of Generalleutnant von Tettau's forces which by then were being ordered to move westwards against 1st Airborne Division's dropping and landing zones. Other units under von Tettau's command included SS-Standartenführer Hans Lippert's Unteroffizierschule Arnheim which, with its headquarters at Schoonrewoerd, was deployed in the western sector of von Tettau's screen along the Waal. This was a training unit consisting of officers and men who were experienced soldiers, many of whom had served on the Eastern Front.

On the afternoon of 17 September, Lippert received orders to report with his unit to von Tettau's headquarters near Rhenen. He went ahead of his men and on his arrival was ordered to move with all haste to Renkum and attack the British troops in that area. As reinforcements, he was given two battalion-sized units: Schiffstammabteilung 10 of the Kriegsmarine (a naval manning unit) and a fliegerhorst (ground crew) battalion of the Luftwaffe. Neither of these was of much use to Lippert, their men being totally untrained in infantry tactics. Placing them on each side of his own unit, Lippert began his advance eastwards along the north bank of the lower Rhine towards Renkum and the positions of the 1st Battalion The Border Regiment.

Meanwhile, similar orders had been issued to SS-Sturmbannführer Eberwein, commander of an SS depot battalion. He was to go to Bennekom, to the west of the British dropping and landing zones, and mount an attack eastwards, also against positions held by the 1st Battalion The Border Regiment. To his north would be the Dutch SS battalion. Other units along the Waal that also found themselves being withdrawn and sent towards Arnhem included the Hermann Göring Training Regiment and an artillery regiment reorganized as an infantry battalion. By nightfall on 17 September the leading elements of von Tettau's force were advancing eastwards to form the western side of the 'box' to contain 1st Airborne Division.

At dawn on 18 September, a number of truckloads of enemy troops drove down the streets dominated by the buildings held by 2nd Parachute Battalion and the other elements of 1st Parachute Brigade which opened fire at close range, killing most of the occupants. Shortly afterwards, a column of armoured cars and half-tracks of 9th SS Panzer Division's reconnaissance battalion, under the command of SS-Haupsturmführer Viktor Gräbner, started to cross the bridge from the south. They were heading northwards to rejoin the rest of the division, having been relieved at Nijmegen by a unit of 10th SS Panzer Division. Pushing aside the wrecked trucks from the previous action, and managing to avoid the necklaces of Hawkins grenades laid by 2nd Parachute Battalion during the night, the first four vehicles drove through at high speed and disappeared into the town. The remaining ten, however, were not so fortunate and were destroyed by a 6pdr anti-tank gun and the battalion's PIATs.

Shortly afterwards, panzer grenadiers of SS-Sturmbannführer Brinkmann's battle group attacked 2nd Parachute Battalion in force and during the next two hours a major battle was fought at close range, buildings being set on fire and destroyed as shells and mortar bombs crashed down into the area. Casualties among the battalion were light, however, and morale was extremely high. The enemy, on the other hand, had suffered heavily, losing four more armoured vehicles and a considerable number of men dead or wounded. Major Freddie Gough, manning the twin Vickers 'K' guns on his jeep, had accounted for many of them. The guns of 1st and 3rd Airlanding Light Batteries, directed by Major Denis Munford from his observation post in the attic of a house, had provided excellent support for the battalion, their accurate fire helping to break up infantry attacks.

At this juncture brief radio contact was established with the leading elements of XXX Corps and shortly afterwards with 'B' Company which succeeded in making its way to the area of the pontoon bridge. After fighting their way through the streets, Major Douglas Crawley and most of his company arrived to join the battalion, but there was still no word of 'C' Company.

During the afternoon the Brigade Major, Major Tony Hibbert, made his way to Major Denis Munford's OP to try to locate an enemy field gun which had been sited on a crossroads 400 yards to the north of 2nd Parachute Battalion's positions. Shortly afterwards it opened fire, causing heavy damage to buildings occupied by the battalion. Munford called down fire on the gun, which by then had demolished the northern end of the house in which his OP was located, giving his own position as a reference. Such was the accuracy of 3rd Airlanding Light Battery's response that after the first salvo had been corrected the field gun was knocked out.

It was during the afternoon that 2nd Parachute Battalion discovered that it was up against troops of 9th SS Panzer Division, as Lieutenant Colonel Johnny Frost recounted:

'Bucky Buchanan brought disturbing news during the afternoon. He had been interrogating prisoners in our cellars and found that among them were several from the 9th SS Panzer Division. They had come in during the morning. On the previous day the prisoners had been from various units of no particular renown. It had been thought that the well-known 9th and 10th SS Panzer Divisions had been written off in the Falaise battle on the far bank of the Seine in France. I told Bucky to find one of them who spoke English. He produced a captain. "What are you doing in these parts?" I asked.

'"We have been resting, re-equipping and getting reinforcements between here and Apeldoorn for several days."

'Well there it was. Further questions elicited the fact that most of the key personnel of the 2nd SS Panzer Corps, which made up the two fine divisions, had got back across the Seine, and now they would soon be able to put ever-increasing pressure against our lightly equipped 1st Airborne Division, which had its back to the Rhine. We had been given absolutely no inkling of this possibility. The odds against an outcome in our favour were heavy indeed.'

Meanwhile, the sounds of fighting could be heard from the west of the town where 1st and 3rd Parachute Battalions were attempting to break through to the bridge.

Dawn found 3rd Parachute Battalion resuming its advance towards Arnhem after spending most of the night near the Hartenstein Hotel in Oosterbeek. Having moved off through Oosterbeek at 0430 hours, it joined the southernmost road running alongside the river. 'B' Company was again in the lead, followed by Lieutenant Colonel Fitch, his battalion headquarters and some sappers. They were accompanied by Major General Urquhart and Brigadier Lathbury. 'B' Company set a fast pace, passing under the railway bridge at 0530 hours; so much so that, in the dark, 'A' Company, Headquarters Company, the Mortar and Machine Gun Platoons, together with some anti-tank guns, became separated and cut off.

On reaching the outskirts of Arnhem, near the St. Elizabeth Hospital, the battalion was held up at the junction where the southernmost road joined the central road. There it encountered tanks and self-propelled guns of SS-Obersturmbannführer Spindler's battle group which brought down heavy fire while infantry sniped at 3rd Parachute Battalion and machine-gunned it from the upper storeys of buildings. Before long, the battalion was surrounded as more enemy troops closed up around it.

1st Parachute Battalion, meanwhile, had set off at 0100 hours for the bridge. After crossing the railway at Oosterbeek station, it turned on to the main road to Arnhem. Shortly afterwards at 0430 hours, 'S' Company, which was in the lead, came under heavy fire from mortars, and sustained fire from machine-guns and armoured cars sited on high ground above a railway bridge to the front. The company responded with a left flanking attack and succeeded in clearing the enemy but suffered thirty casualties in the process.

During this action one of 1st Airlanding Light Regiment's FOOs appeared in a jeep en route to divisional headquarters to report on the situation at the Arnhem bridge. After talking to him, Lieutenant Colonel Dobie decided to continue his move direct to the bridge and by 0630 hours 1st Parachute Battalion was once again heading for the railway bridge on the southern route along which 3rd Parachute Battalion had, unbeknown to him, passed a few hours earlier. Some thirty minutes later it reached the railway bridge where it found 3rd Parachute Battalion's Headquarter Company, including some anti-tank guns and detachments of the Machine Gun Platoon, which it added to its own depleted strength.

By now it was dawn and the enemy brought down mortar fire in the area around the railway bridge. 'T' Company, commanded by Major Chris Perrin-Brown, encountered the enemy in strength in houses and a factory some 400 yards beyond the bridge, and a number of armoured vehicles were seen on Den Brink. The company, supported by the guns of 1st Airlanding Light Regiment RA and the battalion's own mortars, together with some of those of 3rd Parachute Battalion, put in an attack on some houses on the crossroads nearby but was held up by a 20mm cannon which opened fire from the factory.

At this point, 'A' Company 3rd Parachute Battalion, commanded by Major Mervyn Dennison, arrived and another attack was mounted with 'A' Company on the left of the road and 'T' Company on the right, once again supported by mortars, machine-guns and 1st Airlanding Light Regiment RA. The action lasted for about an hour, during which time the enemy launched a counter-attack on 1st Parachute Battalion's left flank. Nevertheless, the battalion fought its way through to the main road junction ahead which it reached at about 1500 hours. By now, however, its strength was down to about 100 men.

The situation by the morning of the second day was looking grim. 2nd Parachute Battalion was managing to hold on at the bridge, but had suffered casualties and was running very low on ammunition. 1st and 3rd Parachute Battalions had both been held up in heavy fighting on the outskirts of Arnhem and were unable to reinforce Lieutenant Colonel Frost and his men.

To make matters worse, Major General Roy Urquhart and Brigadier Gerald Lathbury were both missing from their headquarters, out of contact with their respective formations and their units. The two men had taken cover in a house together with the battalion headquarters of 3rd Parachute Battalion, watching German tanks and self-propelled guns moving along the street outside. During the morning Captain William Taylor, Lathbury's GSO3 (Intelligence) who was with them, succeeded in contacting brigade headquarters at the bridge and learned that it was being held.

During the afternoon the remnants of 'A' Company 3rd Parachute Battalion, numbering only about forty strong under Lieutenant Burwash, appeared with two Bren carriers loaded with ammunition. At this point, Lieutenant Colonel Fitch decided to make a further attempt to reach the bridge by heading north and approaching via the railway. At 1500 hours the battalion moved off but soon found itself hampered by having to clamber over the high fences of gardens and by increasingly heavy machine-gun fire from the direction of the railway.

Major General Urquhart and Brigadier Lathbury decided to make their own way to the bridge. Leaving the house where they had been sheltering, they ran across the garden of the house next door under cover of a smoke grenade thrown by Lathbury. Here they met Lieutenant James Cleminson, with the remnants of his platoon, who warned them not to go any further. Ignoring his advice, Urquhart and Lathbury, followed by Captain Taylor, ran into the Alexanderstraat and headed in the direction of St. Elizabeth Hospital. Somewhat alarmed at the idea of the two senior officers moving through the enemy-occupied area unescorted, Cleminson ran after them, calling on his men to follow.

As the four officers ran down the street, a machine-gun opened fire and Brigadier Lathbury was hit in the back. While the other three were dragging him inside the nearest building, a German soldier followed them but was shot by Major General Urquhart with his pistol through the window. Lathbury was paralysed and unable to walk. Leaving him in the care of a Dutchman and his wife, Urquhart and the two others continued on their way. However, they were soon forced to take refuge in the attic of a house to avoid capture by a company of panzer grenadiers approaching from the opposite direction. Once again Urquhart was forced to lie low, unable to reach his headquarters.

Meanwhile at the dropping and landing zones, 1st Airlanding Brigade had come under attack from the German force advancing from the west. At 0500 hours, the 1st Battalion The Border Regiment found itself engaged by a battalion of SS-Standartenführer Lippert's Unteroffizierschule, the sailors of Schiffstammabteilung 10 and the airmen of the Luft-

waffe fliegerhorst battalion. Farther north, on Ginkels Heath, the four companies of the Dutch SS battalion attacked the positions of the 7th Battalion The King's Own Scottish Borderers. Meanwhile, SS-Sturmbannführer
Eberwein's SS depot battalion advanced north-eastwards, between the
fliegerhorst battalion and the Dutch SS, towards the railway, driving a
wedge between the two British battalions defending the dropping and landing zones.

By 0700 hours, Lippert's battalion had cleared Renkum and the
area to the north, but an attack on a factory to the south of the Wagenin-
gen–Arnhem road by Schiffstammabteilung 10 was beaten off, the sailors
suffering heavy casualties. It was not until 0900 hours, with the support of
mortars and heavy machine-guns, that the defenders were forced out of
the factory buildings. By the early afternoon, the Germans had reached
Heelsum which lay on the southern edge of DZ 'X' and LZ 'Z'. Meanwhile,
the Dutch SS battalion was still attempting to dislodge the 7th Battalion
The King's Own Scottish Borderers from its positions in the woods on the
eastern side of Ginkels Heath.

In the centre, however, the fliegerhorst battalion's advance had been
halted by the 1st Battalion The Border Regiment and consequently the airmen had been reinforced by two companies of the Unteroffizierschule battalion and six Renault tanks. Under the command of SS-Standartenführer
Lippert, an attack was launched but this ground to a halt after all six
tanks had been quickly knocked out. A second attack, in which Lippert
staged a diversion, proved successful and within an hour the Borderers
had been forced to withdraw eastwards from DZ 'X' and LZ 'Z' towards
Oosterbeek.

Meanwhile at HQ 1st Airborne Division, located at the Hartenstein
Hotel in Oosterbeek, Brigadier 'Pip' Hicks, commander of 1st Airlanding
Brigade, had assumed command of the division in the absence of Major
General Urquhart. Realizing 2nd Parachute Battalion's perilous situation,
he sent 'B' and 'D' Companies of the 2nd Battalion The South Staffordshire
Regiment (less two companies which would arrive in the second lift), one of
the three airlanding battalions holding the dropping and landing zones, as
reinforcements. Unfortunately, however, they also became held up as they
attempted to make their way towards the bridge. The division's only hope
therefore lay with 4th Parachute Brigade, which was due to arrive at 1000
hours.

The weather was bright and clear as Major 'Boy' Wilson and the
pathfinders of 21st Independent Parachute Company laid out their
coloured markers and set up their Eureka beacons on DZ 'Y' and LZ 'L'. As
they did so they were attacked from the air by Messerschmitt Bf 109s but
managed to take cover in time and suffered no casualties. However, there
was no sign of the aircraft carrying 4th Parachute Brigade. Unbeknown to

those awaiting their arrival, all the airfields in England were covered in low-lying mist and it was not until late morning that conditions improved sufficiently for the aircraft to take off.

At 1500 hours, the second lift arrived overhead. As on the previous day, the parachutists and gliders were delivered accurately but on this occasion flak was encountered during the final twenty minutes of the run-in, together with considerable opposition on the DZ and LZ. 10th Parachute Battalion in particular suffered casualties from heavy fire brought to bear by the Dutch SS battalion. However, the latter was counter-attacked by the 7th Battalion The King's Own Scottish Borderers who virtually annihilated it.

Despite their casualties all three parachute battalions rallied quickly and headed for their respective rendezvous points. Brigadier John Hackett was in good form, having taken several prisoners soon after landing. Shortly afterwards, he was met by Lieutenant Colonel Charles McKenzie, the GSO1 1st Airborne Division, who briefed him on the situation and on the new orders which had been issued by Brigadier 'Pip' Hicks.

Two hours after the drop, 4th Parachute Brigade was heading towards Arnhem. Brigadier Hicks's orders specified that 10th and 156th Parachute Battalions were to carry out their previously allocated task of taking and holding the high ground north of Arnhem, but, much to Hackett's displeasure, 11th Parachute Battalion was to be detached from the brigade and was to head for the bridge together with the two companies of the 2nd Battalion The South Staffordshire Regiment which had also just landed.

So concerned was Hackett that he drove to HQ 1st Airborne Division with the intention of trying to sort out what he later referred to as a 'grossly untidy situation'. Although Urquhart had nominated Lathbury as his deputy in the event of his becoming hors de combat, Hicks had taken over command of the division in the latter's absence. However, Hackett was in fact his senior. Eventually, having helped Hicks to restore some degree of order, Hackett returned to his brigade after obtaining Hicks's agreement that 4th Parachute Brigade would move next morning to take the area of Koepel, a feature of high ground to the north of Arnhem. From there it would advance into Arnhem north of the railway line. En route, it would collect the 7th Battalion The King's Own Scottish Borderers to replace 11th Parachute Battalion.

By the time that dusk fell, the two South Staffordshire companies were on the march towards Arnhem with Lieutenant Colonel George Lea and his 11th Parachute Battalion following up. Soon afterwards, just after nightfall, they met Lieutenant Colonel David Dobie and the remnants of 1st Parachute Battalion. The three commanding officers between them decided that the advance would be continued at 0400 hours next day, 19

September. 1st Parachute Battalion and elements of 3rd Parachute Battalion would head south to the river and then approach 2nd Parachute Battalion's positions along the northern bank while the South Staffordshire companies and 11th Parachute Battalion moved along the main road.

By now, however, the eastern side of the 'box' had been firmly established by SS-Obersturmbannführer Spindler. To the north of the Arnhem–Ede road was SS-Sturmbannführer Sepp Krafft's 16th SS Panzer Grenadier Depot & Reserve Battalion which had been joined by elements of 9th SS Panzerjäger Battalion, a Wehrmacht infantry battalion, 642nd Marine Regiment, 1st Marine Cadre Regiment and No. 10 Company of 3rd Police Regiment. On Krafft's left was a Wehrmacht battle group under Hauptmann Bruhns. In the centre, and covering the Arnhem–Utrecht road, was a battle group composed of elements of 9th SS Panzer Division's anti-aircraft battalion, its engineer battalion and a detached company of 16th SS Panzer Grenadier Depot & Reserve Battalion. Manning the line in the southern sector, covering the area south of the Arnhem–Utrecht road to the Lower Rhine, were elements of 19th and 20th SS Panzer Grenadier Regiments. In all, the line was held by some seven battalions supported by self-propelled guns, half-tracks and armoured cars.

To the rear was a second blocking line, stretching from the station to the river, manned by another battle group comprising two infantry companies formed from elements of 9th SS Panzer Regiment and a third from naval personnel.

By now, the situation facing 1st Parachute Battalion was very grim. In the early hours of 19 September, after heading for the river, Lieutenant Colonel David Dobie and his men encountered troops of 20th SS Panzer Grenadier Regiment and some fierce close-quarter fighting took place near the area of the pontoon bridge. Major John 'Tim' Timothy led his 'R' Company in a bayonet charge and Major Chris Perrin-Brown did likewise with 'T' Company in attempts to drive the enemy back, but achieved only limited success.

As dawn broke on 19 September, the battalion, with the remaining elements of 3rd Parachute Battalion in support, also came under fire from elements of 9th SS Panzer Division's reconnaissance battalion which had taken up positions in brickworks on the southern bank of the river. A storm of fire from 20mm and 37mm cannon, mounted on half-tracks and armoured cars, was brought down on the battalion which was hopelessly exposed. By 0600 hours, both battalions numbered fewer than forty men, and the arrival of enemy armour made the situation all the more impossible. As Lieutenant Colonel Dobie and the other survivors of both battalions attempted to take cover in nearby houses, enemy troops appeared inside the buildings and opened fire, Dobie himself being wounded by a grenade. Eventually he and six others found shelter in a cellar occupied by Dutch civilians. An hour later they were discovered by enemy troops who took them prisoner.

At 0500 hours, 156th Parachute Battalion launched its attack through the woods of Johanna Hoeve, heading for the Lichtenbeek feature. By 1000 hours, however, it had failed and the battalion had suffered heavy casualties, 'A' Company having lost all its officers. Lieutenant Colonel Ken Smyth's 10th Parachute Battalion had fared little better, having encountered heavy fire from 88mm anti-aircraft guns being used in the ground target role as well as from tanks and self-propelled guns on the main Arnhem–Ede road. The battalion had been ordered to establish a firm base 1,000 yards from a small farmstead at Johanna Hoeve. However, Smyth ordered his men to dig in where they were, astride the Arnhem–Utrecht road, planning to attack and seize his objective after nightfall. Throughout the day the battalion was subjected to heavy fire but stood its ground.

Dawn on 19 September also saw the arrival of further German reinforcements in the form of 280th Sturmgeschutz Brigade with its 75mm assault guns which were deployed at various points along the line held by SS-Obersturmbannführer Spindler's battle groups.

It was not until the morning of 19 September that Major General Roy Urquhart was eventually able to make his way to his headquarters. Having been trapped in the house in which he was sheltering by the presence of a self-propelled gun outside, he was unable to move until 0700 hours when he heard the gun move off. Shortly afterwards, the owner of the house appeared and told Urquhart that British troops were advancing up the street. These turned out to be the two companies of South Staffordshires and 11th Parachute Battalion attempting to make their way to the bridge to reinforce 2nd Parachute Battalion. Commandeering one of their jeeps, Urquhart sped back towards his headquarters.

After assuming command of the division from Brigadier 'Pip' Hicks, Urquhart learned with growing alarm of the chaotic situation reigning in Arnhem. Hicks informed him that 1st and 3rd Parachute Battalions, together with 11th Parachute Battalion and the 2nd Battalion The South Staffordshire Regiment, were advancing independently into the town in an attempt to link up with 2nd Parachute Battalion which was still hanging on at the bridge. 156th and 10th Parachute Battalions, together with the 7th Battalion The King's Own Scottish Borderers, were to the north of Arnhem and it was not known whether they were advancing into the town. The 1st Battalion The Border Regiment was occupying positions on a line running along the western outskirts of Oosterbeek from Westerbouwing to Wolfheze.

Another major problem was that of re-supply. Because the operation was way behind schedule, Supply Dropping Zone 'V', on the north-western outskirts of Arnhem, had not been secured and the situation was such that it was no longer feasible to use it as a re-supply point. Moreover, the same applied to DZ 'K', south of the town and river, on which 1st Polish Independent Parachute Brigade was due to drop that morning. Divisional HQ signalled England, advising the RAF that new dropping zones would have to be selected. There was no response and this was subsequently to have tragic results.

Urquhart was appalled at what he learned from Hicks and his staff and sent Colonel Hilaro Barlow, Deputy Commander 1st Airlanding Brigade, into Arnhem in a radio-equipped jeep to co-ordinate the five battalions operating independently in the town. Unfortunately, Barlow never reached Arnhem. He was never seen again and it was assumed that he had been ambushed and killed en route. Some time later it was learned that he was killed by mortar fire near the Rhine Pavilion Hotel.

Deciding that he must see the situation on the ground for himself, Urquhart drove to HQ 4th Parachute Brigade which was located near Wolfheze. There he found Hackett and his brigade heavily committed on the northern outskirts of Oosterbeek around the woods of Johanna Hoeve and Lichtenbeek. Confronting them were troops of 9th SS Panzerjäger Battalion supported by self-propelled guns and armoured vehicles, including half-tracks and armoured cars of 9th SS Panzer Division's reconnaissance battalion which were acting as mobile fire support units, on call as required.

4th Parachute Brigade had advanced during the night of 18/19 September to take its objective, the high ground to the north of Arnhem. In doing so it had encountered the northern element of the eastern blocking line which would form the lid of the German 'box'. Initially 10th and 156th Parachute Battalions had gained some ground and the enemy were under great pressure. Unfortunately, however, German reinforcements had arrived in the form of an SS unit of self-propelled anti-aircraft guns on half-tracks and a Wehrmacht anti-aircraft battalion equipped with twin and quadruple 20mm guns mounted on half-tracks. Two companies of 156th Parachute Battalion had fallen victim to the very heavy firepower of these two units and shortly afterwards the survivors had been forced to withdraw.

As he reached Hackett's brigade headquarters, Urquhart had a narrow escape when three Messerschmitts suddenly attacked, forcing him to throw himself down a steep bank into the headquarters itself. He discovered that despite every effort to push forward to the high ground at Koepel, the brigade had been unable to make any progress. After conferring with Hackett, he decided to withdraw the brigade south to the middle road leading into Arnhem, but ordered Hackett not to implement the withdrawal plan until ordered to do so. Shortly after Urquhart's departure, however, the 1st Battalion The Border Regiment, which was behind 4th Parachute

Brigade on the western outskirts of Oosterbeek, was attacked from the west. At the same time, SS-Obersturmbannführer Sepp Krafft's and Hauptmann Bruhns' battle groups began advancing southwards, to put the 'lid' on the 'box', while SS-Obersturmbannführer Spindler's forces began to push westwards towards Oosterbeek. Hackett and his brigade were threatened with being cut off, particularly if the enemy took Wolfheze, whose level crossing was the sole means whereby 4th Parachute Brigade's vehicles could cross the railway line which was lined by steep embankments. 10th Parachute Battalion was sent to take and hold the crossing and almost immediately afterwards the order to withdraw was received from HQ 1st Airborne Division.

The withdrawal was carried out in contact with the enemy who harassed the brigade as it pulled back. 10th Parachute Battalion meanwhile had encountered the SS depot battalion battle group under SS-Sturmbannführer Eberwein on approaching Wolfheze and heavy fighting subsequently took place in the village itself. Captain Lionel Queripel, commanding a composite company of men from two other battalions as well as his own, was wounded in the face as he carried a wounded NCO to shelter. Disregarding his wound, he then led an attack on an enemy strongpoint, killing the crews of two machine-guns and a 6pdr anti-tank gun captured previously by the enemy. At this point, enemy infantry counter-attacked and Queripel was wounded again in the face and in both arms. Together with some of the men with him, he took cover in a ditch and stood his ground against the enemy who by now were showering his party with stick grenades. Despite his wounds, Queripel threw several of these back at his attackers. He continued to do so as he ordered his men to withdraw while he covered them. Shortly afterwards, the enemy closed in and killed him. His supreme gallantry was recognized by the posthumous award of the Victoria Cross.

By the time that 10th Parachute Battalion withdrew across the railway line, it numbered only some 250 men. 156th Parachute Battalion had also suffered heavily, numbering only some 270 all ranks and having lost virtually all its transport. Nevertheless, the withdrawal by 4th Parachute Brigade was carried out in such a way that the enemy paid a very heavy price for every yard of ground gained. The brigade headquarters defence platoon carried out a number of counter-attacks, assaulting Krafft's No. 9 Company from the flank, killing the company commander and inflicting heavy casualties.

At 1600 hours, during the withdrawal by 4th Parachute Brigade, some of the glider-borne elements of 1st Polish Independent Parachute Brigade started to land on LZ 'L' over which 10th Parachute Battalion was withdrawing at the time, while being covered by brigade headquarters, and in full view of the enemy. The Poles immediately came under very heavy fire from the Germans on the ground and from Messerschmitt Bf 109 fighters which appeared at the same time. Several gliders caught fire in mid-air and others exploded on landing. Tragically, in the confusion and poor visibility caused by smoke, some of the Poles opened fire on 10th Parachute Battalion and other units of 4th Parachute Brigade, and their fire was returned.

Meanwhile the South Staffordshires had been held up in the main street of Arnhem. As they advanced eastwards from St. Elizabeth's Hospital they came under fire from troops of 9th SS Panzer Division's anti-aircraft and engineer battalions who were supported by a self-propelled gun and two half-tracks. After running out of PIAT ammunition, they were overrun by enemy armour and were forced to withdraw westwards. After reorganizing, they attacked the Den Brink feature so as to allow 11th Parachute Battalion to reach the road running north of the feature. No sooner had they taken it than they came under very heavy mortar fire and were driven off by enemy armour which then turned its attention to 11th Parachute Battalion, causing heavy casualties.

The surviving South Staffordshires, together with survivors of 11th Parachute Battalion, withdrew to Oosterbeek Station. Together with remnants of 1st and 3rd Parachute Battalions, they formed a composite force, which was later called Lonsdale Force, under the command of Major Dickie Lonsdale, the Second in Command of 11th Parachute Battalion. By now the commanding officers of all four battalions represented in Lonsdale Force had become casualties: while Lieutenant Colonel Fitch of 3rd Parachute Battalion had been killed, Lieutenant Colonels Dobie and Lea of 1st and 11th Parachute Battalions and Lieutenant Colonel W. D. H. McCardie of the South Staffordshires had been wounded and taken prisoner.

During the day, the RAF dropped supplies to the beleaguered division. Unfortunately, however, the messages from HQ 1st Airborne Division to England concerning the necessary changes in dropping zones had not been received. Consequently the Dakotas and Stirlings flew in to meet a heavy barrage of anti-aircraft fire and dropped their containers accurately on to Supply Dropping Zone 'V' which by now was behind enemy lines. A new dropping zone was marked out near divisional headquarters and a Eureka beacon was set up nearby. But the coloured marker panels only served to attract the attention of enemy fighters, which strafed the dropping zone. Nevertheless, those on the ground did everything in their power to attract the attention of the aircrew, firing flares, laying out parachutes on the ground and even setting fire to the grass – but all to no avail.

As the troops watched, the aircraft flew on through the barrage of flak. One of them was a Dakota of 217 Squadron, of 46 Group RAF, flown by Flight Lieutenant David Lord. As the aircraft made its run-in over the drop zone, it was hit and caught fire. Despite this, the crew dropped six panniers of ammunition and Flight Lieutenant Lord turned his aircraft for a second run-in. As the last two panniers were being dropped, the flames enveloped the aircraft, which crashed. One member of the crew, Flying Officer Henry King, survived and he later revealed that, after the ammunition had been dispatched, Lord had ordered his crew to bale out while remaining at the controls and holding the burning aircraft steady. Unfortunately all the dispatchers and crew, with the exception of Flying Officer King, had taken off their parachutes. While they were putting them on again, there was an explosion and the starboard wing broke off. Flying Officer King, who had been standing by the door, was flung clear and managed to pull the ripcord of his parachute. Flight Lieutenant Lord was subsequently awarded a posthumous Victoria Cross for his great heroism.

Other aircraft crash-landed in the area, some landing south of the Lower Rhine. Of the total of 390 tons of supplies dropped, only a tiny proportion fell into the division's hands. During the RAF's resolute and gallant efforts to re-supply 1st Airborne Division, its aircraft and crews suffered heavy casualties: thirteen aircraft were shot down and ninety-seven were damaged.

Chaos reigned in most areas throughout the day. Other than in 2nd Parachute Battalion's area, the only place where some form of order reigned was in Oosterbeek where Lieutenant Colonel 'Sheriff' Thompson, the Commanding Officer of 1st Airlanding Light Regiment RA, had established his forward command post with the guns of 3rd Airlanding Light Battery RA. Having already formed a force of glider pilots and anti-tank gunners to protect the battery, Thompson had moved forward to reconnoitre. While doing so he had encountered a number of stragglers from 11th Parachute Battalion and the South Staffordshires withdrawing from Arnhem. Quickly organizing them into a unit, he had placed them under command of Major Robert Cain of the South Staffordshires and ordered him to deploy them on the high ground west of the Den Brink feature, covering the railway line. Cain and his men were later joined by Lieutenant J. L. Williams, 1st Parachute Battalion's Motor Transport Officer, who had collected some fifty men of Headquarter Company and some 200 from other units. Williams had then attempted to break through to 2nd Parachute Battalion but had been held up near the St. Elizabeth Hospital. By the time dusk fell on 19 September, he had decided to withdraw and he and his men, who had been joined by others from 3rd and 11th Parachute Battalions, made their way to the area of the railway south of Den Brink where they met Lieutenant Colonel Thompson's force.

2nd Parachute Battalion, meanwhile, had been under constant heavy fire from tanks and artillery from two battle groups: that of SS-Sturmbannführer Brinkmann and another commanded by Major Hans-Peter Knaust, commander of a Wehrmacht panzer grenadier training and replacement battalion comprising four companies of infantry which had arrived on the morning of the previous day with eight tanks of 6th Panzer Regiment, including two Tiger tanks which crossed the bridge from the south. These were impervious to the 6pdr anti-tank guns and PIATs, the only anti-tank weapons with which 2nd Parachute Battalion was equipped, and the fire from their 88mm guns rapidly reduced buildings to rubble. They were supported by two 88mm guns positioned near the southern end of the bridge, which brought fire to bear on the houses in which 2nd Parachute Battalion was located. Both these enemy battle groups were supported by artillery which included a battery of Nebelwerfer multi-barrelled rocket-launchers.

By the afternoon of 19 September, most of the buildings in which Lieutenant Colonel Frost's men had installed themselves had been set ablaze by phosphorous shells. After each artillery barrage, infantry attacked but were beaten off by the determined defenders who counter-attacked with bayonet charges, some of which were led by Major Digby Tatham-Warter. Morale within the battalion was still high despite the appalling conditions, and the troops carried the war to the enemy whenever they could do so, leaving their positions with PIATs and Gammon bombs to hunt the enemy tanks which crawled through the streets blasting the houses on either side of them. One tank, which had proved to be particularly troublesome, was destroyed with grenades by Lieutenant Pat Barnett, the commander of the brigade headquarters defence platoon, while three others were knocked out by Captain Tony Frank with a PIAT.

However, that evening Tiger tanks appeared again and opened fire on the battalion's positions. Major Digby Tatham-Warter, who had taken over as second in command after Major David Wallis had been killed, and the battalion's Roman Catholic chaplain, Father Egan, were both wounded.

By the evening of 19 September, the remnants of 1st Airborne Division in the area of Oosterbeek were being pushed back on all sides. The majority of them were in an area between Heveadorp and Wolfheze to the west and from Oosterbeek to Johanna Hoeve to the east. Divisional HQ was roughly in the centre, located in the Hartenstein Hotel. Major General Urquhart decided that his only chance of conserving his remaining forces and hanging on until the arrival of XXX Corps was to withdraw his troops and consolidate them inside a defensive box. This would also form a bridgehead on the northern bank of the river for any subsequent crossings from the south via the ferry at Heveadorp which had been found to be still in working order. Although it would in effect mean abandoning 2nd Parachute Battalion and the other units at the bridge, Urquhart knew that it was the only option open to him. That evening, orders were issued for troops to withdraw into the perimeter around Oosterbeek. As night fell, the sky was brilliantly lit by burning buildings throughout Arnhem.

5
TAKING HELL'S HIGHWAY

'Jim, never try to fight an entire corps off one road.' — Lieutenant General Sir Brian Horrocks to Brigadier General James Gavin.

While the saga of 1st Airborne Division was unfolding at Arnhem and Oosterbeek, the two American airborne divisions had been establishing the 'corridor' along which Lieutenant General Sir Brian Horrocks' XXX Corps would advance.

The landings of 101st US Airborne Division, commanded by Major General Maxwell Taylor, had proved successful. Of the 424 transport aircraft carrying the parachute element of 6,809 men on 17 September, 422 succeeded in dropping their 'sticks'. Heavy flak was encountered during the approach to the dropping zones and two aircraft were shot down during the final run-in, but the majority of the paratroopers aboard them managed to jump clear. In all, sixteen aircraft crashed, with the loss of their crews. Casualties on the dropping zones, however, amounted to only 2 per cent, and within an hour of the drop all units had regrouped successfully and were moving off towards their objectives.

The division's tasks were to seize the four road and railway bridges over the River Aa and the Zuid Willems Vaart Canal at Veghel, the road bridge over the lower Dommel at St. Oedenrode, the road bridge over the Wilhelmina Canal at Zon, and the town of Eindhoven with its bridges over the upper Dommel. These objectives were spread over a distance of some fifteen miles, so the division was thinly spread; any threat would have to be met by the movement of troops to critical points along the 'corridor'.

As explained earlier, these tasks were such that Major General Maxwell Taylor had been forced to allocate virtually all the capacity in his first lift to his three parachute infantry regiments, each of which comprised three battalions, two engineer companies and as many jeeps and trailers as possible to give his division some mobility. His glider infantry regiment, artillery and supporting arms would have to be brought in during the following two days.

The drop began at 1300 hours. 501st Parachute Infantry Regiment, commanded by Colonel Howard R. Johnson, less its 1st Battalion but with two platoons of 326th Airborne Engineer Battalion attached, dropped on DZ 'A' two miles west of Veghel and, encountering little resistance, within an hour moved off towards the town. By 1500 hours the regiment had seized all its initial objectives, namely the bridges over the Aa and the Zuid Willems Vaart Canal. Meanwhile its 1st Battalion had landed on DZ 'A-1', in the vicinity of Kasteel, some three miles north-west of the Veghel, where it met some resistance from small units of enemy line-of-communications troops in the vicinity of the dropping zone. The battalion reached Veghel at 1700 hours, encountering scattered groups of enemy who made no serious attempt to defend the town. By nightfall, the regiment was well dug-in and prepared for any attack, all the bridges having been captured intact and secured. The two engineer platoons, meanwhile, began to build a second bridge over the Zuid Willems Vaart Canal so that military traffic could move through the towns in both directions if necessary.

502nd Parachute Infantry Regiment, commanded by Colonel John H. Michaelis, with three platoons of 326th Airborne Engineer Battalion attached, landed on DZ 'B' where it encountered no opposition. By 1500 hours the regiment had regrouped and the 1st Battalion headed for St. Oedenrode which it captured after a skirmish, subsequently seizing intact its objective, the bridge over the Dommel. The battalion then dug-in and by dusk was well established.

Meanwhile, Company 'H' of the 3rd Battalion had made its way four miles to the west, to the road bridge at Best which it was to secure as an alternative crossing over the canal. En route it lost its way and initially only one platoon arrived at the bridge. It was here that the first real resistance was encountered. As the platoon approached the bridge, it met an enemy roadblock. Eventually, the remainder of Company 'H' arrived and a fierce fight ensued against the defenders of the bridge who consisted of troops of 59th Infantry Division, commanded by Generalmajor Walter Poppe, reinforced by an anti-aircraft battalion using its 20mm guns in the ground target role. The company was counter-attacked later and forced to withdraw. On receiving reports of the situation, the regimental commander sent the rest of the 3rd Battalion with the task of seizing the bridge on the following morning.

Meanwhile, 506th Parachute Infantry Regiment, commanded by Colonel Robert F. Sink, landed on DZ 'C' where it encountered no opposition. Companies of the 1st Battalion immediately headed for their individual objectives, the three bridges over the Wilhelmina Canal, to seize them before they were blown by the enemy. Only slight resistance, from scattered groups of enemy, was met and the Americans were within 100 yards of the main bridge at Zon when it was blown by troops of the Hermann Göring Training Regiment who were withdrawing. It later transpired that the two other bridges had been blown two days earlier. Nevertheless, the regiment crossed the canal by other means and by 2359 hours was on the south bank and had established a bridgehead.

Major General Maxwell Taylor's tactical headquarters dropped with 502nd Parachute Infantry Regiment and subsequently set up its command post at Zon. One hour later, gliders brought in more personnel of the divisional headquarters, the reconnaissance platoon, and signals and medical companies. Losses among the gliders had been relatively heavy, only fifty-three of a total of seventy arriving on the landing zone with 75 per cent of the men and equipment dispatched from England. By nightfall, the headquarters was in communication with all the landed elements of the division with the exception of 501st Parachute Infantry Regiment. This was contacted at 0600 hours next day.

The following morning, 18 September, found 501st Parachute Infantry Regiment continuing its defence of Veghel. The enemy mounted several small-scale attacks on the regiment but these were beaten off without difficulty. At St. Oedenrode, the 1st Battalion 502nd Parachute Infantry Regiment held on to the town and repulsed several half-hearted assaults. At Best, meanwhile, the 3rd Battalion mounted an attack on the road bridge at first light but suffered heavy casualties, including the death of its commanding officer, Lieutenant Colonel Robert H. Cole, who had been awarded the Congressional Medal of Honor during the Normandy campaign. The 2nd Battalion was therefore ordered to assist. Carrying out a flanking move to the right, and supported by its own mortars, the battalion advanced across open ground but encountered heavy small arms, mortar and artillery fire and was forced to withdraw. At 1100 hours, while fighting was continuing, the enemy suddenly blew the bridge. The 2nd Battalion subsequently took up defensive positions on the left of the 3rd Battalion and by nightfall the whole of 502nd Parachute Infantry Regiment was in defensive positions east of the road.

506th Parachute Infantry Regiment, led by its 3rd Battalion, began its advance on Eindhoven at first light on 18 September. One mile from the city, however, it was held up by determined resistance at Woensel. The 2nd Battalion moved round to the east, outflanked the enemy positions and captured the city at 1300 hours. Contact had already been made with a British reconnaissance patrol north of Eindhoven at just after midday and at 1915 hours contact was established with the Guards Armoured Division, the leading element of XXX Corps, just south of the city.

At 1530 hours that afternoon, 428 gliders had brought in the 3rd Battalion 327th Glider Infantry Regiment, together with an engineer battalion, the remainder of the division's signals and medical companies, Battery 'B' of 377th Parachute Field Artillery Battalion and some of the divisional supply and administrative transport. The glider-borne infantrymen were given the task of securing and holding the landing zone and the divisional administrative area.

During the night, at about 2100 hours, the leading elements of the Guards Armoured Division reached the south bank of the Wilhelmina

Canal at Zon and began to build a bridge which was completed before dawn on 19 September. At 0615 hours the armoured cars of the leading squadron of the 2nd Household Cavalry Regiment began to cross the Canal and half an hour later were moving through Veghel and St. Oedenrode.

Dawn on 19 September saw a further attack on the Best bridge by the 2nd Battalion 502nd Parachute Infantry Regiment but this was also halted, the enemy having reinforced the area with three infantry companies and two replacement battalions. Another attack was mounted during the afternoon, this time with the 2nd and 3rd Battalions of the 502nd and elements of 327th Glider Infantry Regiment taking part. Support was provided by XXX Corps which attached a squadron of the 15th/19th The King's Royal Hussars to 101st US Airborne Division and provided artillery fire, its guns now being within range. This final attack proved successful and resulted in more than 300 enemy killed, 1,056 prisoners taken and fifteen 88mm guns knocked out.

That afternoon, at approximately 1400 hours, the division's third glider lift arrived, bringing in the 1st and 2nd Battalions 327th Glider Infantry Regiment, 81st Airborne Anti-Tank Battalion, 377th Parachute Field Artillery Battalion (less Battery 'B') and 321st and 907th Glider Field Artillery Battalions. Unfortunately, because of bad weather, a large number of gliders failed to arrive at the landing zones. Some glider-tug combinations were forced to turn back, and in several instances tugs were forced to cast off their gliders early, the latter having to land wherever possible in enemy-held territory. Heavy flak also took its toll, several gliders being shot down. Nevertheless, those elements that were landed safely deployed to their allotted areas. Elements of the two glider infantry battalions joined their 3rd Battalion in protecting the landing zones while at the same time sending some of their number to assist 502nd Parachute Infantry Regiment in its attack on the bridge at Best.

At about 1700 hours on the 19th, enemy armour was reported to be approaching Zon and shortly afterwards forty tanks appeared within a few hundred yards of the bridge which they proceeded to shell, together with the divisional command post and the town itself. Little damage was done, however, and the tanks withdrew on the appearance of detachments of 81st Airborne Anti-Tank Battalion, sent from the landing zone, which succeeded in knocking out two of them.

Farther to the north, Brigadier General James Gavin's 82nd US Airborne Division had also carried out a successful landing with minimal losses of men and equipment, despite having encountered a considerable amount of flak as it approached its dropping zones. Its initial task was to seize and hold the Groesbeek Heights, the feature of high ground to the immediate south-east of Nijmegen which dominated the area. It was then

100

to seize the main road bridge over the Maas at Grave, the smaller railway bridges and crossings over the Maas-Waal Canal and the huge bridge over the Waal at Nijmegen. These objectives covered an area whose perimeter extended some twenty-five miles.

General Gavin had decided to drop two of his three parachute infantry regiments, together with one of his parachute artillery battalions, to the north-east and south-east of Groesbeek, between the Groesbeek Heights and the forests of the Reichswald. His third regiment, tasked with seizing the bridge at Grave, would be dropped north of the Maas, to the north of the village of Overasselt, with one company dropped to the south of the river so that the bridge could be attacked from both directions. The glider-borne element of his division, which would be brought in by fifty Waco gliders, would land on a large LZ to the east of Groesbeek which would also be used by thirty-eight Horsa gliders bringing in HQ 1st Airborne Corps fifteen minutes later.

At approximately 1230 hours on the 17th, the divisional pathfinder teams landed on their respective dropping zones and between 1250 and 1400 hours the division's parachute element was dropped from 482 C-47 Dakotas. At 1350 hours, Waco gliders brought in elements of the divisional headquarters, part of the divisional airborne anti-tank regiment and engineers on to the landing zone south-east of Groesbeek and shortly afterwards General Gavin's command post was established 1,000 yards west of the town. Of fifty gliders which took off from England, forty-six arrived in the divisional area, although some touched down a few miles short of the landing zone.

505th Parachute Infantry Regiment dropped shortly after the pathfinders and quickly seized Groesbeek after which, having cleared the area of enemy, it established defensive positions on the high ground west of the town, extending south to Mook.

504th Parachute Infantry Regiment, commanded by Colonel Reuben H. Tucker, meanwhile dropped at 1313 hours on to three drop zones located west of the Maas-Waal Canal, two to the north and one to the south of the Maas. One of its battalions was dropped north-east of Overasselt and, after encountering strong opposition from the enemy, captured the Maas-Waal Canal bridge at 1600 hours. Both of the canal bridges near Blankenburg and Hatert were blown by the enemy as the battalion approached, but both sites were captured after nightfall. Another battalion dropped west of Overasselt and cut the Grave–Nijmegen road, blocking all movement southwards and clearing all enemy from the western part of the divisional area. Meanwhile the regiment's third battalion dropped one company south of the Maas at Grave while the remainder of the battalion landed north of the river and to the west of Overasselt. Both elements of the battalion then advanced against the bridge at Grave which was captured at 1430 hours. At 2300 hours the regiment occupied the town after the withdrawal of the 400 enemy defenders.

508th Parachute Infantry Regiment, commanded by Colonel Roy E. Lindquist, dropped to the north-east of Groesbeek at 1328 hours and established positions on the northern part of the Groesbeek Heights. After receiving reports from local people that both were only lightly held by the enemy, General Gavin ordered Colonel Lindquist to send one battalion immediately to Nijmegen to seize the road bridge over the Waal. The 1st Battalion, commanded by Lieutenant Colonel Shields Warren, was given the job and moved off immediately. At 2000 hours it launched an attack but this met stiff opposition some 400 yards from the bridge. Taking up positions due east of the Maas-Waal Canal, the battalion set up roadblocks to cut off any enemy moving southwards, and one of its companies was sent to clear any enemy from the glider landing zone north-east of Groesbeek but met considerable resistance. One battalion established positions on the vital high ground in the area of Berg en Dal, encountering little opposition while doing so. One of its companies was then detached and ordered to head for the Nijmegen bridge from the south-east. By 2359 hours it had reached and occupied a feature known as Hill 64.4 north-east of Ubbergen.

As mentioned earlier, elements of 82nd US Airborne Division's supporting arms also dropped with it on 17 September. The 376th Parachute Field Artillery Battalion, commanded by Lieutenant Colonel Wilbur Griffith, dropped at 1335 hours on its allotted dropping zone south of Groesbeek with ten 75mm pack howitzers and moved 1,000 yards to its first gun line position. At 1800 hours, the battalion carried out its first fire mission in support of 508th Parachute Infantry Regiment. Companies 'B', 'C' and 'D' of 307th Airborne Engineer Battalion also dropped south of Groesbeek. Two of them, 'B' and 'D', covered the divisional headquarters' move to its initial deployment location and thereafter provided local protection for General Gavin's command post. Company 'C' meanwhile linked up with 504th Parachute Infantry Regiment west of the Maas-Waal Canal. Anti-aircraft support also arrived in the form of Battery 'A' of 80th Airborne Anti-Aircraft Battalion which was deployed with two of its 57mm guns allotted to each parachute infantry regimental group and two in reserve at the divisional command post.

Next day, 18 September, 504th Parachute Infantry Regiment was still holding the bridges over the Maas at Grave and over the Maas-Waal Canal at Heuman. At the same time, the regiment was carrying out extensive patrolling to the west and north-west of its area along the Grave–Nijmegen road. At midday, one platoon was sent northwards along the west bank of the Maas-Waal Canal to assist a platoon from 508th Parachute Infantry Regiment in the capture of a bridge on the

Grave–Nijmegen road near Honinghutie. As the two platoons advanced on the bridge, the enemy blew it. Although not destroyed, the bridge was so weakened that it could not be used by vehicles which had to be diverted eastwards to the bridge at Heuman.

Within 505th Parachute Infantry Regiment's area, meanwhile, the enemy mounted a counter-attack at 0630 hours with four battle groups, each of approximately battalion strength and supported by five armoured cars and three half-tracks armed with 20mm anti-aircraft guns, which advanced north-westwards from the northern Reichswald towards Groesbeek. This took 82nd US Airborne Division by surprise and for a time it was under pressure as it was already overstretched. Nevertheless, attacks were beaten off at Horst, Grafwegen and Riethorst. The main problem facing the Division was that its dropping and landing zones had been overrun and the second lift was due to land at 1300 hours. So clearance of the zones became a priority and 505th Parachute Infantry Regiment was given the job, which it began at at 1240 hours. The battle was still in progress as the 450 gliders began landing twenty minutes later, the 1st Battalion attacking downhill across the northernmost landing zone under heavy fire from small arms and 20mm guns. At this point the enemy broke and withdrew in confusion. Casualties among the 1st Battalion were very light, totalling eleven; the enemy lost fifty killed, 150 taken prisoner and sixteen 20mm guns captured. Losses among the gliders had been light and most of their loads, including thirty 75mm pack howitzers and eight 57mm guns, were unloaded intact.

At Nijmegen, 508th Parachute Infantry Regiment withdrew its battalion from the town, but at 0900 hours Company 'G' re-entered it and succeeded in advancing to the same location as had been reached on the previous day. A strong force of enemy was encountered and fighting lasted until 1500 hours when the company was withdrawn to the area of Berg en Dal. Meanwhile, at 1310 hours, other units of the regiment carried out an attack to clear the enemy from the area of the glider landing zone north and north-east of Groesbeek, in preparation for the arrival of the division's second lift which had been delayed by fog in England. Surprise was complete and by 1400 hours the area was clear, the 508th having killed fifty enemy and taken 149 prisoners and sixteen anti-aircraft guns. Throughout the day, the regiment continued to hold the high ground in the area of Berg en Dal, a town on the north of the Groesbeek Heights, suffering sporadic artillery shelling and probing attacks from patrols.

The clearing of the landing zones around Groesbeek enabled further support elements of 82nd US Airborne Division to be brought in. Taking off from airfields in England between 1000 and 1100 hours, 450 gliders and their tugs flew the same route as those on the previous day, bringing in 80th Airborne Anti-Aircraft Battalion (less Battery 'A'), 319th and 320th

Glider Field Artillery Battalions, 456th Parachute Field Artillery Battalion and 307th Airborne Medical Company. Some gliders overshot their landing zones and landed over the border in Germany, but most of their passengers with their equipment succeeded in reaching the divisional area. Twenty minutes after the gliders had landed, a resupply drop from 135 B-24 Liberator bombers took place on the dropping zone south of Groesbeek.

After rallying and regrouping, 319th Glider Field Artillery and 456th Parachute Field Artillery Battalions were placed in direct support of 508th and 505th Parachute Infantry Regiments respectively, and 320th Glider Field Artillery Battalion was tasked with providing support to the rest of the division.

The morning of 19 September saw the arrival at Grave of the leading elements of the Guards Armoured Division which linked up with 504th Parachute Infantry Regiment at 0820 hours. Leaving a company to guard the bridge at Grave, two other companies to guard the Maas–Waal Canal bridges at Heumen and Honinghutie, and another to patrol and guard the road between Grave and the Honinghutie bridge, the regiment moved east of the Maas–Waal Canal where it relieved the 2nd Battalion 505th Parachute Infantry Regiment and occupied the Jonker Bosch woods. Its 3rd Battalion moved to the area of Malden to become divisional reserve.

On being relieved by the 504th, the 2nd Battalion 505th Parachute Infantry Regiment was placed under command of the Guards Armoured Division and moved northwards to take part in an attack on the two Nijmegen bridges with the division's Grenadier Group which comprised 1st (Motor) and 2nd (Armoured) Battalions Grenadier Guards. This would be carried out in three columns. The right-hand one, comprising Companies 'E' and 'F' of the parachute battalion, most of No. 2 Company of the Grenadiers' 1st Battalion and part of No. 3 Squadron of their 2nd Battalion, would head for the main bridge. The centre column, consisting of a troop of tanks and a platoon of Grenadier infantry, would make its way to the town's post office where, it had been reported, demolition apparatus for blowing the bridge had been found. The left-hand column, comprising a platoon of the Grenadiers' No. 2 Company, the rest of their No. 3 Squadron and Company 'D' of the parachute battalion, would head for the town centre and then north-west for the railway bridge.

The road and railway bridges at Nijmegen are situated to the north-east and north-west of the town respectively and are the only two crossings of the Waal for some twenty miles. The road bridge, situated on high ground, was 2,000 feet long with a centre span of 800 feet. The approaches to both bridges were difficult for the two columns attacking them and favoured the defenders.

Facing the Americans and the Grenadiers was a battle group of 10th SS Panzer Division. The approaches to the road bridge were defended by a battalion of 100 men reinforced by Wehrmacht troops, under the command of SS-Hauptsturmführer Karl-Heinz Euling, which had until the previous week formed part of 9th SS Panzer Division. The railway bridge and the area to the south of it was held by four companies of 6th Ersatz Battalion commanded by Oberst Henke, commander of a Luftwaffe parachute training regiment who had been in overall charge of the defence of the two bridges until the arrival of the SS battle group. North of the river was a battalion of panzer troops, fighting in the infantry role, under command of SS-Hauptsturmführer Leo Hermann Reinhold, who was the commander of the SS battle group and was responsible for the defence of Nijmegen.

The first unit of 10th SS Panzer Division to arrive in Nijmegen on the morning of 18 September was a company of engineers who had been tasked with preparing both bridges for demolition as well as improving the defences at the southern end of the bridge. At about midday, Euling's battalion had arrived and taken up its positions around the road bridge. By now fighting was already taking place in the southern outskirts of the city. During the afternoon, Reinhold's battalion arrived and established positions on the north bank. The Guards' three columns set off at about 1600 hours and moved through the outskirts of the town, encountering only artillery fire. On reaching the centre, they headed for their individual objectives. The centre column occupied the post office after meeting little resistance and the Grenadier 1st Battalion's commanding officer, Lieutenant Colonel Edward Goulburn, established his command post there. The right-hand column made for the road bridge, guided by members of the Dutch Resistance who travelled in the leading tanks. However, on approaching a large roundabout about 400 yards short of the bridge, it encountered considerable opposition from enemy troops in buildings that had been converted into strongpoints.

The Grenadiers' leading tank was engaged by anti-tank guns and set on fire as soon as it approached the roundabout. A large number of enemy infantry, supported by two 88mm self-propelled guns, covering a large barricade which blocked the road, brought a heavy volume of fire to bear and two more tanks were knocked out. A platoon of Grenadier infantry was sent on a flanking move to the right but was unable to make much headway. Eventually, as dusk was approaching and little progress was being made, the attacking force took up positions for the night.

Meanwhile, the left-hand column was heading for the railway bridge. As it approached, it came under very heavy shelling and machine-gun fire and the leading tank was knocked out. The railway line itself proved to be an obstacle for the tanks and the combined infantry force of the parachute company and Grenadier platoon was insufficient to take the objective without armoured support. In view of this, the column withdrew and concentrated around a crossroads north of Nijmegen's railway station. There it would remain, cut off by enemy forces which infiltrated past it back into the town during the night.

The fighting had been fierce and the Americans had already suffered heavy casualties. Since landing, these numbered 150 killed and 600 wounded, with an unspecified number missing. The enemy, however, were in strength; their numbers at the southern end of the road bridge alone being estimated at some 500.

By nightfall, 32nd Guards Brigade had arrived at a concentration area between Grave and the Maas–Waal Canal. Its Coldstream Group, comprising 1st (Armoured) and 5th Battalions Coldstream Guards, was placed under command of 82nd US Airborne Division and moved to Dekkerswald in divisional reserve, ready to protect the division's right flank from any threat from enemy armour emanating from the Reichswald to the east.

6
ADVANCE TO CONTACT

'I am proud to meet the commander of the greatest division in the world today.'
— Lieutenant General Sir Miles Dempsey to Brigadier General James Gavin.

While the three airborne divisions had been fighting in Arnhem and along the 'corridor' stretching from Eindhoven to Nijmegen, XXX Corps had been moving northwards on the first stage of its advance. However, all had not gone well as it headed for its link-up with 101st US Airborne Division at Eindhoven.

At 1435 hours on 17 September, the Guards Armoured Division, in the van of XXX Corps, had begun the breakout from the bridgehead over the Meuse–Escaut Canal which was being held by 50th (Northumbrian) Infantry Division. In the lead was 5th Guards Armoured Brigade, commanded by Brigadier Norman Gwatkin and led by the Irish Group comprising 2nd (Armoured) and 3rd Battalions Irish Guards commanded respectively by two cousins: Lieutenant Colonels Giles and Joe Vandeleur. No. 3 Squadron, commanded by Captain Mick O'Cock, with No. 1 Company mounted on its Sherman tanks, was the spearhead of the advance with Lieutenant Keith Heathcote's troop leading the way. Following behind the Irish Guards was the Grenadier Group, consisting of 1st (Motor) and 2nd (Armoured) Battalions Grenadier Guards. Behind 5th Guards (Armoured) Brigade came 32nd Guards Brigade, commanded by Brigadier George Johnson, which comprised the Coldstream Group, together with the Welsh Group comprising 1st Battalion and 2nd (Armoured) Battalions Welsh Guards.

Ahead of the Irish Guards' tanks, a massive rolling barrage, laid down by six field and three medium regiments of the Royal Artillery, crashed down on the enemy positions. This had begun ten minutes prior to 'H-Hour' and would continue for twenty minutes after it, the line of the barrage being rolled forward in front of the tanks at the rate of 200 yards per minute and extending 1,000 yards either side of the axis of advance. On completion of the barrage, the gunners would re-lay their guns and, if necessary, the entire barrage would be fired again. Meanwhile, further timed concentrations of artillery fire would be fired by three field and one heavy regiment on known enemy positions, and by a heavy anti-aircraft regiment firing airburst shells. Dutch and Belgian artillery would also provide supporting fire.

The enemy forces lying in wait to the front of the advancing tanks had been estimated as numbering some six infantry battalions supported by about twenty armoured vehicles and approximately a dozen field and medium artillery pieces together with a few 88mm anti-aircraft guns deployed in the ground target role. The presence of tanks was suspected but there had been no confirmation.

In fact, the enemy numbered ten understrength infantry battalions supported by some artillery and twelve self-propelled anti-tank guns. These comprised a battle group under the command of Oberst Walther, a paratroop officer who had previously commanded the Luftwaffe's 4th Fallschirmjäger Regiment, and consisted of the following: Fallschirmjäger Regiment von Hoffmann which was a reinforcement training unit consisting of a headquarters, three battalions and an anti-tank company with eight 75mm guns; 6th Fallschirmjäger Regiment comprising four battalions, numbering 200 to 300 men each, the fourth battalion consisting of a reconnaissance company, an engineer company, an anti-tank company, a medium mortar company with 81mm mortars, and an air defence company equipped with machine-guns and four quadruple-mounted 20mm guns; two panzer grenadier battalions from 9th and 10th SS Panzer Divisions respectively; six 105mm field howitzers from 10th SS Panzer Division; four companies of 6th Luftwaffe Penal Battalion; and an air defence unit equipped with two 88mm and three 20mm anti-aircraft guns.

The entire battle group was deployed around the XXX Corps bridgehead over the Meuse–Escaut Canal at Neerpelt. To the east were the two SS panzer grenadier battalions; in the north, opposite the centre of the bridgehead, was Fallschirmjäger Regiment von Hoffmann which had been reinforced by an SS engineer company. To the west was 6th Fallschirmjäger Regiment commanded by Oberstleutnant von der Heydte, a well-known veteran of German airborne actions at Eben Emael and in North Africa and Crete.

On each side of the road to Eindhoven (the axis of advance for the tanks and infantry of Guards Armoured Division) were sited the anti-tank guns of the 1st Battalion Fallschirmjäger Regiment von Hoffman. Further on, a platoon of thirty panzerfaust-equipped infantry were sited in a tank ambush, supported by machine-guns.

As the Irish Guards' tanks rolled forward behind the barrage, rocket-firing Typhoon fighter-bombers dived and attacked the German positions while others loitered overhead 'on call' to engage targets indicated to them from the ground. The anti-tank company of the 1st Battalion Fallschirmjäger Regiment von Hoffmann, which was sited in in-depth positions along the road, was completely annihilated by the artillery barrage before it had any opportunity to come into action. Lack of tractor units to tow them meant that the guns had been sited only a few yards from the road and so were very vulnerable. The rest of the battalion escaped virtually unscathed, including the platoon with panzerfausts awaiting the tanks and the machine-gunners who would engage the motorized infantry.

As the Irish Guards' No. 3 Squadron approached the ambush the dug-in enemy troops held their fire until the rear elements were level with them. Three of the squadron's rearmost tanks and the six leading tanks of No. 2 Squadron were knocked out as the ambush was sprung. Ditches on each side of the road and marshy terrain prevented the tanks from deploying off the road, but the infantry of the 3rd Battalion dismounted rapidly and took cover in the ditches while other tanks returned fire. The situation was chaotic until a self-propelled gun was knocked out by one of the Irish Guards' Fireflies (Shermans equipped with 17pdr guns as opposed to the standard 76mm), whereupon the gun crew surrendered and were joined by the crew of another nearby. At this point RAF Typhoons swooped low again, called in by an RAF forward controller travelling alongside Lieutenant Colonel Joe Vandeleur, firing their rockets at enemy positions that had survived the artillery barrage.

On each side of the road, guardsmen of the 3rd Battalion moved forward to clear the enemy from their positions in woods and ditches. They were assisted in this by two battalions from 50th (Northumbrian) Infantry Division which were tasked with clearing the Guards Armoured Division's flanks until it broke through the enemy screen. Meanwhile, the hulks of the knocked-out tanks were pushed off the road by an armoured bulldozer which had been called forward. Gradually the road and surrounding area were cleared. On-the-spot interrogation of prisoners revealed the locations of further positions which were promptly engaged and destroyed by the tanks of the 2nd (Armoured) Battalion.

The artillery barrage started again and the advance was resumed, with No. 2 Squadron leading, and once again the barrage was brought down in front of the leading tanks. Resistance slackened and good progress was made until 1930 hours when the Irish Group reached Valkenswaard, the first town on the route to Eindhoven, which they occupied without opposition. It had been expected that Eindhoven would be reached within two to three hours of the breakout, but only seven miles had been covered that day. There were still fifty-seven miles to go to Arnhem, and the question arose of continuing the advance to Eindhoven that night. However, Lieutenant Colonel Joe Vandeleur, commander of the Irish Group, was informed by the commander of 5th Guards Armoured Brigade, Brigadier Norman Gwatkin, that the bridge beyond Eindhoven at Zon had been destroyed and that bridging would have to be carried out during the night before the advance could be continued. Meanwhile, the brigade was to carry out much needed replenishment of fuel and ammunition and servicing of its tanks. Vandeleur was ordered to resume the advance at 0630 hours on 18 September.

Next morning the division's two brigades assumed two separate axes of advance: 5th Guards Armoured Brigade, with the Irish Group in the lead, remained on the main axis of the Eindhoven road; 32nd Guards Brigade detoured eastwards via Leende, Geldrop and Helmond. But the going proved almost as difficult as before, and it was not until nightfall that Leende and Heeze had been cleared after fierce fighting. Reconnaissance patrols sent out at first light on the 19th confirmed reports that Geldrop was held in strength, and during the night local inhabitants had reported that Helmond was a main enemy stronghold, so the brigade was ordered to rejoin the main axis of advance.

Meanwhile, during the morning of 18 September, from the wooded country on each side of the road the Irish Group had encountered strong opposition from troops supported by Panther tanks and anti-tank guns. On reaching the southern edge of the village of Aalst, they were held up completely by infantry elements of the 1st and 3rd Battalions Fallschirmjäger Regiment von Hoffmann supported by eleven 75mm anti-tank guns and a flak platoon equipped with 20mm guns. To the east of the road were sited eight Panzerjäger self-propelled 75mm anti-tank guns of 10th SS Panzer Division's anti-tank battalion which engaged the Irish Group from the flank.

While the Irish Group was trying to fight its way through, the Grenadier Group was ordered to follow the 2nd Household Cavalry Regiment which was already trying to work its way round to the west of Eindhoven so as link up with 101st US Airborne Division. But the Grenadiers found that while the bridges on their new route would accommodate armoured cars, tanks were too heavy for them and eventually they were forced to return to the main axis.

The Household Cavalry then reported that it had broken through to link up with elements of 101st US Airborne Division, and shortly afterwards the Irish Group overcame resistance in Aalst and pushed on towards Eindhoven. It was held up again two miles further on, at a bridge over the River Dommel, by a force of infantry and 88mm anti-tank guns in houses and strongpoints that formed the southern defences of Eindhoven. Unable to deploy off the road, and with the rest of the divisional column stretching back behind them, the leading tanks of No. 2 Squadron, under Major Edward Tyler, could only try to move forward, but one 88mm gun proved particularly troublesome by firing straight down the road. Requests for air support were refused because fog had grounded the Typhoons at their airfields in Belgium.

While Lieutenant Colonel Joe Vandeleur was calling for artillery support, No. 1 Company of the 3rd Battalion Irish Guards, commanded by

Major Edward Fisher-Rowe, made a detour to the west via Gestel and reported that the route was clear. Meanwhile a troop of the Household Cavalry, which had succeeded in infiltrating round the enemy positions and was reconnoitring the country further north, unexpectedly made contact with troops of 506th Parachute Infantry Regiment north of Eindhoven.

In the meantime the commander of another Household Cavalry reconnaissance patrol had succeeded in advancing on foot to a point from where he could observe the enemy positions blocking the axis. Shortly afterwards he reported that the enemy were withdrawing and the Irish Guards continued their advance, passing six 88mm guns abandoned by their crews. They entered Eindhoven to a tumultuous welcome from the inhabitants. Pushing on through the cheering crowds, they advanced as quickly as possible to Zon where they linked up with 506th Parachute Infantry Regiment during the evening of 18 September.

The priority task now facing the Guards Armoured Division was to put a Class 40 Bailey bridge across the Wilhelmina Canal to replace the bridge blown by the enemy. Fortunately, the division's Commander Royal Engineers, Lieutenant Colonel C. P. Jones, had ensured that the necessary bridging equipment was travelling sufficiently far forward in the column for it to be brought up quickly. By 0600 hours on 19 September, 14th Field Squadron Royal Engineers had completed the task and ten minutes later the leading tanks of the Grenadier Group crossed the Canal.

The division, which by now was thirty hours behind schedule, sped rapidly along the 'corridor' cleared and secured by 101st US Airborne Division, and by 0700 hours on the 19th the Grenadier Group had passed through Veghel, crossing the bridge over the Maas at Grave at 0830 hours, closely followed by the rest of 5th Guards Armoured Brigade and 32nd Guards Brigade. Here the division halted because the commanding officers of the two Grenadier battalions received a message that the commander of 1st Airborne Corps wished to see them at his headquarters on the southern part of the Groesbeek Heights, about five miles south of Nijmegen. For Lieutenant General Browning it must have been doubly a pleasure to see Lieutenant Colonels Edward Goulburn and Rodney Moore, not only because they represented the spearhead of XXX Corps en route to relieve 1st Airborne Division, but also because he himself was a Grenadier and had previously commanded the 2nd Battalion.

Browning informed Goulburn and Moore that the bridge over the Maas–Waal three miles south-west of Nijmegen had been damaged and would not take the weight of tanks, but that there was an alternative route to the east via Overasselt and Heumen. The Grenadier Group followed this diversion and by 1200 hours had halted and regrouped in the vicinity of a monastery at Marienboom, just south of Nijmegen. The 2nd Household Cavalry Regiment, meanwhile, had reached the Waal.

By now Lieutenant General Horrocks and the commander of the Guards Armoured Division, Major General Allan Adair, together with Brigadier Norman Gwatkin, commander of 5th Guards Armoured Brigade, had also arrived at HQ 1st Airborne Corps where they met Lieutenant General 'Boy' Browning and Brigadier General James Gavin. Until then Horrocks and Adair had received very little information as to the situation regarding the three airborne divisions and the degree of success, or otherwise, of their respective missions. At this meeting they discovered that 82nd US Airborne Division had succeeded in all of its tasks except the capture of Nijmegen and its two bridges which were being strongly defended. They also learned of the difficulties facing Gavin: his division was overstretched because bad weather had delayed his second lift, and the constant threat to his landing zones had forced him to withdraw units from Nijmegen to protect them. Of 1st Airborne Division, Browning could tell them little other than that the landings on the first day had been successful. He was to receive no firm information regarding 1st Airborne Division's predicament until the following day.

At 1600 hours on the 19th, the Grenadier Group, with the 2nd Battalion 505th Parachute Infantry Regiment under command, moved off to carry out the first attack on the road and railway bridges. But, as has already been recounted, the attack failed in the face of resolute defence by Reinhold's SS battle group and the Americans suffered 150 killed and 600 wounded.

An alternative plan had to be produced quickly. Browning and Gavin in particular were well aware that further delay in the advance could spell disaster for 1st Airborne Division at Arnhem and that even after Nijmegen there were still eleven miles to be fought through before they got there. Indeed, the terrain after Nijmegen posed even more problems than that through which XXX Corps had already advanced: the road ran along an embankment across low-lying, marshy terrain; the tanks would present an easy target for anti-tank guns.

During the evening of the 19th, Browning, Horrocks, Adair and Gavin produced a plan for a second assault on Nijmegen and its bridge. The first phase, the clearing of the town, would start at first light next day. This would be followed later in the day by the second phase: an attack with artillery support on the 2,000-foot-long road bridge. The third element of the operation, proposed by Gavin, would be an assault river crossing west of Nijmegen; once across, the troops would head east to attack the bridge from the north. The only problem was that the nearest available boats – thirty-three collapsible wood and canvas craft – were on vehicles in XXX Corps' rear echelons. These would have to be brought forward along the single road that was already choked with long lines of vehicles and could not be delivered before dawn next day, which would mean that the assault crossing would have to be carried out in daylight.

The problems posed by being restricted to a single road for support and resupply were exacerbated during the night when 120 Luftwaffe bombers carried out a raid on Eindhoven which caused delay and confusion, particularly among XXX Corps' supply echelons. Some roads in the city were blocked, which made the traffic problems even worse. The line of communications was already exposed and under pressure from the enemy because of the apparent inability of XII and VIII Corps, on the left and right flanks respectively, to advance at the same rate.

At 1715 hours on the 19th, forty Panther tanks of 107th Panzer Brigade, supported by infantry of 1034th Grenadier Regiment, attacked Zon where HQ 101st US Airborne Division was located. The attack took the Americans completely by surprise and was only beaten off after fierce fighting. A critical situation was saved by the timely arrival of anti-tank detachments of 327th Glider Infantry Regiment from the landing zone where they had landed earlier.

At 0800 hours on 20 September, 107th Panzer Brigade tried once more to cut XXX Corps' line of communications; again it attacked Zon, and again surprised the Americans who had assumed that any further attacks would take place elsewhere. This second attack was beaten off by a counter-attack mounted by a combined force of 501st Parachute Infantry Regiment, the 15/19th The King's Royal Hussars, 44th Royal Tank Regiment, the Sherwood Rangers Yeomanry and troops from Main HQ XXX Corps. By the time that it withdrew, 107th Panzer Brigade had lost 10 per cent of its tanks.

Such was the situation to the rear that no additional forces would be available for the assault on Nijmegen for at least twenty-four hours. Consequently, the two divisions would have to cope on their own with the task of capturing Nijmegen and its bridges, despite the fact that they were already thinly stretched over a large area. 5th Guards Armoured Brigade, with the 2nd Battalion 505th Parachute Infantry under command, was allotted the task of clearing Nijmegen and capturing the bridge. The assault river crossing would be carried out by one of the two battalions of 504th Parachute Infantry which would be relieved of their task of defending the bridge at Grave. The crossing would be supported by infantry and tanks of the Irish Group and the guns of the Guards Armoured Division's two field regiments and those of corps artillery units. Close air support would be provided by RAF Typhoons.

32nd Guards Brigade, which had concentrated between Grave and the Maas–Waal Canal, would detach the Coldstream Group which would come under command of 82nd US Airborne Division to provide protection against an increasing threat from the Reichswald where it had become apparent that the enemy forces were building up. The Welsh Group would meanwhile take over the defence of the Grave area and would form a reserve. The 2nd Household Cavalry Regiment would detach a squadron in support of 82nd US Airborne Division while at the same time reconnoitring westwards between the Maas and the Rhine, and on the flanks of the main axis of advance to the south of the Maas.

At 0800 hours on 20 September the Grenadier Group, supported by elements of the 2nd Battalion 505th Parachute Infantry Regiment, began the arduous task of clearing the enemy from Nijmegen. This was a slow process in the teeth of stiff opposition, and streets had to be cleared building by building. By early afternoon, however, Lieutenant Colonel Edward Goulburn of the Grenadiers' 1st (Motor) Battalion, who was in command of the operation, decided that his troops were now in a position to launch the attack on the road bridge.

On the left, the King's Company, reinforced by a platoon of No. 2 Company, a section of Vickers medium machine-guns and two tanks, was given the task of clearing the houses in its area and then pushing forward to the river bank near the bridge. In the centre, No. 4 Company would seize an old fort that dominated the approaches to the bridge, and the surrounding area of parkland before moving on to the bridge itself. On the right, elements of the American parachute battalion would clear the area to the east of the bridge and then advance on the bridge.

Meanwhile, the 3rd Battalion 504th Parachute Infantry, which was to carry out the inital crossing, had been waiting for the assault boats to arrive. The convoy of three trucks carrying them had had difficulty coming forward along the overcrowded single road and had been delayed at Eindhoven by the damage and chaos caused by the enemy bombing during the night. 'H-Hour', which had already been postponed, was set for 1500 hours. At 1430 hours, exactly on cue, squadrons of RAF Typhoons appeared and began to attack the enemy positions on the far bank. Shortly afterwards, the Sherman tanks of the 2nd (Armoured) Battalion Irish Guards moved forward and lined up along the south bank of the Waal. Alongside them was the 2nd Battalion 504th Parachute Infantry which would also cross the river if needed.

Ten minutes later the trucks carrying the boats appeared. Engineers quickly unfolded and assembled the canvas and wooden flat-bottomed craft which were immediately hauled away by the parachute infantrymen to the water's edge where they were loaded with equipment. Meanwhile the tanks had begun firing smoke shells to provide cover for the crossing, and in the rear the supporting artillery opened fire. As soon as his men were ready, the commanding officer of the 3rd Battalion, Major Julian Cook, gave the order for the first wave to begin the crossing. Dragging their heavily laden boats into the water, Companies 'H' and 'I', together with some engineers, scrambled aboard them and started making their way towards the far bank 400 yards away.

Before long, however, the smoke-screen laid down by the tanks began to be dispersed by wind. Despite the heavy amount of suppressive firepower brought down on them during the previous thirty minutes by artillery, tanks and aircraft, the enemy brought fire to bear on the two companies as they frantically paddled their cumbersome craft across the Waal. Shells and mortar bombs started to rain down around the 3rd Battalion, some boats received direct hits and others were swamped and capsized. Some of the boats, caught by the current, were spinning round as their occupants desperately tried to bring them under control.

About half the boats reached the north shore; the troops disembarked and with fixed bayonets cleared the foremost enemy trenches within half an hour. The first wave of the 3rd Battalion then regrouped and provided covering fire for the second wave which had started to cross in the thirteen boats that had survived the first crossing. Although enemy artillery fire was still directed on the river, only two boats were hit in the second crossing. The remaining eleven survived to make a further five crossings, bringing across the rest of the battalion.

Such was the ferocity of the American parachute battalion's assault that before long the surviving enemy withdrew, pursued by Cook's men. While the main body of the battalion headed eastwards for the bridge, one company was detached to attack and seize the strongly defended Hof van Holland fort. Swimming the moat which surrounded it, the parachute infantry succeeded in scaling the walls and set about the fort's defenders, who quickly surrendered.

At about 1700 hours, Companies 'H' and 'I', which had comprised the first wave of the assault crossing, arrived at the northern ends of the railway and road bridges respectively and launched attacks on the defenders who put up a stout resistance. But the Grenadier Guards and the 2nd Battalion 505th Parachute Infantry Regiment were also pushing forward. Suddenly the pressure proved too great and the enemy at the southern end of the railway bridge broke and withdrew across the bridge in confusion. Company 'H' opened fire and within the space of a few minutes nearly 500 of the enemy lay dead or wounded, or had been taken prisoner.

At the southern end of the road bridge, meanwhile, the enemy had virtually been annihilated. Two platoons of the Grenadiers' King's Company, commanded by Captain The Honourable V. P. Gibbs, had succeeded in gaining entry to the Valkhof, the ancient fort on the edge of the river which dominated the approaches to the bridge, and two platoons were inside before the enemy were aware of them. A short but fierce fight ensued, during which the King's Company suffered casualties, including Captain Gibbs who was killed. The Company soon gained the upper hand, however, and within a few minutes had overwhelmed the enemy and installed itself in the latter's positions on the eastern side of the Valkhof from where it was able to bring fire to bear on the enemy at the southern end of the bridge.

During this time No. 4 Company had been held up in the centre by heavy fire from the fort, but having managed to get within thirty yards of it, one platoon charged and succeeded in entering and dealing with the defenders while another platoon cleared the houses in the area. This success enabled the 2nd Battalion 505th Parachute Infantry Regiment to push forward and by 1830 hours the Americans and the Grenadiers' No. 4 Company had reached the embankment which led to the bridge.

In the meantime No. 1 Squadron of the 2nd (Armoured) Battalion Grenadier Guards had moved up and tried to advance on the road bridge only to be met by anti-tank gun fire. Just before 1900 hours it received a report that an American flag had been seen at the far end of the bridge. Its leading troop, commanded by Sergeant Robinson, had already been ordered by the squadron leader, Major John Trotter, to be ready to rush the bridge. Without further ado Sergeant Robinson ordered his four tanks to advance across the bridge. Led by Sergeant Pacey, who was followed by Sergeant Robinson, the four tanks thundered across while engaging an 88mm anti-tank gun at the far end, which Sergeant Robinson's gunner knocked out with his second round. They were followed by Captain The Lord Carrington, the squadron's second in command, and the reconnaissance officer of 14th Field Squadron RE, Lieutenant Anthony Jones. Despite heavy fire, Pacey and Robinson crossed unscathed, but the third tank, commanded by Sergeant Knight, and the fourth were both hit. On discovering that their tank had not caught fire, Knight and his crew remounted and followed the rest of the troop which took up covering positions where they were joined shortly afterwards by Companies 'H' and 'I' of the 3rd Battalion 504th Parachute Infantry Regiment and a troop of 17pdr self-propelled anti-tank guns of 21st Anti-Tank Regiment RA.

Shortly afterwards, the rest of No. 1 Squadron also arrived and pushed forward to the northern edge of the village of Lent, immediately to the north of the bridge, where it took up positions to form a bridgehead. An hour later it was reinforced by Nos. 1 and 3 Companies of the 3rd Battalion Irish Guards which arrived on foot. Meanwhile, Lieutenant Anthony Jones and his sappers were busy disarming the explosive charges and firing circuits which they found on the bridge. As they did so, they captured enemy troops whom they found hiding in the internal compartments of the bridge.

The railway bridge had also fallen to the Grenadiers and the Americans earlier on and so XXX Corps was able to establish its bridgehead over the Waal before launching its final push for Arnhem to relieve 1st Airborne Division. Unknown to Horrocks and the other senior British and American commanders at Nijmegen, a major factor that had contributed to their success was the orders given by Generalfeldmarschall Model that the bridges at Nijmegen and Arnhem must not be blown. Model was convinced that both could be defended and, more importantly in his view, that they would be required in any subsequent counter-attacks. In this he had been strongly opposed by Bittrich who on more than one occasion had begged to be allowed to blow both bridges if it proved necessary. But his pleas had fallen on deaf ears.

It was only at the very last minute, as Sergeant Robinson's troop was crossing the bridge, that it was decided to disregard Model's order. SS-Brigadeführer Heinz Harmel, commander of 10th SS Panzer Division, was watching the action around the bridge from a forward command post which was also the location of the demolition firing box connected to the explosive charges on the bridge. On seeing the tanks halfway across, Harmel gave the order to detonate the charges but nothing happened, despite the frantic efforts of the engineer beside him, and the Grenadiers' tanks reached the far end of the bridge safely. The reason why the charges failed to explode has never been determined and must be put down to the fortunes of war.

In Nijmegen fighting continued as groups of the enemy tried desperately to get back to the river and escape over the bridges northwards. In the area of the Valkhof fort dominating the southern approach to the road bridge, SS and Wehrmacht troops under SS-Hauptsturmführer Krüger, commander of 21st Battery 5th SS Artillery Training Regiment, tenaciously resisted all efforts to oust them from their positions. Eventually, at 2030 hours on 20 September, they were overrun by troops of the 2nd Battalion 505th Parachute Infantry Regiment. By that time, only twelve men were left and they were eventually forced out by white phosphorous grenades.

Meanwhile, SS-Hauptsturmführer Karl-Heinz Euling and sixty survivors of the 1st Battalion 22nd SS Panzer Grenadier Regiment had regrouped in a house. Little notice was taken of them until one of their number with a panzerfaust knocked out a tank which had halted in front of the building and fired a round into it. Another tank retaliated by firing three rounds into a trench in front of the house as Euling and his men fought back. At 2230 hours Euling decided to try to break out. He led his men out of the back of the house, which was now ablaze, and headed north to the Waal. Eventually, having survived a contact with a British patrol, he and his men met a group of Fallschirmjäger with whom they succeeded in crossing the river and reaching German lines.

In the village of Lent, survivors of No. 1 Company of 10th SS Panzer Division's engineer battalion also made a last stand until overrun by tanks of the 2nd (Armoured) Battalion Grenadier Guards. Meanwhile, 21st Battery of 5th SS Artillery Training Regiment, located in the village of Oosterhout, on the northern bank of the Waal to the west of Nijmegen, continued to shell the town while continuing to defend its own positions.

The two days spent in taking Nijmegen and the bridges meant that XXX Corps' advance was severely behind schedule and junior commanders who had spearheaded the assault, and were fully aware of the urgency to reach Arnhem and 1st Airborne Division, were anxious that the advance should continue immediately. 504th Parachute Infantry Regiment in particular had sustained severe casualties during the assault crossing to seize the bridge, its 3rd Battalion having lost 134 men killed or wounded. So its commander, Colonel Reuben Tucker, could scarcely contain his rage when he heard that the Grenadier and Irish Groups had been ordered to halt for the night instead of pushing on over the final eleven miles to Arnhem.

The main problem facing the commander of the Guards Armoured Division, Major General Allan Adair, however, was that his division was already fully committed. The bulk of the infantry of his Grenadier and Irish Groups were still heavily involved in winkling out elements of the enemy in Nijmegen, and both infantry battalions had suffered very heavy casualties. The 3rd Battalion Irish Guards had previously lost a considerable number of men during the fighting in the Meuse–Escaut Canal bridgehead and had not received any replacements; by the time the battalion crossed the bridge to deploy in Lent, the strength of its three rifle companies was no more than five platoons and there was only one surviving subaltern officer. Moreover, both regimental groups were very short of ammunition and fuel and it would take time for the supply echelons to come forward to replenish the squadrons and companies.

The Coldstream Group of 32nd Guards Brigade was meanwhile deployed to the east, covering the right flank of 82nd US Airborne Division where it was busily employed fending off counter-attacks from the direction of the Reichswald, continually moving to whichever part of the Americans' perimeter was under threat. Indeed, the afternoon of 20 September saw the heaviest of these counter-attacks which comprised a main assault south of Groesbeek with two others thrusting north-west through Mook and south-west via Beek.

The only available reserve was the Welsh Group at Grave, but it was already committed to defending the vital bridge there. If that had been recaptured and destroyed by the enemy, it would have caused even more severe disruption to XXX Corps' line of communications, which was under pressure from both flanks, and caused even more problems to the operation as a whole.

The requirement for the next stage of the advance was, in any case, for infantry rather than armour. The ill-chosen terrain was not suited to tanks, being flat and featureless with marshy ground and large ditches on each side of the embanked road, making it impossible for deployment off it.

On both sides of the main axis were orchards and woods which would provide cover for enemy infantry and anti-tank guns.

More troops, and infantry in particular, could have been supplied by the formation following the Guards Armoured Division: 43rd (Wessex) Infantry Division, commanded by Major General Ivo Thomas. Indeed, Lieutenant General Horrocks had already decided that it should move through and mount a divisional attack on Arnhem. Once again, however, the problems caused by using a single road to supply and support a corps were rearing their heads. Those vehicles bringing up essential supplies required so urgently in the forward area were already experiencing great difficulty in making their way along the overcrowded road which was constantly under enemy fire. It would take time for more troops to move forward. One element of 43rd Infantry Division, however, was only a relatively short distance from Nijmegen. Although it had experienced some delay through enemy action at Zon, 130th Infantry Brigade had arrived just south of Grave by nightfall. However, instead of being ordered forward to relieve the Welsh Group as quickly as possible, or indeed to move on through Nijmegen and spearhead the next stage of the advance, it was permitted for reasons still far from clear, to halt there for the night.

So, while 1st Airborne Division was fighting for its life in Arnhem and Oosterbeek, the advance of XXX Corps came to a halt. On the morning of 20 September, 1st Airborne Corps had succeeded in establishing radio contact with 1st Airborne Division and received an up-to-date report on its situation, which was becoming increasingly desperate. At 1505 hours the following signal was sent to 1st Airborne Corps Main by Major General Roy Urquhart: 'Enemy attacking main bridge in strength. Situation serious for 1 Para Brigade. Enemy also attacking position east from Heelsum and west from Arnhem. Situation serious but am forming close perimeter defence around Hartenstein with remainder of division. Relief essential both areas earliest possible. Still retain ferry crossing Heveadorp.'

7
FIGHTING FOR TIME

'I'm afraid it's not been a very healthy party and it don't look like getting any health-ier as time goes by.' — Lieutenant Colonel Johnny Frost.

Dawn in Arnhem on 20 September had seen the resumption of heavy shelling of 2nd Parachute Battalion. By now, most of the buildings in the battalion's area had been destroyed and the survivors of Lieutenant Colonel Johnny Frost's troops had been forced to evacuate them and dig-in around those sheltering HQ 1st Para-chute Brigade and Battalion HQ. In the cellars of the ruined houses, wounded men were crammed together and medical officers and orderlies were working under appalling conditions.

At about 1000 hours, radio contact was suddenly established between HQ 1st Parachute Brigade and that of 1st Airborne Division. On being summoned to the radio, Frost was told by Major General Roy Urquhart that XXX Corps was expected to arrive within a matter of hours. When told of the perilous situation at the bridge, Urquhart replied that there was little or no chance of any of the division being able to fight its way through to 2nd Parachute Battalion.

That afternoon, Frost was wounded by a mortar bomb while talking to Major Douglas Crawley. On being taken to the battalion's Regimental Aid Post, he found that he had been wounded in both legs. Major Digby Tatham-Warter, himself also wounded, took over command of the battalion while Major Freddie Gough, commander of 1st Airborne Reconnaissance Squadron, assumed command of the entire force at the bridge.

It was during this time that Lieutenant Jack Grayburn of 'A' Com-pany once again distinguished himself. His platoon had been holding a keypoint position in the battalion's defensive perimeter. Despite several attacks in strength supported by tanks and self-propelled guns, Grayburn and his men had held out at the cost of severe casualties. Subsequently, although wounded in the shoulder, he had led several fighting patrols that caused such concern that the enemy brought up their tanks again. Later, German sappers were spotted placing demolition charges under the bridge. Grayburn responded by leading out another patrol which held the enemy off while the fuzes were removed from the charges. Wounded again, he refused to leave his men or to desist in carrying the fight to the enemy.

That evening, however, he was killed by fire at close range from a tank while standing up in full view of it and directing the withdrawal of the remnant of his platoon to the battalion's main defensive position. For his great gallantry he was awarded a posthumous Victoria Cross.

In the evening, the sole remaining unburnt building which housed HQ 1st Parachute Brigade caught fire several times but the flames were extinguished. Its cellars were crammed with more than 200 wounded and Captain Jimmy Logan, 2nd Parachute Battalion's Regimental Medical Officer, told Lieutenant Colonel Frost that they would have to be evacuated and surrendered to the enemy or they would perish. Frost discussed the matter with Major Freddie Gough and told him to be ready to move those troops still able to fight to new positions. Shortly afterwards the building caught fire again and, as the flames began to spread, Frost ordered Gough to move his men out. The wounded remained behind in the cellars, awaiting the arrival of enemy troops. Just after nightfall, under a flag of truce, they were carried up from the cellars by SS troops who removed them from the area. Subsequent opinion in 1st Airborne Division of the behaviour of the SS troops in the battle was generally high.

During the two hours of the truce, additional enemy reinforcements arrived in the shape of 21st SS Panzer Grenadier Regiment, elements of which had already been involved in the fighting. More troops were also expected, including a battalion of heavy tanks. Meanwhile, the battle group commanded by SS-Sturmbannführer Brinkmann was ordered to complete the annihilation of 2nd Parachute Battalion on the following morning.

Thereafter, the battle was resumed with tanks, including heavy Tigers, and 88mm guns blasting the battalion's positions. By now the northern end of the bridge was no longer held and ammunition was so low that each man had only a few rounds. At this point the Brigade Major, Major Tony Hibbert, gave orders that the force was to break up into small groups for the night and then, at first light next day, infiltrate back to the buildings in the area of the bridge. In the event, this proved impossible and, as best he could, Hibbert ordered those whom he could contact to withdraw westwards to the divisional headquarters. However, most of those who tried to do so were killed or wounded and the remainder were hunted down and taken prisoner.

By dawn on 21 September, only 150 men of 2nd Parachute Battalion were left. These fought back as SS panzer grenadiers advanced once again to clear the area, which they did only after all the parachutists had been killed or wounded. By 0900 hours the surviving remnants of 2nd Parachute Battalion and elements of other units of 1st Parachute Brigade in the area of the bridge had been overrun. Ordered to hold the bridge for two days, they had done so against heavy and increasing pressure for three days and three nights.

Meanwhile, 4th Parachute Brigade had also been virtually destroyed. At about 0600 hours on 20 September, having been ordered by Major General Urquhart to move to the main divisional area, Brigadier John Hackett and his much depleted battalions made their way towards the divisional perimeter. What remained of 156th Parachute Battalion was in the lead. The twenty-five surviving men of 'A' Company came under fire from machine-guns and self-propelled guns as they moved through woods near the Wolfheze Hotel. 'C' Company, commanded by Major Geoffrey Powell, attempted to put in a flanking attack but this failed and his company suffered heavy casualties.

Bearing in mind his orders to rejoin the rest of the division, and realizing that he must try to avoid any major encounter with the enemy, Brigadier Hackett ordered 10th Parachute Battalion to take an alternative route to the east and bypass the enemy, leaving 156th Parachute Battalion to follow as a rearguard while in contact with the enemy. The battalion fought its way through the woods, harried by machine-guns and snipers all the way. On receiving a message from Hackett to 'pull the plug out' and speed up his advance, Lieutenant Colonel Ken Smyth ordered his men to fix bayonets. Charging through the woods, the remnants of 10th Parachute Battalion fought their way through to the divisional perimeter which they reached just after 1300 hours. Besides himself and one of his company commanders, Major Peter Warr, Smyth's battalion numbered only sixty men. Despite the fact that they were exhausted, filthy and covered in blood, Smyth and his men formed up in column and marched to the divisional headquarters where they were met by Major General Urquhart. 'We have been taken on Sir,' said Lieutenant Colonel Ken Smyth to the divisional commander, 'but here we are.' They subsequently took up defensive positions in buildings by the main crossroads in Oosterbeek.

Meanwhile, Brigadier Hackett and the remnants of his headquarters and 156th Parachute Battalion were being hard pressed by enemy infantry supported by tanks, but he and his men on several occasions counter-attacked and drove the enemy back, though suffering casualties in the process. At one point, several men of 156th Parachute Battalion were killed after being lured out of cover by German troops wearing parachute smocks. These disappeared into a hollow as machine-guns opened fire and cut down the unsuspecting paratroops who had mistaken the Germans for members of the glider-borne element of 1st Polish Independent Parachute Brigade. On an order from Hackett, Major Geoffrey Powell and 'C' Company carried out a bayonet charge and drove the enemy from the hollow which was then occupied by Hackett and the rest of his force. There they regrouped and beat off more attacks. During the afternoon, the German armour pulled back for some unknown reason but the action continued.

By now, ammunition was running very low and heavy losses had been suffered. The survivors of 156th Parachute Battalion numbered fewer than thirty, and the remainder of Hackett's small force consisted of twelve men from his brigade headquarters, ten from 10th Parachute Battalion and twenty to thirty from other units. Among those officers who had been killed during the day's fighting were the Commanding Officer of 156th Parachute Battalion, Lieutenant Colonel Sir Richard des Voeux, the Brigade Major, Major Bruce Dawson, the GSO 3 (Intelligence), Captain George Blundell, and the commander of the brigade headquarters defence platoon, Captain Jimmy James.

With some thirty of his men now wounded, Brigadier Hackett decided that rather than stay in the hollow and be overrun, he and his men would break through the enemy to reach the divisional perimeter about half a mile away. At 1800 hours, charging with fixed bayonets and screaming at the tops of their voices, they swept the Germans aside and ran the few hundred yards to join the rest of 1st Airborne Division.

The perimeter enclosed a horseshoe-shaped area, in the centre of which was divisional headquarters. After the arrival of the remnants of 4th Parachute Brigade, Major General Urquhart divided the area into eastern and western sectors, commanded by Brigadiers Hackett and Hicks respectively. The northern curved end of the perimeter was manned by men of 21st Independent Parachute Company and the 7th Battalion The King's Own Scottish Borderers. The eastern side was defended by the survivors of 10th and 156th Parachute Battalions, with some glider pilots and gunners of 1st Airlanding Light Regiment RA. On the western side were the 1st Battalion The Border Regiment, glider pilots, sappers, Poles from the glider-borne elements of 1st Polish Independent Parachute Brigade and men from several other units. The southern end of the area was held by Lonsdale Force, consisting of men of 1st, 3rd and 11th Parachute Battalions, the 1st Battalion The Border Regiment, the 2nd Battalion The South Staffordshire Regiment and divisional troops. At the base of the divisional area was the gun line of 1st Airlanding Light Regiment RA.

As the battle continued throughout Oosterbeek, enemy reinforcements from Germany continued to pour into the area. On 19 September a powerful anti-aircraft brigade of five battalions equipped with 88mm guns and 20mm and 37mm cannon had arrived and deployed throughout the area to counter Allied aircraft supporting 1st Airborne Division. Additional air defence was provided by the Luftwaffe which appeared in strength for the first time, to the surprise of all those on the ground, particularly the Germans who had become used to operating without air support. Some 300 fighters were detailed for operations in the area and soon made their presence felt, attacking the glider-borne element of 1st Polish Independent Parachute Brigade during its landing, and 4th Parachute Brigade as it withdrew towards Oosterbeek. They also attacked transport aircraft attempting to resupply 1st Airborne Division.

On 20 September, 191st Artillery Regiment also arrived, although its lack of transport meant that 9th SS Panzer Division had had to supply some of its own vehicles to tow the guns to their positions. On 21 September, two SS batteries of 320mm Nebelwerfer multi-barrelled rocket-launchers also appeared. Some of these reinforcements arrived by air: on 21 September 9th Pionier-Lehr Battalion, an assault pioneer unit equipped with flame-throwers and specially trained in fighting in urban areas, arrived at the airfield at Deelen. That day saw also the arrival in Arnhem of more enemy units, namely 171st *Auffrischung* Light Artillery Regiment, a panzer grenadier battalion, and several companies of Luftwaffe ground staff reformed as infantry.

The enemy kept up constant pressure on the perimeter. After 20 September there was a virtually continuous bombardment of mortar fire which at times reached a rate of about fifty bombs a minute. Added to this was the threat of snipers, although many of these fell victim to the airborne troops, two or three of whom would move out from their positions and clamber to the rooftops of nearby buildings from where they picked off the snipers with unerring accuracy. The men of 21st Independent Parachute Company were particularly adept at this tactic; one man accounted for eighteen of them. Conditions within the divisional area were appalling. All the houses had been badly damaged; many of them were demolished or burned down. Those men still capable of firing a weapon manned slit trenches dug in once-immaculate gardens and streets. Dutch civilians crowded into cellars with the wounded whom they nursed to the best of their ability. Throughout the area some of the dead lay unburied among the shell craters, burned-out vehicles and general flotsam of battle. There was little or no food and water was scarce. The replenishment situation was not helped by the fact that some supplies were mistakenly dropped behind the German lines. In the dressing-stations in the Hotels Schoonoord, Vreewyck and Tafelberg, the medical officers and orderlies worked tirelessly on an endless stream of wounded who at one point numbered nearly 1,200.

Throughout the entire battle, the Dutch inhabitants of Arnhem and the surrounding villages showed unbelievable courage, frequently risking their lives to save wounded men. One person in particular will always be remembered in the annals of British airborne forces and no account of the battle of Arnhem would be complete without mention of her: Kate ter Horst. This remarkable woman, a mother of five children, became a source of great comfort and inspiration to those who were brought to her house next to Oosterbeek Church. Not only did she assist Captain Randall Martin, the Medical Officer of 1st Airlanding Light Regiment RA, and his orderlies to nurse the casualties, but she moved constantly among the wounded and dying men, praying with them and reading to them the 91st Psalm from her prayerbook. Her house had suffered appalling damage and it was crammed to overflowing from attic to cellar with wounded men; her garden eventually contained fifty-seven graves. Despite her undoubted fears for herself and her family, she remained outwardly calm and her composure had a marked effect on those around her.

The battle for the Oosterbeek perimeter raged on. On 21 September the enemy attempted to break through but were driven back by a bayonet charge of men of the 1st Battalion The Border Regiment. Much of the fighting took place at very close quarters, and in the weaker sectors of the perimeter enemy tanks and infantry, sometimes with flame-throwers, succeeded in infiltrating between individual positions where they caused heavy casualties.

On the morning of 21 September, the first indications that XXX Corps had managed to fight its way to within supporting range of Arnhem came when salvoes of shells crashed down a hundred yards or so in front of the airborne troops. Controlled by Lieutenant Colonel Robert Loder-Symonds, the Commander Royal Artillery 1st Airborne Division, the 5.5in and 7.2in howitzers of the Corps' 64th Medium Regiment RA broke up enemy attacks with unerring accuracy. Meanwhile the gunners of 1st Airlanding Light Regiment RA continued to serve their own 75mm pack howitzers while under fire, as they had done throughout the battle, in some cases engaging tanks over open sights.

During the afternoon of 21 September, the western sector of the perimeter was attacked but the enemy were again driven off by men of the 1st Battalion The Border Regiment. Simultaneously, an assault was made on Lonsdale Force in the south while at the northern end the 7th Battalion The King's Own Scottish Borderers was driven out of its positions. Fixing bayonets, the Lowlanders counter-attacked and routed the enemy. By the end of the action, however, the battalion's strength numbered only 150 all ranks. At 1900 hours, on the east of the perimeter astride the main road through Oosterbeek, 10th Parachute Battalion, now only some fifty men strong, was attacked by tanks and self-propelled guns. The houses in which Lieutenant Colonel Ken Smyth and his men were located were set on fire by phosphorous shells and they were forced to withdraw. Smyth himself was fatally wounded, dying a few days later, and the last of his remaining officers were killed.

Urquhart's main hope for re-supply and reinforcement had rested on the Heveadorp ferry, a cable-operated craft capable of carrying vehicles and personnel. On 20 September, a patrol of sappers had carried out a reconnaissance of the crossing, taking soundings of the river and measuring the current. On the night of the 20th, a patrol of twelve men was sent to secure the northern end of the ferry, which was to be used to take the men and equipment of 1st Polish Independent Parachute Brigade across next day. In the darkness the patrol was unable to find the craft itself, despite searching for a quarter of a mile on each side of the landing stage. At dawn on the 21st, the patrol returned to the perimeter. It was believed at the time that the ferry had been sunk by artillery fire but it was eventually discovered by some Dutch civilians, washed up intact on the bank downstream near the Arnhem railway bridge. The loss of the ferry was a bitter blow to Urquhart as it removed the only effective means of bringing vehicles across the Lower Rhine.

Meanwhile, during the early afternoon of 21 September, 1st Polish Independent Parachute Brigade, much delayed by fog, had taken off from its airfields in England and was en route for its dropping zone east of Driel, a village just south of the Lower Rhine. Unfortunately, the Luftwaffe and the flak units throughout the area had been alerted in advance to the columns of transport aircraft as they crossed the French coast near Dunkirk. In addition, bad weather forced forty-one aircraft, carrying one of Major General Sosabowski's battalions, numbering 500 men, to turn back for England.

At 1700 hours, as they made their final approach to the dropping zone, the transport aircraft were attacked by two squadrons of Messerschmitt Bf 109s. Major General Stanislaw Sosabowski and his men jumped into a barrage of anti-aircraft fire which, together with the fighters, shot down thirteen of the Dakotas. On landing, the Poles suffered relatively light casualties despite heavy fire being brought to bear on the dropping zone by machine-guns, mortars, rocket-launchers, artillery and tanks. The 9th SS Panzer Division's reconnaissance battalion, which by now was deployed near the village of Elden, also joined the fray with its 20mm guns. By the time they had fought their way to cover in nearby dykes and embankments and subsequently regrouped by nightfall, Sosabowski's men numbered only about 750 including the wounded.

The appearance of 1st Polish Independent Parachute Brigade raised German fears of the possibility of the road being cut south of Arnhem and 10th SS Panzer Division, which was heavily committed around Nijmegen, being cut off. Accordingly a separate battle group was put in, under SS Obersturmbannführer Walter Harzer, commander of 9th SS Panzer Division. This was a hastily assembled ad hoc formation comprising five battalion-sized units drawn from 3rd Dutch SS *Landsturm Niederland* Battalion, a battalion of Kriegsmarine naval personnel, 642nd Marine Regiment, a Luftwaffe battalion and 47th Fortress Machine Gun Battalion. It was supported by 20mm, 37mm and 88mm flak detachments, as well as elements of 191st Artillery Regiment. The commander of 2nd SS Panzer Corps, SS-Obergruppenführer Willi Bittrich, was so concerned by this new threat that he committed his reserve, comprising 10th SS Panzer Division's reconnaissance battalion and the Wehrmacht panzer grenadier training and replacement battalion commanded by Major Hans-Peter Knaust, from their location at the village of Elst, approximately halfway between Arnhem and Nijmegen, to redeploy in support of Harzer's battle group.

While the Poles regrouped and established defensive positions around Driel, Harzer established his force along the embankment of the railway line which ran northwards from Nijmegen, through Elst across the river to Oosterbeek, thereby blocking the Poles from advancing eastwards to the road. That afternoon, Knaust's battalion was ordered to carry out a counter-attack through Elst against some of the leading elements of XXX Corps which by now were making their appearance to the south. The battalion reached the area south of the village where, the flat featureless terrain providing no cover for any further advance, it was forced to withdraw to the cover of the village.

That night, 10th SS Panzer Division's reconnaissance battalion pushed forward in its armoured cars and half-tracks to engage the Poles. The terrain being unsuitable for armour, the vehicles were restricted to tracks as they headed westwards north of Elst towards the area of Driel. As it drew close to its objective, the battalion was attacked by armoured cars of a reconnaissance unit of 43rd (Wessex) Infantry Division which was probing forward in the area. One of the vehicles was captured, its radios subsequently being employed to monitor the British radio net, before the battalion withdrew to the railway embankment. Meanwhile, the supporting artillery and mortars were bringing down fire on the Polish positions.

At 2100 hours on the night of 21 September Captain Zwolanski, the Polish liaison officer attached to HQ 1st Airborne Division, arrived at Sosabowski's headquarters after swimming the Rhine. He told Sosabowski that rafts would be sent across the river later that night to ferry him and his brigade to the northern bank. The Poles moved up to the southern bank and waited for the rafts, but none came. At 0300 hours on the 22nd Sosabowski withdrew his men.

Before dawn that morning, Major General Urquhart reduced the size of the northern sector of the perimeter which by now had become very weak in places. 21st Independent Parachute Company, the remnants of 1st Airborne Reconnaissance Squadron and some sappers were moved to the north-eastern sector of the perimeter and some of the divisional RASC troops were transferred to the south-eastern sector.

Early that morning, radio contact with XXX Corps was established and its commander, Lieutenant General Brian Horrocks, informed Urquhart that 43rd Infantry Division had been ordered to relieve 1st Airborne Division. However, Horrocks was apparently unaware that the

Heveadorp ferry was no longer held by 1st Airborne Division, despite two messages to that effect having been sent to Second British Army.

Urquhart was convinced that Horrocks and Browning were not fully aware of the desperate situation. Accordingly, on the morning of 22 September he sent his GSO 1, Lieutenant Colonel Charles McKenzie, and Lieutenant Colonel Eddie Myers, the Commander Royal Engineers 1st Airborne Division, to make contact with Lieutenant Generals Horrocks and Browning and brief them. At the same time, Myers was tasked with organizing arrangements for ferrying men and supplies across the river.

The two officers crossed the Lower Rhine in an inflatable dinghy and made their way to the headquarters of 1st Polish Independent Parachute Brigade which at the time was under attack by enemy troops supported by artillery north of the river. There they discussed with Major General Sosabowski the idea of ferrying some of his men across in small rubber boats. At the same time they sent a signal to Lieutenant General Horrocks, asking for reinforcements and supplies.

To the south, meanwhile, Major General Ivo Thomas's 43rd Infantry Division was attempting to push its way northwards towards Arnhem. Unfortunately, its progress had been hampered by traffic jams in Nijmegen, which it had reached on the morning of 21 September, and it had subsequently been misrouted over the wrong bridge. As a consequence, leading elements of the division did not reach the village of Oosterhout, some seven miles south of Arnhem, until 0930 hours.

The capture on 21 September of one of the division's reconnaissance patrols had revealed to the enemy that an infantry, rather than an armoured, formation was now spearheading XXX Corps' thrust towards Arnhem. Well aware that the terrain between Nijmegen and Arnhem favoured the use of infantry, Model and Bittrich realized that it was imperative that 1st Airborne Division be overrun and destroyed before 43rd Infantry Division could link up with it. While placing even more pressure on Urquhart and his beleaguered men, Model's forces also had to make every effort to halt the advance of XXX Corps. This meant that not only would Horrocks' spearheads have to be blocked, but his lengthy and vulnerable line of communications, extending through the two 'corridors' protected by the two American airborne divisions, would have to be attacked and disrupted, if not severed completely.

During the night of 21 September, Oberstgeneral Kurt Student, commander of 1st Parachute Army, received orders for his forces to move against XXX Corps' line of communications. This would take the form of a pincer movement on Veghel by two formations: from the west, a battle group of 59th Infantry Division, comprising two battalions supported by armour and artillery; from the east, a battle group under the command of Oberst Walther, comprising 107th Panzer Brigade, the 1st Battalion 16th

Top: A knocked-out Tiger Mk II heavy tank 100 metres north of the Benedendorpskerk in the Weverstraat in Arnhem. (Photo: Airborne Forces Museum)

Above: A defensive position of Headquarters 1st Airlanding Brigade. (Photo: Imperial War Museum)

Above: A Bren gun group in a position on the divisional perimeter. The two individuals seen here are Ptes Jury and Malcolm. (Photo: Imperial War Museum)

Below: Jeeps and trailers wrecked by shellfire. (Photo: Imperial War Museum)

Above: A re-supply drop landing on the Utrechtseweg in Oosterbeek on 19 September. (Photo: Imperial War Museum)

Below: Wounded at a forward dressing-station near Wolfheze. (Photo: Imperial War Museum)

Above: Major General Roy Urquhart outside his divisional headquarters at the Hartenstein Hotel. (Photo: Imperial War Museum)

Opposite page, top: A Sturmgeschutz III self-propelled gun parked behind a house in Oosterbeek. (Photo: Imperial War Museum)

Opposite page, bottom: Part of a much-needed re-supply drop is retrieved and unpacked. Most drops fell outside the divisional perimeter and into enemy hands. (Photo: Imperial War Museum)

Opposite page, top: A wounded man is carried away on a stretcher to a regimental aid post on 24 September. (Photo: Imperial War Museum)

Opposite page, bottom: A member of 1st Airborne Division engaging a sniper from the cover of the Hartenstein Hotel. (Photo: Imperial War Museum)

Above: Two glider pilots, Sergeants J. Whawell and J. Turrell, clear a ruined school building in Oosterbeek. (Photo: Imperial War Museum)

Above: A defensive position near the Hartenstein Hotel. Members of 1st Airborne Division enjoy a rare opportunity to cook a meal and clean their weapons. (Photo: Imperial War Museum)

Below: German troops advance cautiously through the outskirts of Arnhem. (Photo: Imperial War Museum)

Above: A group of SS troops in a heavily camouflaged truck in the woods on the outskirts of Oosterbeek. (Photo: Airborne Forces Museum)

Below: Armoured cars of the 2nd Household Cavalry Regiment on the road to Valkens- waard. (Photo: Imperial War Museum)

Above: A 'Firefly' and a Sherman of the 2nd (Armoured) Bn. Irish Guards pass two of their number knocked out on the road to Eindhoven on 17 September. (Photo: Imperial War Museum)

Opposite page: The 2nd Household Cavalry Regiment passing through the crowded streets of Eindhoven. (Photo: Imperial War Museum)

Below: A Sherman tank of the Guards Armoured Division passes a knocked-out enemy tank near Uden. (Photo: Imperial War Museum)

Opposite page, top: A vehicle of the Guards Armoured Division is hit and explodes while heading north along 'Hell's Highway' after XXX Corps' line of communication was cut for the third time on the evening of 24 September. (Photo: Imperial War Museum)

Left: A 'Firefly' and Shermans of the Guards Armoured Division crossing the Nijmegen bridge on the 21 September, the day after its capture by 2nd (Armoured) Battalion Grenadier Guards and the 3rd Battalion 504th Parachute Infantry Regiment. (Photo: Imperial War Museum)

Above: A 3-inch mortar detachment of the 1st Battalion The Border Regiment in action at Oosterbeek. (Photo: Imperial War Museum)

Above: A 75mm pack howitzer of 1st Airlanding Light Regiment RA in action. (Photo: Imperial War Museum)

Opposite page, top: Troops of 1st Airborne Division, in the grounds of the Hartenstein Hotel, trying in vain to attract the attention of RAF aircraft dropping supplies on 20 September. (Photo: Imperial War Museum)

Right: The Heveadorp ferry, seen from the Westerbouwing Heights looking south over the Lower Rhine towards Driel and the dropping zone of 1st Polish Independent Parachute Brigade. This picture shows the exposed nature of the flat terrain, which offered little cover for troops approaching the Lower Rhine from the south. (Photo: Imperial War Museum)

Above: Members of 1st Airborne Division being escorted away after capture. (Photo: Imperial War Museum)

Below: Exhausted but unbowed – men of 1st Airborne Division are marched away into captivity. (Photo: Imperial War Museum)

Grenadier Regiment, a battalion of 180th Artillery Regiment, elements of 10th SS Panzer Division, the 1st Battalion 21st Fallschirmjäger Regiment, 10th SS Panzerjäger Battalion, two more infantry battalions and a heavy anti-aircraft battery.

That night, Model's headquarters received news of a further powerful element to reinforce Bittrich's 2nd SS Panzer Corps; during the afternoon forty-five Tiger tanks of 506th Panzer Battalion had departed by rail from Germany and would arrive in the area of Arnhem on the morning of 24 September.

Meanwhile, within 1st Airborne Division's area the mortar and shell-fire continued and casualties mounted. By now the pressure was beginning to have serious effects on many of the defenders, some of whom were shell-shocked and on the verge of mental breakdown, but the defence was conducted as doggedly as ever by others who fought tenaciously and refused to give an inch against overwhelming odds. In Oosterbeek church Major Dickie Lonsdale roused his exhausted men with a stirring speech delivered from the pulpit while, not far from divisional headquarters, Sergeant Calloway of 3rd Parachute Battalion charged a Tiger tank single-handed with a PIAT and succeeded in immobilizing it as it gunned him down. Major Robert Cain of the 2nd Battalion The South Staffordshire Regiment, who was later awarded the Victoria Cross for his gallantry, personally hunted down and knocked out with a PIAT six tanks and a number of self-propelled guns.

Sergeant Baskeyfield, also of the South Staffordshires, engaged a troop of three enemy tanks with his 6pdr anti-tank gun as they approached along a track. Having knocked out the leading tank with his first round, he engaged and badly damaged the second. As he was about to engage the third, his gun was hit and disabled. Undeterred, Sergeant Baskeyfield moved to another gun, whose crew were dead, and continued to engage the remaining tank until he too was killed. He was later awarded a posthumous Victoria Cross for his great gallantry and self-sacrifice.

During the battle, moving among the positions throughout the perimeter, some of which were only yards from those of the enemy, the figures of Major General Urquhart and Brigadiers Hicks and Hackett could be seen constantly braving the shell and mortar fire to visit their men and give encouragement.

At 2100 hours on the night of 22 September, men of 1st Polish Independent Parachute Brigade moved silently up to the southern bank of the Lower Rhine. Sappers on both sides of the river had set up a hawser on pulleys which would pull four inflatable dinghies and a number of hastily constructed wooden rafts back and forth across the river, ferrying six men and a quantity of supplies at a time. For a while all went well until suddenly the night sky was illuminated by parachute flares. Almost immedi-

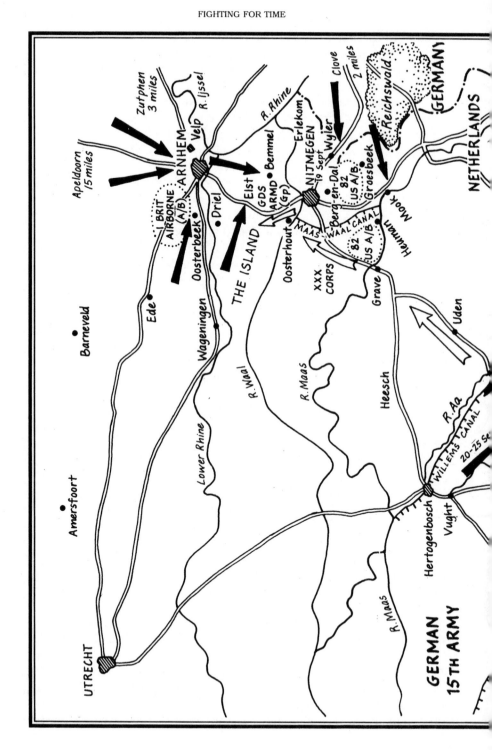

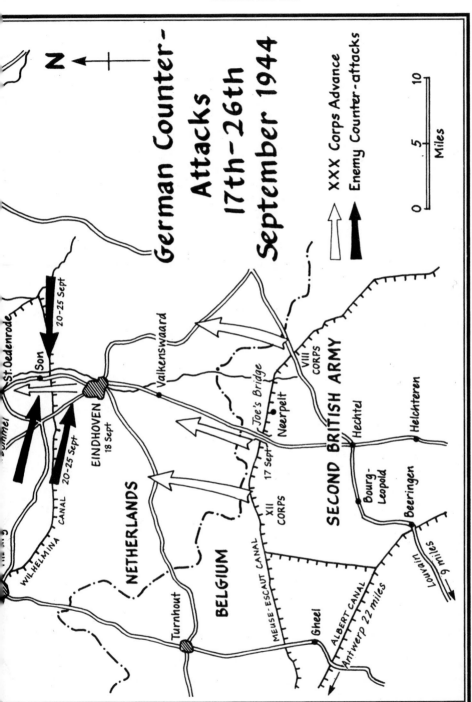

German Counter-Attacks 17th–26th September 1944

XXX Corps Advance
Enemy Counter-attacks

Miles
0   5   10

131

ately, the crossing point came under heavy mortar fire. Two of the rubber dinghies were destroyed and the Poles on the southern bank took cover. As soon as the flares burned out, the Poles resumed crossing. Throughout the night the desperate attempt to ferry men and supplies across the river continued, despite heavy casualties being suffered by Sosabowski's men. Only fifty men of 1st Polish Independent Parachute Brigade succeeded in reaching the northern bank and 1st Airborne Division.

Not until Lieutenant Colonel Charles McKenzie eventually reached HQ 1st Airborne Corps at Nijmegen on the morning of 23 September was Lieutenant General 'Boy' Browning able to gain a truly accurate picture of 1st Airborne Division's appalling predicament. Until then, plagued by the absence of radio communications with 1st Airborne Division, he had had only a vague idea of events in Arnhem. There was, however, little that Browning could do because all troops in the Nijmegen–Arnhem area were under the control of XXX Corps and ultimately of Second British Army. However, Browning assured McKenzie that every effort would be made that night to ferry reinforcements and supplies to Urquhart and his beleaguered force.

That night, 1st Polish Independent Parachute Brigade once again began to ferry some of its men across the river to join 1st Airborne Division. Again, the enemy brought the crossing point under heavy fire and only 250 men reached the northern bank. Of those, only 200 reached 1st Airborne Division. Meanwhile, 43rd Infantry Division was pushing forward as best it could, but its leading element, 130th Infantry Brigade, did not reach Driel until after the Poles had withdrawn once again from the southern bank of the river.

Throughout Saturday 23 September, the hell continued. The enemy continued to attack in force at several points along the perimeter and the mortar and shell fire continued without abating. Still the defenders held on, watching hopelessly as the RAF continued desperately to drop supplies while being shot out of the skies at virtual point-blank range by anti-aircraft fire. All the while, as they fought back against increasingly overwhelming odds, the men of 1st Airborne Division hoped against hope that relief from XXX Corps would be forthcoming.

8
SO NEAR, YET SO FAR

'I now began to feel as though I was in a boxing ring, fighting a tough opponent with one arm tied behind my back. I was in fact trying to fight three battles at the same time.' — Lieutenant General Brian Horrocks.

At 1230 hours on 21 September, XXX Corps' advance recommenced as the Guards Armoured Division's Irish Group set off from Lent along the single, embanked road towards Arnhem. Despite the obvious desperate urgency to reach 1st Airborne Division, a full nineteen hours had elapsed since the road bridge at Nijmegen had fallen to the tanks of the 2nd (Armoured) Battalion Grenadier Guards and the two companies of the 3rd Battalion 504th Parachute Infantry Regiment. Not only had this prolonged the agony for 1st Airborne Division, but it had given the enemy time to regroup and make his dispositions for the inevitable advance from Nijmegen. Unknown to XXX Corps, the road to Arnhem was only weakly defended for much of the night of 20/21 September, the enemy presence consisting only of small detachments in the area of Elst and on the southern outskirts of Arnhem.

Lieutenant General Brian Horrocks' orders to the Guards Armoured Division were that it should advance as early as possible at maximum speed to Arnhem. If it met strong resistance, it was to make every effort to fan out westwards and reach the lower Rhine area west of Arnhem in order to make contact with 1st Airborne Division. Its Coldstream Group would meanwhile remain on the right flank of 82nd US Airborne Division to counter the threat from the area of the Reichswald.

The 43rd (Wessex) Infantry Division, meanwhile, was to relieve the Guards Armoured Division's Welsh Group from its task of protecting the bridges at Grave, enabling it to rejoin the advance. In addition, it was to send two battalions from 130th Infantry Brigade to help the Guards Armoured Division clear the western part of Nijmegen and secure the railway bridge. Meanwhile, the leading elements of the division were to advance as quickly as possible in a two-pronged advance: 129th Infantry Brigade along the main road, following up in support of the Irish Guards, while 214th Infantry Brigade moved west of the Guards Armoured Division and headed north towards the Lower Rhine. The remainder of the division would concentrate at Grave.

During the night of 20 September, 5th Guards Armoured Brigade had established a close bridgehead at the northern end of the Nijmegen road bridge with the Irish Group and 153rd Field Regiment RA. At 1230 hours next day 130th Infantry Brigade, commanded by Brigadier Ben Walton, less two companies of the 4th Battalion The Dorsetshire Regiment, took over the road bridge from 5th Guards Armoured Brigade; the 7th Battalion Royal Hampshire Regiment was responsible for the southern, and the 5th Battalion The Dorsetshire Regiment for the northern approaches.

As they set off along the road to Arnhem, Captain Stephen Langton's No. 1 Squadron in the lead, the Irish Guards had few illusions about the likely opposition awaiting them: RAF tactical reconnaissance had already reported a column of twenty tanks heading south from Arnhem. They also knew that they would be operating on a one-tank front along a road six feet higher than surrounding terrain, lined on each side with deep ditches that would prevent deployment off it, and flanked by marshy ground that would favour the enemy. Moreover, ammunition was very low as a result of replenishment problems which had increased during the advance from the bridgehead over the Meuse–Escaut Canal to Nijmegen. Artillery support would be limited initially to one medium battery although this be would increased to a field regiment as soon as the advance had progressed sufficiently for the guns to be deployed. Equally serious was the fact that the absence of advanced landing strips would restrict air cover to a limited number of Typhoons on call.

The enemy had made full use of the breathing space afforded by XXX Corps' pause in Nijmegen during the night of 20/21 September. By nightfall on the 20th, a weak blocking line had been established one mile north of Lent by SS-Brigadeführer Heinz Harmel's 10th SS Panzer Division. During the night other units arrived, including a battle group comprising one and a half battalions of 22nd SS Panzer Grenadier Regiment and a Wehrmacht reserve battalion, plus a few tanks of 10th SS Panzer Regiment. The latter two units had been ferried across the Lower Rhine at Pannerden by 10th SS Panzer's engineers on the 19th, but had been unable to reach Nijmegen in time to take part in its defence. By dawn on the 21st, the blocking line had been firmly established in the area of the crossroads south of Ressen, extending westwards to Oosterhout and south-east to the north bank of the Waal. In Oosterhout, elements of 21st SS Artillery Regiment and the whole of 5th SS Artillery Training Regiment were progressively relieved by elements of Major Hans Peter Knaust's battle group and withdrew to Elst. By 1600 hours, the main body of Knaust's battle group had arrived from Arnhem and had established itself in positions around Elst.

To the east of the road, Harmel established three battalion-sized units supported by sixteen Mk IV tanks to attack the leading elements of XXX Corps as they advanced along the road. A battalion of 21st SS Panzer Grenadier Regiment was expected but had not yet arrived, having been delayed in crossing the Lower Rhine. Harmel used the flat, featureless terrain to his advantage, siting his tanks and self-propelled guns to cover the embanked road along which XXX Corps' tanks would advance.

Captain Stephen Langton's squadron of the 2nd (Armoured) Battalion Irish Guards had travelled less than a mile when all three tanks of his leading troop were knocked out as they rounded a bend in the road. The infantry of the 3rd Battalion Irish Guards dismounted rapidly from the tanks of the following two squadrons and deployed to positions in the deep ditches on either side of the road, coming under severe mortar and shell fire which caused heavy casualties. Lieutenant Colonel Giles Vandeleur arrived shortly afterwards and, on realizing that further advance along the road was impossible, ordered the tanks to remain where they were and sent reconnaissance patrols from the 3rd Battalion to reconnoitre both flanks for an alternative route. Meanwhile, the supporting medium battery brought fire to bear but this proved inadequate. The situation was exacerbated by the inability of the RAF forward controller to establish radio contact with the cab rank of Typhoons on call.

The Welsh Group, which had moved up to replace the Grenadiers, advanced on another road to the east, the companies of the 1st Battalion Welsh Guards mounted on the tanks of all but the leading troop of the 2nd (Armoured) Battalion. No. 1 Squadron led the way and was soon involved in heavy fighting; its leading troop knocked out three enemy tanks. By now darkness was falling and the Welsh Group was ordered to harbour up for the night. Meanwhile the Irish Group had succeeded in pushing forward to within striking distance of the station at Bemmel, but little further progress had been made because of the terrain and the well-sited enemy defences. It was joined there twenty-four hours later by 69th Infantry Brigade, which had been detached earlier from 50th Infantry Division and sent forward.

At dawn on 22 September, a troop of 'C' Squadron of the 2nd Household Cavalry Regiment, under Captain Richard Wrottesley, succeeded in moving through the enemy line to the west under cover of the early morning mist and made contact with 1st Polish Independent Parachute Brigade. The squadron had been tasked with pushing ahead to link up with units of 1st Airborne Division ahead of the rest of XXX Corps. On hearing of Wrottesley's success, his squadron leader, Major A. W. P. P. Herbert, sent another troop, commanded by Lieutenant Arthur Young, and this too got through to join Wrottesley's troop.

The two troops then skirted to the west of Oosterhout and moved along the north bank of the Waal before heading northwards for Driel where they met the Poles at 0800 hours. The remainder of the squadron attempted to join them but the mist started to lift and the armoured cars were spotted by enemy troops in a village 300 yards ahead. The enemy, supported by several tanks, opened fire and knocked out the leading vehicle, but the squadron managed to disengage under cover of smoke and withdrew. Nevertheless, Young and Wrottesley's troops continued to carry out reconnaissance tasks, sending back much valuable information and directing artillery fire on to targets. They also distinguished themselves by engaging and sinking a German steamer towing four barges.

By now, Second British Army had been forced to alter its plans. The firm grip by the enemy on Arnhem and the area to the north meant that XXX Corps' original task of seizing the town and the surrounding area, subsequently using it as a springboard for an assault across the Rhine, could not be undertaken. 1st Airborne Division had been unable to establish a bridgehead as originally intended, and the area encompassed by its shrinking perimeter was too small to be used as a bridgehead for an assault crossing. Moreover, the area of the south bank of the Lower Rhine opposite 1st Airborne Division's positions was such that the movement of assault craft to a launch site would be very difficult from the point of view of access, and very vulnerable to enemy fire from the north bank. Any assault crossing would have to be undertaken farther west, out of range of enemy artillery in the Arnhem area.

The task of XXX Corps was therefore modified. Originally, it was to have advanced north to the Zuider Zee with the Guards Armoured Division, while 43rd (Wessex) and 50th (Northumbrian) Infantry Divisions held the area of high ground north of Arnhem. 43rd Infantry Division was now directed to capture the Arnhem bridge and establish a bridgehead, and the Guards Armoured Division subsequently to move through to take and secure the high ground north of the town.

Lieutenant General Horrocks, accepting that the terrain was unfavourable to armour, had already ordered 43rd Infantry Division to take over as the leading formation; it was to move up to the west of the Guards Armoured Division which would remain in its positions and protect 43rd Infantry Division's right flank. But it was making very slow progress forward: 130th Infantry Brigade did not arrive south of Grave until the afternoon of 20 September and it was not until 1230 hours next day that it relieved the Welsh Guards of the defence of the road bridge and took over the job of clearing the enemy from Nijmegen.

214th Infantry Brigade, commanded by Brigadier Hubert Essame, concentrated to the south of Nijmegen in the early hours of the 22nd, having been delayed in Eindhoven during the night, its leading unit, the 7th Battalion Somerset Light Infantry, having taken the wrong route. On its arrival, the brigade received orders to move immediately through Nijmegen and advance to the west of the Guards Armoured Division via Oosterhout. Unfortunately, it experienced difficulty in getting through the town – some companies of the Somerset Light Infantry were directed over the wrong bridge – so its advance did not commence until 0830 hours on 22 September.

Shortly after it began advancing westwards out of the Nijmegen bridgehead, however, the Somerset Light Infantry encountered stiff opposition from the area of Oosterhout which was being held by a battalion-sized element of Major Knaust's battle group supported by tanks, self-propelled guns and mortars. It being impossible for armoured vehicles to be deployed off the roads in this terrain, the battalion had no option but to attack without support from the brigade's armoured regiment. The attack failed, as did a second, flanking attack. The brigade commander ordered a third attack with all of 43rd Infantry Division's artillery in support, and by 1700 hours a gap had been punched in the enemy line.

Brigadier Essame seized this opportunity to send a mobile column, which had already been formed and prepared for such an eventuality, through the gap with orders to advance northwards at speed to Driel to link up with 1st Polish Independent Parachute Brigade. The column comprised the 5th Battalion Duke of Cornwall's Light Infantry, commanded by Lieutenant Colonel George Taylor, a machine-gun platoon of the 8th Battalion The Middlesex Regiment and a squadron of the 4th/7th Royal Dragoon Guards. Accompanying the column were two DUKW amphibious vehicles heavily laden with ammunition, medical stores and other supplies for 1st Airborne Division.

Setting out just before dusk, Taylor's two leading companies travelled on the 4th/7th Royal Dragoon Guards' tanks and were followed by the two other companies in the battalion's own trucks, which escorted the two DUKWs. En route for Driel, however, the two halves of the column became separated. An enemy force of five Tiger tanks and some infantry inadvertently joined the same route behind the two leading companies which sped on ahead to Driel where they linked up with Major General Sosabowski's brigade. Fortunately the enemy were spotted by the crew of a Bren gun carrier, at the rear of the leading half of the column, which rammed the leading Tiger and killed its commander. Two platoons, equipped with PIATs, engaged the enemy and succeeded in knocking out the remaining four Tigers. The rest of the column eventually reached Driel without further difficulty and it was followed by the 1st Battalion The Worcestershire Regiment which had established itself in Valburg by 2359 hours on 22nd September.

Meanwhile, 129th Infantry Brigade had been attempting to advance along the main road in support of 5th Guards Armoured Brigade's Irish Group. There it was held up by Knaust's battle group, whose panzer grenadiers and tanks were blocking the road at Elst, and by the counter-attack force to the east of the road which was threatening the right flank of the brigade and that of the Guards Armoured Division's Irish and Welsh Groups which had already repelled a number of counter-attacks.

On the morning of the 22nd, XXX Corps' problems became even more serious when the enemy struck at its line of communications which was very exposed on both flanks because of the lack of progress of VIII and XII Corps whose leading elements had succeeded in getting no further than Eindhoven. Logistical problems had resulted in both corps being slow to begin their respective advances. Progress had been impeded by the difficult terrain and severe fighting in their sectors as the enemy continued to put up stiff resistance. In particular VIII Corps was suffering from lack of support on its right from First US Army which had been pulled farther to the south than had been envisaged by the advance eastwards of Patton's Third US Army.

On 21 September, Generaloberst Kurt Student's HQ 1st Parachute Army had received its orders from Generalfeldmarschall Model's HQ Army Group B to cut the 'corridor' being held by US 101st Airborne Division. This operation would take the form of a simultaneous pincer attack at Veghel by battle groups already located on each side of the St. Oedenrode–Grave road.

To the south-east of the road, drawn up in the area of the village of Erp, was a battle group commanded by Oberst Walther whose troops had borne the brunt of the initial breakout of the Guards Armoured Division on 17 September. Walther's group, which was tasked with seizing Veghel and destroying the bridge over the Zuid Willems Vaart Canal, comprised two elements. On the left of the axis, which was the road approaching Gheel from Gemert to the south-east, was a force commanded by SS-Hauptsturmführer Friedrich Richter, consisting of three companies of the 1st Battalion 16th Grenadier Regiment, an ad hoc company of administrative troops, 107th Panzer Engineer Company in half-tracks, three self-propelled guns and six Panther tanks. On the right was 107th Panzer Brigade, commanded by Major Freiherr von Maltzahn, comprising a panzer and a panzer grenadier battalion. Additional forces, in the form of two more infantry battalions, a battalion of 180th Artillery Regiment, the 1st Battalion 21st Fallschirmajäger Regiment, 10th SS Panzerjäger Battalion and a heavy anti-aircraft battery would also be re-deployed to Walther's group.

Richter's objective was the bridge at Veghel. Two companies of 16th Grenadier Regiment, supported by the six Panthers, would spearhead the attack, advancing through Erp to the bridge, the third company following up with the three self-propelled guns. To the rear would be 107th Panzer Engineer Company which would prepare the bridge for demolition, covered by the two forward companies and the tanks. The third company and the self-propelled guns would cover the southern approach to the bridge from the bank of the Zuid Willems Vaart Canal. Meanwhile 107th Panzer Brigade would attack Veghel, itself which was defended by the 2nd Battalion 501st Parachute Infantry Regiment whose other two battalions had been committed to a task in the area of Schijndel, some five miles to the west of Veghel.

To the north of the St. Oedenrode–Grave road was another battle group, commanded by Major Huber, which comprised three battalions of infantry, an artillery battalion with 105mm howitzers, a battery of 20mm light anti-aircraft guns, seven anti-tank guns and four Jagdpanther tank destroyers. Its task was to attack Veghel from the west.

The forming up of the two enemy battle groups, however, had not gone unnoticed. HQ 101st US Airborne Division had received several reports from the Dutch Resistance and local people of their presence. Accordingly, Major General Maxwell Taylor ordered 506th Parachute Infantry Regiment to move with all speed from Zon to Veghel to assist in dealing with this threat.

At 0900 hours on 22 September, Oberst Walther's battle group began its advance. Moving through Erp it reached the edge of Veghel and the village of Uden, on the road to the north-east, at 1100 hours. As the tanks and panzer grenadiers of 107th Panzer Brigade reached the road and wheeled left towards Veghel, they encountered the leading company of 506th Parachute Infantry Regiment as it arrived in Uden. Meanwhile, on the eastern outskirts of Veghel, the 2nd Battalion 501st Parachute Infantry Regiment was under pressure as it fought to stem the enemy advance from the direction of Erp.

To the west, meanwhile, Huber's battle group had reached the village of Eerde, a little way south-west of Veghel, at 1100 hours and at 1400 hours began shelling the bridge over the Canal while continuing to move up to the road. At that point a company of 506th Parachute Infantry Regiment appeared, supported by a squadron of 44th Royal Tank Regiment, which beat off Huber's attack. Having withdrawn, Huber decided to attack and cut the road further south, but was again thwarted, this time by two battalions of 327th Glider Infantry Regiment which appeared on the scene. Meanwhile, the 2nd and 3rd Battalions 501st Parachute Infantry Regiment were heading for Veghel from Schijndel to reinforce their comrades in 1st Battalion. Heading south, the two battalions encountered the rear of Huber's battle group which soon found itself cut off.

As 107th Panzer Brigade headed down the main road towards Veghel, further support for the beleaguered defenders arrived in the form of a battalion of 327th Glider Infantry Regiment with an anti-tank platoon equipped with 57mm guns. The leading tank was swiftly knocked out and the remainder withdrew temporarily.

The fighting around Veghel grew fierce during the day as the defenders repulsed attacks from both sides. The town was held by six parachute and glider battalions of 101st US Airborne Division under the command of

Brigadier General Tony McAuliffe, commander of the division's artillery, supported by two squadrons of 44th Royal Tank Regiment. The latter had been part of an armoured brigade detached from 7th Armoured Division and sent forward to assist in countering the threat to XXX Corps' line of communications.

Reinforcements for the Americans were already on their way in the form of 32nd Guards Brigade, commanded by Brigadier George Johnson, elements of which had until now been protecting the right flank of 82nd US Airborne Division. When Lieutenant General Horrocks heard of the attack, he ordered Johnson to turn his brigade round and head south to attack the enemy from the north.

The Grenadier Group, which had been swapped for the Welsh Group after its operations in Nijmegen, led the advance south and reached Uden during mid-afternoon. There it found the town full of halted convoys, staff officers and other headquarters personnel marooned by the fighting. A troop of tanks of the Grenadiers' 2nd (Armoured) Battalion and a platoon of the 1st (Motor) Battalion were sent forward to reconnoitre the road farther south, but after two miles they came under fire and the leading tank was knocked out by a panzerfaust. The remainder of the small force regrouped and established defensive positions but was recalled shortly afterwards as night had fallen.

Next morning, 23 September, an attack was launched on the enemy force astride the road. This began with a heavy artillery concentration laid down by 130 Battery 153rd Field Regiment (Leicestershire Yeomanry) RA, part of the Guards Armoured Division's own artillery, and the 4.2in heavy mortar platoon of No. 1 Independent Machine Gun Company Royal Northumberland Fusiliers which also belonged to the division. Such was the effect of this bombardment that the enemy withdrew eastwards, almost without firing a shot. At 1500 hours the Grenadiers linked up with 44th Royal Tank Regiment squadrons at Veghel.

The Coldstream Group, less a squadron and company group which had been sent to secure a large food dump at Oss, had followed the Grenadiers. Its tasks were to clear Volkel, south-east of Uden, and the airfield there before heading south to clear Erp and the surrounding area of any threat to the main road from that direction. On the morning of 23 September, the Coldstream attacked Volkel and a short but fierce battle ensued. Several tanks on both sides were knocked out and casualties mounted. By early afternoon, however, Volkel and the area around it had been cleared of enemy.

Farther south, however, the enemy attempted once again to cut the road. On the nights of 21/22 and 22/23 September, Oberstleutnant von der Heydte's 6th Fallschirmjäger Regiment had marched from its previous location east of Tilburg to Boxtel, west of Veghel, where it was to support

Huber's battle group in its attack on the road. This involved a march of thirty-nine miles, by the end of which von der Heydte's heavily laden troops, who had no transport, were exhausted. In the event, they did not reach their forming-up place in time to take part in the attack on Veghel on 22 September.

With the demise of Huber's battle group, von der Heydte was ordered to carry out an attack south of Veghel to seize the canal bridge and cut the road. It was to be mounted as soon as his regiment arrived at Boxtel, so as to coincide with a further attack by Oberst Walther's battle group which had attacked Veghel unsuccessfully during the night. Walther was expecting to be reinforced by the 1st Battalion Fallschirmjäger Regiment von Hoffmann, a panzer grenadier battalion of 9th SS Panzer Division and 10th SS Panzerjäger Battalion which were due to arrive during the afternoon.

At 0700 hours on 23 September, von der Heydte's regiment crossed its start line and advanced eastwards towards the road and the canal bridge. It was not long, however, before its three battalions of inexperienced and ill-trained troops, very different from those who had taken part in the airborne actions at Eben Emael and Crete, came under heavy and accurate fire from two battalions of 501st Parachute Infantry Regiment. Casualties mounted on both sides as the fighting escalated, but by 1300 hours the attack had failed and Von der Heydte's men began to dig in.

To the east, Oberst Walther's battle group had enjoyed similar lack of success and broke off their attack on Veghel at 1200 hours, eventually withdrawing to an area just east of Gemert. During the afternoon some of its units encountered the Coldstream Group at Volkel and the 44th Royal Tank Regiment squadron north-east of Veghel, the latter joining up with 32nd Guards Brigade during the afternoon. In addition, Walther faced another threat from the leading elements of VIII Corps which had crossed the Zuid Willems Vaart Canal on the previous day and were advancing northwards towards Helmond. To the west, XII Corps' leading elements were advancing north-east of Eindhoven.

By 1300 hours it was apparent that the enemy attack had lost its momentum, and two battalions of 506th Parachute Infantry were ordered to move north to link up with the Grenadier Guards who by now were advancing south down the road from Uden towards Veghel. By 1530 hours, the road had been opened and vehicles were sent northwards towards Nijmegen in blocks of ten every thirty minutes. However, the road was still threatened by the enemy who carried out occasional shelling and fired on convoys with panzerfausts and small arms.

The afternoon of 23 September saw the arrival by glider of the remaining elements of 101st US Airborne Division, including the 3rd Battalion 327th Glider Infantry Regiment and those elements of the divisional artillery that had not been brought in on the earlier lifts.

Twenty-four hours later, however, the Germans struck again and cut the road once more. Early in the morning of the 24th a strong attack was launched at Koevering, on the road just north of St. Oedenrode, by a battle group of four understrength battalions. One of these was an ad hoc unit commanded by Major Hans Jungwirth, a veteran Fallschirmjäger officer, which had been formed from a motley collection of parachutists, troops from 1035th Fusilier Regiment and stragglers. The others were the three battalions of von der Heydte's 6th Fallschirmjäger Regiment which included the 1st Battalion 2nd Fallschirmjäger Regiment and another parachute battalion which had previously been deployed at s'Hertogenbosch. Armoured support for this battle group was limited, consisting of the remaining Jagdpanther tank destroyers of No. 1 Company 559th Panzerjäger Battalion.

The attack began at 0900 hours on 24 September and approximately an hour later 6th Fallschirmjäger Regiment engaged the 1st Battalion 501st Parachute Infantry Regiment in its defensive positions in Eerde. Supported by artillery, von der Heydte's men overran the Americans' forwardmost positions outside the village. At that point a squadron of 44th Royal Tank Regiment appeared but was engaged by the tank destroyers which rapidly knocked out three of its tanks. 501st Parachute Infantry Regiment counter-attacked and fierce fighting took place at close quarters. Meanwhile, two of 559th Panzerjäger Battalion's Jagdpanthers caused mayhem after making their way to the road and attacking convoys of vehicles. Soft-skinned vehicles and a troop of tanks fell victim to their 88mm guns, bursting into flames and blocking the road as they were abandoned by their crews. Traffic came to a halt for miles to the rear, causing chaos.

Meanwhile, during the early evening, Major Jungwirth's ad hoc battalion had advanced southwards towards the small village of Koevering which was situated on the main road approximately one and a half miles north-west of St. Oedenrode. From thorough reconnaissance carried out earlier, Jungwirth knew the locations of the Americans' positions and was able to avoid them. As the battalion neared the village, a long column of stationary vehicles, parked nose-to-tail, could be seen on the road. Having deployed into assault formation, Jungwirth's men opened fire with panzerfausts and small arms and within minutes had reduced fifty vehicles to blazing wrecks which lit up the evening sky.

The first response came from two companies of 502nd Parachute Infantry Regiment which prevented Jungwirth and his men from entering Koevering itself, but the latter succeeded in establishing blocking positions astride the road. Despite heavy artillery fire, a battalion of 6th Fallschirmjäger Regiment reinforced Jungwirth's force during the night, but American counter-attacks were not long in coming. 506th Parachute Infantry Regiment, supported by a squadron of tanks, attacked from the north-east while a battalion of 502nd Parachute Infantry Regiment, supported by a brigade from 50th (Northumbrian) Infantry Division, advanced and attacked from the direction of St. Oedenrode. Despite being almost surrounded, Jungwirth's battalion maintained its grip on the road, knocking out three tanks and capturing intact three more. At the same time, it took the opportunity to mine the road and areas on each side.

As a consequence of the chaotic traffic jams, 50th (Northumbrian) Infantry Division was unable to move up to clear the road until the afternoon of the following day. Eventually, however, the enemy realized that it would be only a matter of time before Jungwirth's battalion was overrun and he was ordered to withdraw at dusk on 25 September. Under cover of darkness, the battalion moved off to the north-west while being subjected to heavy fire from artillery and tanks. By mid-morning on the 26th it had reached an area south of Schijndel but had suffered heavy casualties en route.

The enemy attacks blocked XXX Corps' line of communications for two days, and resulted in severe congestion farther south, vast amounts of transport being halted nose-to-tail from Eindhoven to St. Oedenrode. Convoys carrying urgently needed supplies were hindered by divisional and corps transport. Moreover, troops intended to link up with 1st Airborne Division had to be diverted back down the line of communications to mount counter-attacks against the enemy battle groups blocking the road. Once again, further delay had been imposed on XXX Corps, and by 26 September it was too late to save 1st Airborne Division.

While the fighting was raging around Veghel and Uden, further strenuous efforts were being made south of the Lower Rhine to ferry men and supplies through to 1st Airborne Division.

At 0200 hours on 23 September the two DUKWs, brought forward during the night by 5th Battalion Duke of Cornwall's Light Infantry, moved towards the river. The only approach was via a narrow, ditch-lined road immersed in mud caused by heavy rain which had fallen during the previous day. Time after time, the cumbersome and heavily loaded vehicles slid off the road and had to be manhandled on to it again. Within a few yards of the river, however, both DUKWs crashed into the ditch where they remained immovably stuck. At 0300 hours, all further attempts to ferry men and supplies across the river that night ceased.

The forward elements of XXX Corps were still battling their way forward against very stiff opposition. With the Grenadier and Coldstream Groups still heavily committed to the south, the Guards Armoured Division's Irish and Welsh Groups, supported by 69th Infantry Brigade, were still trying to clear the enemy from the village of Bemmel. Meanwhile, 129th and 214th Infantry Brigade were having a very tough fight at Elst where elements of Major Knaust's battle group were grimly resisting all attempts to dislodge them. The remainder of 130th Infantry Brigade, in the meantime, had succeeded in reaching Driel and linking up with 1st Polish Independent Parachute Brigade.

9
THE FINAL DAYS

'The operation was not one hundred per cent successful and did not end quite as we intended. The losses were heavy but all ranks appreciate that the risks involved were reasonable. There is no doubt that all would willingly undertake another operation under similar conditions in the future. We have no regrets.' — Major General Roy Urquhart.

As XXX Corps struggled forward towards Arnhem, at the same time fending off attacks on its line of communications, the surviving elements of 1st Airborne Division were still putting up a fierce resistance against pressure on their perimeter. Enemy artillery, comprising more than 100 guns plus heavy and medium mortars, kept up an unceasing bombardment and reinforcements continued to pour into Arnhem and Oosterbeek as Model's orders to crush 1st Airborne Division, and thus prevent its linking up with XXX Corps, were put into effect. Among these was a company of 506th Panzer Battalion whose fifteen Tiger tanks arrived in the Arnhem area on the morning of 24 September, the other two companies having been sent to Elst to reinforce 10th SS Panzer Division in its attempts to stem the advance of the Guards Armoured and 43rd Infantry Divisions. Although slow and cumbersome, lacking manoeuvrability in the streets of Arnhem and Oosterbeek, the heavy Tigers possessed formidable firepower, their 88mm guns demolishing buildings with ease.

By now, however, artillery support from XXX Corps was forthcoming and was helping to alleviate the pressure on 1st Airborne Division by breaking up enemy attacks on different parts of the perimeter. On the morning of 21 September, contact had been established between the Commander Royal Artillery 1st Airborne Division, Lieutenant Colonel Robert Loder-Symonds, and 64th Medium Regiment RA which had just arrived at Nijmegen and was within range to provide support with its 5.5in and 7.2in howitzers. Thereafter, further support had become available in the form of a battery of 7th Medium Regiment RA and two of 43rd Infantry Division's field regiments.

Throughout the battle, 1st Airborne Division's own artillery had provided magnificent support. With their gun lines almost constantly under fire, the batteries of Lieutenant Colonel W. F. K. 'Sheriff' Thompson's 1st Airlanding Light Regiment RA continued to answer calls for fire support from the brigades and battalions of which they were in support. In the best traditions of the Royal Artillery, the regiment's forward observation parties were located with the forwardmost elements of the division, with 2nd Parachute Battalion in Arnhem and throughout the perimeter in Oosterbeek, on occasions bringing down fire from the regiment's 75mm pack howitzers within yards of their own positions. The regiment's performance was later summed up by the division's Brigade Major RA, Major Philip Tower:

'It must never be forgotten that on the 1st Airlanding Light Regiment during those last few days fell much of the glory of Arnhem. They were mortared almost continuously, the whole gun area was under observation and swept by machine-gun fire. They were subject to attacks, usually backed with tanks, at least twice a day. Finally, their troop positions were overrun and the whole regiment concentrated in 3rd Light Battery's area on the north bank of the river around Oosterbeek Church.

'They fought as gunners, normal field gunners firing indirectly in support of the whole division, though like everyone's their ammunition was very short. They fought as anti-tank gunners, over open sights at ranges down to fifty yards, manhandling their 75mm guns round the positions until they could get a shot. They fought as infantry – in defence from the gunpits and command posts – and in attack and counter-attack led by battery commanders and troop commanders alike.'

An improvement in the weather meant that close air support, which had been notably absent so far, was also available and the RAF's Typhoon fighter-bombers attacked enemy armour as well as artillery and mortar positions. But the lack of forward controllers with radios meant that calls for air support had to be routed via divisional headquarters through the artillery radio net to HQ 1st Airborne Corps, and this inevitably resulted in longer than normal response times. At the time of 'Market Garden', there were somewhat surprisingly no British forward control units trained to operate with airborne forces, so two American forward control teams, each comprising an officer and four other ranks, had been attached to the division and landed with it on the first day. Each team was equipped with a jeep fitted with a high frequency (HF) radio set, which provided communications to 1st Airborne Corps and Second British Army, and a very high frequency (VHF) SCR 193 set for ground-to-air communication with aircraft. For some inexplicable reason, none of the men in either of the teams was familiar with the radio equipment and, furthermore, it transpired that neither of the two officers was trained in signals. In any event, both jeeps and their radios were destroyed soon after arriving at the divisional headquarters location early in the battle. The officers and men of both teams, having nothing else to do, fought on with 1st Airborne Division.

The unceasing bombardment of 1st Airborne Division was claiming more and more casualties, and the overstretched medical units, assisted by Dutch doctors and nurses, worked unceasingly to cope with the unending flow of wounded. At 0930 hours on Sunday 24 September, Colonel Graeme Warrack, the Assistant Director Medical Services 1st Airborne Division, told Major General Roy Urquhart that all the dressing stations were under fire and that he wished to arrange a truce with the Germans for the evacuation of all the wounded. Urquhart agreed but emphasized that Warrack must make it clear to the Germans that the approach was being made purely on humanitarian grounds. The truce was subsequently effected through the senior German medical officer at the Schoonoord Hotel dressing station which by now was being manned by both German and British medical staff.

Warrack, accompanied by an interpreter and a German medical officer, was driven to the headquarters of SS-Obersturmbannführer Walter Harzer, commander of 9th SS Panzer Division. Shortly afterwards SS-Obergruppenführer Willi Bittrich, commander of 2nd SS Panzer Corps, arrived and after discussing the plan with Warrack agreed to the evacuation of the wounded.

At 1500 hours that afternoon, the truce and the evacuation began. An unearthly hush settled over the area as the firing stopped. Convoys of vehicles arrived and the wounded were loaded aboard them. During the next two hours the convoys drove out of Oosterbeek towards Arnhem, carrying more than 250 men, and more than 200 walking wounded were led out of the area to St. Elisabeth's Hospital in Arnhem.

At 1700 hours the battle was resumed in earnest. The enemy had taken advantage of the truce to infiltrate troops into many areas throughout the perimeter and the situation was such that front lines now scarely existed; occasionally German and British troops found themselves in positions only yards apart. Once again, the divisional area was subjected to a constant bombardment by mortars and artillery. The 1st Battalion The Border Regiment, now reduced to little more than an understrength company, was attacked by a force of enemy trying to penetrate the perimeter from the west. Members of the Mortar Platoon, whose mortars had all been knocked out, counter-attacked and drove them back.

The Germans had also suffered terrible punishment at the hands of the airborne troops. In some units, companies had been reduced to no more than thirty or forty men. By 25 September casualties were such that the battle group forming the eastern side of the encircling 'box', under SS-Obersturmbannführer Ludwig Spindler, had to be reorganized from remnants of 19th and 20th SS Panzer Grenadier Regiments, 9th SS Panzer Artillery Regiment and the divisional anti-aircraft regiment. These were divided into four combat teams together with sappers of 9th

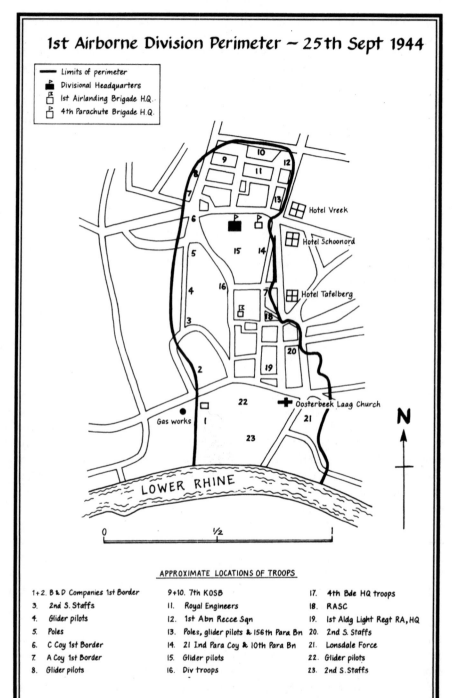

1st Airborne Division Perimeter ~ 25th Sept 1944

- ▬ Limits of perimeter
- Divisional Headquarters
- 1st Airlanding Brigade H.Q.
- 4th Parachute Brigade H.Q.

Hotel Vreek

Hotel Schoonord

Hotel Tafelberg

Oosterbeek Laag Church

Gas works

LOWER RHINE

N

0   ½

APPROXIMATE LOCATIONS OF TROOPS

1+2. B & D Companies 1st Border	9+10. 7th KOSB	17. 4th Bde HQ troops
3. 2nd S. Staffs	11. Royal Engineers	18. RASC
4. Glider pilots	12. 1st Abn Recce Sqn	19. 1st Aldg Light Regt RA, HQ
5. Poles	13. Poles, glider pilots & 156th Para Bn	20. 2nd S. Staffs
6. C Coy 1st Border	14. 21 Ind Para Coy & 10th Para Bn	21. Lonsdale Force
7. A Coy 1st Border	15. Glider pilots	22. Glider pilots
8. Glider pilots	16. Div troops	23. 2nd S. Staffs

SS Panzer Division's engineer battalion and those of 9th Pionier Lehr Battalion. These were commanded by Spindler, SS-Hauptsturmführer Hans Moeller, SS-Hauptsturmführer Klaus von Allworden and SS-Obersturmführer Harder respectively. To the north of them, forming the 'lid', were SS-Sturmbannführer Sepp Krafft's 16th SS Depot & Reserve Battalion and Hauptmann Bruhns' Wehrmacht panzer grenadier battalion. To the west were the three SS units, commanded by SS-Sturmbannführers Eberwein and Schulz and SS-Hauptsturmführer Oelkers respectively, and a battalion of the Hermann Göring Training Regiment. Those units to the north and east of 1st Airborne Division's perimeter were under the command of SS-Obersturmbannführer Walther Harzer, while those on the west remained under that of Generalleutnant Hans von Tettau.

Attached to Spindler's four combat teams were the Tiger tanks of the 506th Panzer Battalion company. Further support was provided by the self-propelled guns of 280th Sturmgeschutz Brigade.

Casualties among the armour had also been high: 224th Panzer Company had lost all its eight Renault tanks (captured from the French in the opening stages of the war), a company of 6th Panzer Replacement Battalion had had five of its eight Mk IV tanks knocked out and 280th Sturmgeschutz Brigade had lost four of its self-propelled guns. Other tanks, half-tracks and armoured cars had been knocked out earlier, and by 24 September it was estimated that almost half the armour committed to the battle up to that time had been lost.

On the afternoon of 25 September, however, the enemy mounted a strong attack on the eastern sector of 1st Airborne Division's perimeter. The combat team commanded by SS-Hauptsturmführer von Allworden, supported by that of SS-Obersturmführer Harder, succeeded in breaking through the line held by the 2nd Battalion The South Staffordshire Regiment and Major Dickie Lonsdale's composite force, and reaching the gun line of 1st Airlanding Light Regiment RA. Indeed, the divisional area was nearly cut in two as von Allworden's force succeeded in reaching a point some 500 yards to the rear of the positions in the western sector of the perimeter. At one point, the gunners of 1st Airlanding Light Regiment RA were engaging the enemy over open sights at a range of only fifty yards. However, help was on hand from XXX Corps' guns which broke up the attack and forced the enemy to withdraw.

By now the predicament of 1st Airborne Division was so dire that serious consideration was being given to its withdrawal. Accounts differ as to when and by whom the decision to withdraw was taken. At St. Oedenrode during the afternoon of 24 September, Lieutenant General Horrocks attended a conference with the commander of Second British Army, Lieutenant General Sir Miles Dempsey, and Lieutenant General 'Boy' Browning.

Horrocks had already planned, and given orders for, a crossing of the Lower Rhine which would be carried out opposite 1st Airborne Division's perimeter by a battalion of 130th Infantry Brigade and elements of 1st Polish Parachute Brigade, taking with them the maximum possible amount of ammunition and other stores. The rest of 43rd Infantry Division would cross the river farther to the west and carry out a flanking attack into the rear of the enemy forces forming the western side of the 'box' enclosing 1st Airborne Division. Earlier during the day, however, Browning had expressed doubts about Horrocks' plan to Dempsey, who had called at HQ 1st Airborne Corps for a meeting with Browning before proceeding to St. Oedenrode for the conference with Horrocks. Browning was of the opinion that 1st Airborne Division should be withdrawn.

In his memoirs, entitled *Corps Commander*, Horrocks states that he outlined his plan and that it was agreed by Dempsey and the others that the crossing would be made that night to reinforce 1st Airborne Division, but with a proviso that if it proved unsuccessful Urquhart and his men would be withdrawn. This is borne out by the entry for 24 September in Dempsey's war diary:

> 'Met Cmdr 30 Corps at St. Oedenrode. Contact with 1st Airborne Division. Depending on next 24 hours 30 Corps on night 25/26th will either: (a) Pass complete Bde of 43 Div across river, West of Arnhem, and build a bridge, and establish a bridgehead; (b) Withdraw 1st Airborne Div. South of Rhine and give up bridgehead.'

Other accounts of the conference at St. Oedenrode have it that Dempsey considered Horrocks' plan but rejected it and ordered the latter to withdraw 1st Airborne Division as soon as possible.

Whatever the truth of the matter concerning the decision to withdraw, that night approximately 400 men of the 4th Battalion The Dorsetshire Regiment, commanded by Lieutenant Colonel Gerald Tilly, crossed the Lower Rhine in assault craft. Even before the operation commenced, problems had arisen because of the late arrival of the boats. H-Hour had been set for 2230 but the boats had not appeared in time and the crossing had had to be postponed. Unbeknown to those waiting on the south bank of the river, the convoy of five trucks carrying the boats had been delayed by the severing of XXX Corps' line of communications by the enemy. When one single truck appeared three hours late, carrying nine collapsible boats, it was discovered that two of the vehicles had taken a wrong turning and driven into enemy positions at Elst, and the other two had skidded on the slippery road and crashed. Nine boats, which were found to be without paddles, were obviously insufficient, but more were obtained from 1st Polish Independent Parachute Brigade which had retained some from its earlier efforts to cross the river.

In the darkness, made worse by the cold and rain, the Dorsets helped sappers to carry the cumbersome and heavy assault boats across the mudflats to the river. By the time they were ready to embark it was after 0200 hours on 25 September and the enemy had been fully alerted and was bringing down a heavy concentration of fire from machine-guns and mortars on the south bank and river. Nevertheless, the Dorsets set off across the river, a platoon at a time, under covering fire from the 5th Battalion The Dorsetshire Regiment and supporting artillery. Several boats were hit and sunk, others were gripped by the strong current and swept away downstream. The operation continued despite these setbacks and by dawn on 25 September 239 men had reached the far bank. On landing, however, they encountered troops of the 1st Battalion 26th Sicherung Regiment which had been moved up to the river from Renkum after reports of the crossing had been received, and another regiment which had been reinforced by two companies of Luftwaffe troops. These two units were supported by a battalion of Luftwaffe personnel reinforced by a company of SS troops.

The majority of the Dorsets landed in small, scattered groups out of contact with one another. Many of them were killed, wounded or captured outside the base line of 1st Airborne Division's perimeter, and only a small number succeeded in reaching the hard-pressed airborne troops. Of the 400 or so who crossed the Lower Rhine, 140 were captured including their commanding officer, Lieutenant Colonel Gerald Tilly.

At the same time as the Dorsets were struggling to gain a hold on the north bank, Lieutenant Colonel Eddie Myers, Commander Royal Engineers 1st Airborne Division, crossed over farther upstream during the early hours of 25 September and made his way back to the perimeter and the divisional headquarters. He was carrying two letters addressed to Major General Roy Urquhart, one from Lieutenant General Browning and the other from Major General Ivo Thomas, commander of 43rd Infantry Division. The latter informed Urquhart that plans to establish a bridgehead at Arnhem had been abandoned and that 1st Airborne Division would be withdrawn. Shortly afterwards, Urquhart made contact with Thomas by radio and told him that the withdrawal, code-named Operation 'Berlin', must take place that night.

Urquhart's plan for the withdrawal depended on being able to deceive the enemy for as long as possible. Groups of men, including those wounded still capable of handling weapons, would keep up a show of force by firing from different positions while the main body of the remainder of the division withdrew under cover of darkness. Those in the north of the perimeter would withdraw down the eastern and western flanks to the river, across which they would be evacuated in boats manned by British and Canadian sappers. Radio transmissions would be maintained as normal and the guns of 1st Airlanding Light Regiment RA would carry on firing until the last possible moment. Medical officers and orderlies would remain with the wounded. Glider pilots would form a human chain along the escape route which would be marked at intervals with strips of white tape.

On the south bank of the Lower Rhine, meanwhile, preparations were being made. A total of thirty-seven craft, manned by Royal Engineers and Canadian sappers, had been assembled. Supporting fire would be provided by 43rd Infantry Division's own artillery plus that of XXX Corps. Farther west along the river, diversions would be created to distract enemy attention from the crossing point.

At 2100 hours on 25 September, the artillery opened fire in a massive barrage which rained down on the German positions and would continue to do so until 0800 hours on the following morning. This bombardment, combined with the heavy wind and rain which lashed the area, provided cover for the withdrawal which began at 2145 hours. With their boots muffled and their equipment secured against rattling, the remnants of 1st Airborne Division made their way through the darkness and pouring rain.

On the river bank at the southern end of the perimeter, the sappers and their assault boats were waiting. To the west of the perimeter, units of 130th Infantry Brigade were carrying out a diversionary operation. Farther west, Second British Army's artillery was firing a barrage as part of another diversion.

The night was dark and the weather, fortunately in this instance, bad with strong winds and heavy rain which helped to conceal the movement of the survivors of 1st Airborne Division as they began to withdraw towards the river. As they did so, those wounded incapable of walking but still able to handle a weapon kept up a steady stream of fire to give the impression that positions were still occupied. Others maintained signals traffic over radios to help in the deception. Medical officers and orderlies remained with the wounded, as did the chaplains. Eventually, those with the boats spotted long lines of men making their way slowly towards them through the darkness, guided by the chain of glider pilots. Others had not been so fortunate: some had lost their way and been captured, others had encountered enemy patrols and been killed. The lucky ones embarked as quickly as possible and the first boats headed for the south bank at about 2200 hours.

At this juncture the enemy were totally unaware that a withdrawal was in progress. Those airborne troops encountered in the darkness and pouring rain were assumed to be members of patrols or taking part in counter-attacks. Even when the boats were spotted, it was assumed that further attempts were being made to reinforce 1st Airborne Division.

Artillery and mortar fire was brought to bear and within an hour 50 per cent of the boats had been sunk. The operation continued, however. On the river bank and in the woods and fields leading back to the divisional area, hundreds of men waited their turn to cross to safety. All the while, machine-gun and mortar fire swept the embarkation point and the river itself as the boats crossed to and fro.

By dawn on the 26th, only a few boats remained, but their crews continued to ferry men across the river. By the time the operation ceased at 0550 hours, 2,398 men had been evacuated – this figure comprising 1,741 all ranks of 1st Airborne Division, 160 men of 1st Polish Independent Parachute Brigade, 420 glider pilots and seventy-five officers and men of the 4th Battalion The Dorsetshire Regiment. Others had swum across, but 300 men were left on the northern side.

Dawn found enemy forces advancing on all three sides, but it was not until mid-morning that they neared the perimeter area, and even then they were still encountering small pockets of resistance. When they reached the Hartenstein Hotel, they found the positions deserted except for corpses. In the hotel's tennis courts they found some of their number who had been taken prisoner earlier by the airborne troops and thereafter guarded by men of 1st Airborne Division Provost Company until the latter slipped away at 0230 hours with the last of those heading for the river. It was only then that the Germans realized that their quarry had got away during the night. They experienced considerable relief that the fighting was at last over; in ten days of fighting their losses had been heavy. The majority of German units involved in the fighting in Arnhem and Oosterbeek had lost on average 50 per cent of their strengths; in one or two instances losses were as high as between 80 and 90 per cent, with one unit numbering only seven men by the end of the battle. The cost of victory at Arnhem and Oosterbeek had been high indeed.

By 1200 hours on 26 September, the exhausted but still unbowed survivors of 1st Airborne Division had been moved to Nijmegen where they met the division's administrative 'tail' which had landed by sea and travelled overland. Four days later they returned to England, leaving behind them 7,212 of their number killed, wounded, captured or missing.

10
REFLECTIONS IN HINDSIGHT

'If you were not going to get all the bridges, it was not worth going at all.'
— Brigadier General John Hackett.

It is all too easy to be wise in hindsight, particularly when one is in possession of information which was not available at the time in question, and any criticism in this book is in the main limited to the errors in the concept and planning of Operation 'Market Garden' which, in the author's opinion, were largely responsible for the tragedy at Arnhem and Oosterbeek that led to the destruction of 1st Airborne Division.

Opinions differ greatly as to the degree of success achieved by 'Market Garden'. Perhaps somewhat understandably, one or two of the senior commanders involved seem to have tended later to gloss over those parts of the operation that had failed and to highlight those that had been successful, as is perhaps illustrated by the following extract from Lieutenant General Lewis Brereton's post-operation report:

'Despite the failure of 2nd Army to get through to Arnhem and establish a permanent bridgehead over the Lower Rhine, Operation MARKET was a brilliant success. The 101st Division took all of its objectives as planned; the 82nd Division dominated the southern end of the bridge at Nijmegen until noon of D+1, by which time it had been planned for the Guards Armoured to be there; the 1st British Division similarly dominated the Arnhem bridge from its northern end until noon of D+3, 24 hours later than the time set for the arrival of the 2nd Army. Hence the airborne troops accomplished what was expected of them. It was the breakdown of the 2nd Army's timetable on the first day – their failure to reach Eindhoven in six to eight hours as planned – that caused the delay in the taking of the Nijmegen bridge and the failure at Arnhem.'

In fact, neither of the American airborne divisions achieved total success. The 101st US Airborne Division did succeed in taking all its objectives but did not prevent the enemy from blowing the bridge at Zon, and 82nd US Airborne Division certainly did not dominate either of the bridges at Nijmegen and was only able to capture them with the assistance of the Guards Armoured Division on the third day of the operation. The architect of 'Market Garden', Field Marshal Montgomery, claimed that the operation had been 90 per cent successful. But when one considers the principal aim of the operation, the establishment of a bridgehead over the Rhine for a thrust through Germany's back door into the heartland of the Ruhr, with the ultimate purpose of finishing the war by the end of 1944, it is clear that 'Market Garden' failed – but only just. The fact that it so very nearly succeeded is a remarkable tribute to the officers and men of the units within the three airborne divisions and XXX Corps that bore the brunt of the fighting.

The seeds of failure were sown initially during the latter days of August, when the Allied forces were advancing through northern France. As has already been described, discord and disagreement had festered continually between Montgomery and Generals Omar Bradley and George Patton. They disliked and were suspicious of him, and it appears that they did not regard him as being a commander of any great ability. Even the normally mild-mannered Bradley, on receiving the news of Montgomery's promotion to field marshal on 1 September, stated waspishly that 'Montgomery is a third-rate general and he never did anything or won any battle that any other general could not have won as well or better'. By the same token Montgomery, with his customary arrogance, appeared to have equally little regard for the abilities of his American counterparts when he declared: 'The real trouble with the Yanks is that they are completely ignorant as to the rules of the game we are playing with the Germans. You play so much better when you know the rules.'

Such a relationship between senior commanders could only cause problems when future operations were under consideration. Eisenhower favoured the broad front policy, but was not supported in this concept by the other three, all of whom favoured a strong thrust but at different points. Bradley and Patton advocated an eastward thrust via Metz and the Saar, while Montgomery persistently propounded his plan for a northern thrust through Holland and then eastwards over the Rhine towards the Ruhr. Jealousy and personal ambition undoubtedly played a part in the dispute, the Americans being suspicious of Montgomery's motives. Each was determined to be the first to seize the glittering prize of Berlin, so each was anxious to obtain the resources needed to make this possible.

American resentment burgeoned during the latter part of August when Montgomery increased the pressure on Eisenhower to agree to his plan and therefore accord him priority of re-supply. Tact was never a prominent feature of Montgomery's character and he made no attempt to conceal his disregard of Eisenhower's broad front policy, constantly criticising it and demanding additional resources of troops and supplies for his own purposes. Furthermore, Montgomery was strongly opposed to Eisenhower's assumption of direct control of his and Bradley's Army Groups.

Eisenhower was in a difficult position. Having assumed the mantle of Commander-in-Chief of land forces on 1 September, he found himself acting as conciliator between the two feuding factions. Bradley and Patton at times suspected him of supporting Montgomery, while the latter thought the opposite. Moreover, Eisenhower was well aware of public opinion in the United States, communicated to him on a number of occasions by General George C. Marshall, Chief of Staff of the US Army, which was predisposed against any apparent favouring of Montgomery. On 23 August, after his meeting with Montgomery during which the latter was highly critical of the Supreme Allied Commander's decision to take over command of the land forces, and of his broad front policy, Eisenhower issued a directive in which he compromised to such an extent that both Montgomery and Bradley thought that he had favoured the other: while Montgomery was permitted to advance northwards, Patton could continue to advance to the east.

Such indecision and vacillation on the part of Eisenhower inevitably decreased the time available for firm planning of future operations, and this situation was exacerbated by the rapid advance of British and American formations along their respective axes and the consequent problems caused by lengthening lines of communication and supply. Neither Army Group was receiving the requisite amount of supplies to enable it to operate at full capacity.

Eisenhower's dilatoriness in giving his full support to 'Market Garden' served only to grant the Germans the respite they needed to regroup. Montgomery was well aware of this threat and emphasized it in his letter to Eisenhower on the day after their meeting in the latter's personal aircraft at Brussels airport on 10 September:

> 'Your decision that the Northern thrust towards the Ruhr is NOT repeat NOT to have priority over other operations will have certain repercussions which you should know. The large scale operations by 2nd Army and the Airborne Corps northwards towards the Meuse and Rhine cannot now take place before 23 September at the earliest and possibly 26 September. This delay will give the enemy time to organize better defensive arrangements and we must expect heavier resistance and slower progress ...'

Although 'Market Garden' was launched on 17 September, it was already by then too late. The opportunity to drive north through a disorganized and retreating enemy had been lost. Had Second British Army not halted after establishing its bridgehead over the Meuse–Escaut Canal at Neerpelt but pushed on, it could probably have advanced all the way to Arnhem. But its leading formations had been forced to halt because they were very short of ammunition, fuel and other supplies. Within the space of a few days, the Germans managed to regroup sufficiently to organize a defence which, although cobbled together largely from makeshift formations and units, would succeed in preventing the link-up between XXX Corps and 1st Airborne Division.

Much has been written previously about the failure to open up the port of Antwerp, captured intact on 3 September by 11th Armoured Division, to solve the problem of overstretched lines of supply. But the Scheldt estuary had been heavily mined and the port could not be used until the estuary had been swept. Moreover, German forces on the South Beveland isthmus and the island of Walcheren had to be cleared before the Allies had control of the estuary, and this was only effected after fierce fighting which lasted until 6 November. Minesweeping began on 4 November and was not completed until 26 November. Two days later, the first supply convoy of ships sailed up the estuary to dock at Antwerp. As Horrocks realized later, he would have been better advised to order 11th Armoured Division to bypass Antwerp and advance a further fifteen miles beyond the city to the north-west, thus cutting off the remnants of General der Infanterie Gustav von Zangen's Fifteenth Army and preventing them from subsequently joining up with Generaloberst Kurt Student's 1st Parachute Army.

The degree of success after the breakout from the Normandy bridgehead, and the astonishingly rapid rate of advance through France into Belgium, had resulted in a feeling of overconfidence and euphoria. This was prevalent at all levels and in turn led to under-estimation of the fighting state of the enemy who were at that time retreating in some disorder. Even Montgomery, who had more than once expressed his respect for the fighting ability of the German soldier, appeared to have been guilty of this, as was pointed out subsequently by Lieutenant General Brian Horrocks:

'Montgomery, for the first and last time in his long and brilliant career as a tactical commander, completely under-estimated the opposition which we were likely to encounter during our advance to Arnhem when he started his orders by saying that the disorganized German Army was straggling back to the Fatherland, or words to that effect.

'I was astonished to hear this, because we knew that the Germans had made a remarkable recovery, and during our advance to the Meuse–Escaut Canal we had been fighting hard against General Student's paratroops, under the command of the redoubtable von der Heydte, plus SS panzer formations. I had been heavily involved in a desperately hard fight carried out by the Guards Armoured Division and later on by the 50th Division. Fortunately, these were two of the best divisions in the British Army, but even they had had a struggle to overcome this tough resistance.'

The commanders of the enemy forces in Holland were some of Germany's most able officers, many of them veterans of the campaigns in Russia, Europe and North Africa: Model, Student, Bittrich and von der Heydte to name just four. They were served at corps, divisional and regimental level by staffs who were experienced and well trained and, when required to do so, were capable of responding rapidly to a crisis. An example of this is the rapidity with which troops and equipment were dispatched to fill the 50-mile-wide gap between Antwerp and Maastricht during the first week of September. Within forty-eight hours of orders being issued on 4 September to Oberstgeneral Kurt Student to form 1st Parachute Army, the leading elements of his parachute regiments, previously based at various locations throughout Germany where they had been resting and re-equipping after fighting in France, arrived in the forward areas where they would take up positions facing XXX Corps. Meanwhile, trainloads of arms and equipment were also sent from Germany at the same time, arriving at railheads where they were collected by troops en route to the front.

Intelligence concerning the enemy was available from ULTRA and other sources, and was supplied to Army HQ level, but was disregarded, particularly by Montgomery who was dismissive of it. It is true that the 9th *Hohenstaufen* and 10th *Frundsberg* SS Panzer Divisions were shadows of their former selves, but their remaining troops were well trained and very experienced, and both formations still possessed sufficient firepower to cause major problems for 1st Airborne Division at Arnhem and Oosterbeek, and for XXX Corps from Nijmegen northwards. Furthermore, both divisions had been thoroughly trained in anti-airborne operations during the summer of 1943: their troops had been taught to attack airborne forces while they were still landing and at their most vulnerable. Much emphasis had been placed on swift reactions, even the most junior commanders being trained to make decisions and act on their own initiative. Each of the nineteen quick-reaction units, into which 9th SS Panzer Division was reorganized after arrival in the area between Arnhem and Apeldoorn, was located in a village in an area well served by excellent roads giving rapid access to Arnhem. Moreover, the division still possessed some of its armoured vehicles, self-propelled guns and tank-destroyers.

Although it resembled no more than a weak brigade, the reorganized 10th SS Panzer Division included a reconnaissance battalion mounted in armoured half-tracks, a company of tanks and three battalions of panzer grenadiers – again, a force to be reckoned with when deployed against lightly equipped airborne troops with no supporting armour. Like their comrades in 9th SS Panzer Division, the men of the 10th were all veterans of the fighting in Normandy and a good number had seen service on the Eastern Front.

Allied intelligence assessments during the build-up to 'Market Garden' had tended to concentrate on enemy forces in the Low Countries, but the Germans had resources outside Holland on which they were able to draw quickly for reinforcements during the battle. These included 506th Panzer Battalion from Ohrduf, 171st *Auffrischung* Light Artillery Regiment, 9th Pionier Lehr Battalion from Glogau, 6th Panzer Replacement Battalion from Bielefeld, 280th Sturmgeschutz Brigade from Aachen, and 37th and 41st Fortress Machine Gun Battalions. These units and others were moved rapidly by rail from Germany to the Arnhem area during the battle, illustrating again the Germans' capability of responding swiftly to any serious threat. As Brigadier John Hackett, commander of 4th Parachute Brigade, with considerable experience of fighting the Germans in the Middle East and Sicily, had commented earlier, 'However weak they seem on the ground, if you threaten a vital point their response is swift and violent'.

Lieutenant General Brian Horrocks was one of those who questioned later why XXX Corps in particular had received no intelligence about the enemy forces assembling to his front. He believed that it was probably due to a determination at high level to commit First Allied Airborne Army to battle in an operation designed to finish the war before the end of 1944.

Indeed, Montgomery later maintained that expediting the end of the war was a principal factor in his mind when proposing a strong thrust northwards through Holland. By 1944 Britain was economically almost exhausted and her reserves of manpower heavily depleted. The lack of the latter was reflected in the serious situation regarding reinforcements for 21st Army Group during its advance though northern France: the Guards Armoured Division, for example, which had suffered heavy casualties during the fighting in Normandy and the advance through Northern France, received replacements drawn from Royal Artillery anti-aircraft units and the Royal Air Force Regiment. After the fierce fighting around Beeringen, however, it did not receive any more. 59th Infantry Division, plus twenty-five other infantry and armoured formations, had to be disbanded so that their troops could be transferred to other divisions as sorely needed replacements.

Montgomery apparently resented the lack of understanding by the Americans on the issue of a speedy end to the war, as he made clear in his memoirs when referring to Eisenhower's broad front policy:

> The more I considered what we were setting out to do, the more certain I was that it was wrong. The British economy and manpower situation demanded victory in 1944: no later. Also, the war was bearing hardly on the mass of people in Britain; it must be brought to a close quickly. Our "must" was different from the American must: a difference in urgency, as well as a difference in doctrine. This the American generals

did not understand; the war had never been brought to their home country. Why should we throw everything away for reasons of American public opinion and American electioneering [1944 was the Presidential election year]? The strategy we were now to adopt would mean more casualties in killed and wounded. The armies were not being deployed on a broad front for any reasons of safety; our southern flank was quite secure and could almost be held by air power alone, with a small military backing. If Dragoon [Operation 'Dragoon': the Allied landings in the South of France] had done nothing else, at least it had achieved that. There was no real risk in doing what I suggested. Indeed my plan offered the only possibility of bringing the war to a quick end.'

Montgomery's plan depended primarily for success on the ability of his ground forces to link up successfully with 1st Airborne Division, but it proved to be flawed in that it was inherently inflexible because of its extremely tight time schedule and the limitations imposed on XXX Corps by the use of a single route through terrain that favoured the enemy, was unsuitable for armour and featured major water obstacles. When problems arose in the early stages and the ground forces were delayed, the entire operation was thrown into jeopardy.

XXX Corps' ability to maintain momentum in the rate of its advance depended on the security of its line of communications and supply. The task of defending the foremost sector of this was initially given to 101st US Airborne Division, but Lieutenant General Sir Richard O'Connor's VIII Corps, protecting XXX Corps' right flank and rear, was also tasked with taking over the responsibility as far as Grave as soon as it had advanced sufficiently far to do so. Lieutenant General Neil Ritchie's XII Corps was responsible for protecting XXX Corps' left flank.

Two factors, however, interfered with this aspect of the plan. The first was the lack of logistical support which Eisenhower had refused to accord 21st Army Group until it was too late. Montgomery had therefore to rely on his own limited resources to produce the build-up of supplies required for the operation, but shortage of transport meant that priority had to be given to supplies rather than troops. This delayed the movement forward of VIII Corps which had already had most of its transport commandeered by HQ Second British Army to help supply XII and XXX Corps. As a consequence, VIII Corps, which comprised 11th Armoured and 3rd Infantry Divisions, was unable to move forward from the Seine until 16 September, the day before 'Market Garden' began. 3rd Infantry Division therefore did not cross the Meuse–Escaut Canal until the early morning of 19 September, by which time XXX Corps should have linked up with 1st Airborne Division at Arnhem, and its armour could not cross until 1930 hours when a Class 40 bridge had been completed. XII Corps, comprising 7th Armoured, 15th (Scottish) and 53rd (Welsh) Infantry Divisions, experienced similar problems: shortage of transport meant that it had only established a single bridgehead across the Meuse–Escaut Canal before 17 September. So it took time for its leading formations to cross the Canal and deploy for the advance.

Having crossed the Meuse–Escaut Canal, both VIII and XII Corps thereafter were hampered by adverse terrain, consisting of swampy heathland with very few tracks, which made progress and deployment of armour difficult and favoured defence. This factor, combined with the slow start by both corps and surprisingly fierce opposition from the scratch formations of Student's 1st Parachute Army, resulted in XXX Corps' line of communications becoming dangerously exposed and able to be cut by the enemy.

The exposure of XXX Corps' right flank in particular caused problems throughout the duration of 'Market Garden', forcing Horrocks on 20 September to place the Coldstream Group of 32nd Guards Brigade under command of 82nd US Airborne Division as a mobile reserve to counter the threat from the Reichswald and so reduce the capability of the already weakened Guards Armoured Division to continue as spearhead of the advance. Furthermore, the disregard of Eisenhower's orders by Generals Bradley and Patton also affected VIII Corps' progress. As the latter's Third US Army advanced further eastwards, Lieutenant General Courtney Hodges' First US Army was forced to pull away southwards to protect Patton's northern left flank, thereby exposing VIII Corps' right flank which it was supposed to be covering. It is worthy of note that throughout 'Market Garden', VIII and XII Corps between them suffered a total of 3,874 casualties, and XXX Corps 1,480.

Whereas disregard of available intelligence had a direct effect on the operation as a whole, incorrect intelligence played its part in causing the failure of 1st Airborne Division at Arnhem.

The major flaws in Major General Roy Urquhart's plan were the distance between his division's objectives and its dropping and landing zones, and their location west of Arnhem and north of the Lower Rhine. But Urquhart had little choice. The RAF vetoed his initial selections on grounds of the threat from enemy flak defences in the vicinity of Arnhem itself and the air base at Deelen to the north. His idea of a glider-borne coup de main force had to be discarded because of an RAF veto on the use of terrain south of the river despite the spectacular success of the Orne Bridge attack in Normandy: this was reported as being unsuitable for parachutists or gliders, being heavily defended by flak. In both instances, the intelligence proved incorrect: the anti-aircraft guns at Deelen had been removed after the bombing on 3 September and those in the area of the town were in any case suppressed by the escorting fighters and fighter-bombers. Furthermore, photographic reconnaissance was carried out on 19 September south of the Lower Rhine and the results showed no presence of flak defences in areas where they had been reported during the first week of the month.

In his book *It Never Snows in September*, which tells the story of 'Market Garden' from the German viewpoint, Robert Kershaw refutes the argument that the operation could have been successful if 1st Airborne Division had been dropped and landed near its objectives. He believes that it would have made little difference because of the deployment of 2nd SS Panzer Corps' two divisions throughout the entire area. But the bulk of Bittrich's forces were north of the Lower Rhine. Had accurate intelligence on the flak defences and terrain been available, 1st Airborne Division could have been landed south of the river close to the bridge, where they could have established a bridgehead and cut the Arnhem–Nijmegen road, blocking any movement south by the enemy and cutting off enemy forces further south at Nijmegen. The time factor of the link-up might not perhaps have been so crucial and the arrival of XXX Corps would have provided sufficient forces to carry out an assault crossing and continue the advance to the Zuider Zee as planned. Even if the bridge had not been captured, the road could still have been blocked to the enemy forces north of the river and XXX Corps could have crossed west of Arnhem if necessary. The commitment of 1st Airborne Division to objectives north of Arnhem now appears unwise in that it over-extended 'Market Garden' as a whole.

Another major flaw in the overall plan was the flying in of 1st Airborne Division in three lifts over three days, which meant that the crucial element of surprise was lost when a large part of the division had yet to arrive. Urquhart was very unhappy about this and made representations to Browning but to no avail. This was entirely due to the decision taken by Major General Paul Williams, commander of US 9th US Troop Carrier Command, and endorsed by Lieutenant General Lewis Brereton, not to fly two sorties on the first day. Browning seems to have voiced no objection and although Montgomery did so on receiving a copy of 1st Airbone Corps' operational plan, it was by then too late to change the air plan.

So Urquhart was forced to leave the most powerful of his three brigades in terms of men and equipment, 1st Airlanding Brigade, tied to the dropping and landing zones until the arrival of 4th Parachute Brigade on the second day, which reduced the forces available to take his objectives on the first day. He had opted to take only six of his nine battalions, three parachute and three airlanding (the latter minus two companies), together with a fair proportion of his supporting arms. His two American counterparts had each chosen to land nine battalions, plus limited support elements, on the first day so as to be able to cope with the number of objectives, and bring in their glider-borne infantry and supporting arms on the second and third lifts. The two American airborne divisions, however, were larger than their British equivalent, comprising nine parachute and three glider-borne infantry battalions, as opposed to the six parachute and three airlanding units of 1st Airborne Division.

Problems caused by delivery in three lifts were increased for all three divisions by bad weather: 1st Airborne Division's 1st Polish Independent Parachute Brigade was not dropped until the fifth day of the operation, and 82nd US Airborne Division had to wait until the seventh day before it received its sorely needed 325th Glider Infantry Regiment and remaining elements of its supporting arms. The 101st US Airborne Division was similarly affected, the final elements of 327th Glider Infantry Regiment and 907th Glider Field Artillery Battalion not arriving until the seventh day.

Criticism of the air plan was later voiced by a senior RAF officer who was directly concerned with the planning of airborne operations. An entry in his diary was reproduced by Geoffrey Powell in his book *The Devil's Birthday*:

'The air plan was bad. All experience and common sense pointed to landing all three airborne divisions in the minimum period of time so that they could form up and collect themselves before the Germans reacted. All three divisions could have been landed in the space of twelve hours or so but FAAA [First Allied Airborne Army] insisted on a plan which resulted in the second lift (with half the heavy equipment) arriving more than twenty-four hours after the Germans had been alerted.'

Despite the shortcomings of the air plan, the actual execution of delivering the major part of the three airborne formations on the first two days of 'Market Garden' went almost without a hitch and must be considered a major feat in itself if account is taken of the enormous number of transports, gliders and escorting aircraft involved.

Urquhart would have been able to land more, if not all, of his infantry and anti-tank elements on the first day if Browning, in his determination to lead his airborne troops into battle, had not insisted on flying in 1st Airborne Corps Main. The forward element of the corps headquarters was transported in thirty-eight Horsa gliders that could have brought in an airlanding battalion or an anti-tank unit: Urquhart had been forced to leave behind two companies of the 2nd Battalion The South Staffordshire Regiment which arrived with the second lift. The forward deployment of this element of Browning's headquarters, 1st Airborne Corps Rear having remained at its base in England, at an early stage in 'Market Garden' was unnecessary. 101st US Airborne Division was under command of XXX Corps once on the ground and there was little or no operational role for

Browning and his headquarters on the ground vis-à-vis the other two airborne formations. It would have been of more use if they had remained in England to act as rear link for 1st Airborne Division, liaise with HQ First Allied Airborne Army, Nos. 38, 46 and 83 Groups RAF and 9th US Troop Carrier Command, ensure that the second and third lifts were dispatched on schedule, ensure that the three airborne divisions received resupply and air support as required, and commit any further forces, such as 52nd (Lowland) Division, when necessary.

Moreover, Browning's headquarters was not properly trained and equipped to command formations in the field. It had been hastily formed from HQ Airborne Troops which was Browning's base in his previous appointment, a non-operational organization concerned almost solely with administration and training. It possessed fewer staff and none of the support and services that normally form part of a corps headquarters. Furthermore, its staff had never trained together in the field or carried out exercises with the headquarters of the divisions that would be under 1st Airborne Corps' command.

One vital element which had been missing from the fledgling headquarters was a signals unit, without which Browning would have no communications with the airborne divisions or with Second British Army. It was not until early September that attempts were made to form one and, in the very short time available, it was inevitably an ad hoc arrangement: American signallers unfamiliar with British equipment and procedures had to be employed in the absence of sufficient Royal Signals personnel, and these received only brief training in the form of one exercise before 'Market Garden'.

Shortage of time was a major limitation placed on those responsible for planning 'Market' (the airborne part of 'Market Garden'), despite the fact that much of the preparation for Operation 'Comet' could be incorporated, and this inevitably was to result in serious shortcomings which affected its outcome. Whereas the operations carried out by 6th Airborne Division in Normandy were the result of months of detailed planning and rehearsals, 'Market' had to be prepared and mounted in just seven days. This inevitably resulted in a lack of flexibility. Once decisions had been made they had to be adhered to, otherwise the result would have been chaos. Unfortunately, some were made in haste and subsequently proved to be unsound. Lieutenant General Lewis Brereton, perhaps understandably, adhered rigidly to his edict, forbidding any changes, and this in itself caused problems when it became apparent that some alterations were necessary.

As a personality Brereton was difficult and could be intransigent. His relationship with Browning, his deputy, was not good and the latter disliked him intensely. Like Browning, he had served in the First World

War where he had gained experience in battle and on the staff before later becoming an airman. Before assuming command of 1st Allied Airborne Army, he had commanded 9th US Air Force before and during the invasion of Normandy, prior to which he had been successively commander of the US Far East and US Middle East Air Forces. He was a very experienced airman but he had no knowledge or experience of airborne operations. A better candidate for his post would have been Lieutenant General Matthew Ridgway, the highly experienced and much respected commander of XVIII US Airborne Corps, who had commanded 82nd US Airborne Division in Normandy.

Once the leading elements of 1st Airborne Division had landed, one of the first major problems they encountered was that of failure of communications. The absence of the radio link with 1st Airborne Reconnaissance Squadron, which was under command of 1st Parachute Brigade and thus not on the divisional radio net, meant that Urquhart was out of contact with the one element that was supposed to provide him with up-to-date information forward of the division. Had Urquhart retained the squadron in its normal role, and so maintained radio contact with it, it could well have proved invaluable in relaying information and orders where signals had failed.

In fact, the use of the squadron in the coup de main role was wholly incorrect because it was unsuitably equipped for the task. Its jeeps, armed with Vickers 'K' machine-guns, were fast and manoeuvrable, but they were unarmoured and very vulnerable to ambush of the type which the leading troop met by the railway line at Wolfheze. Major Freddie Gough had been unhappy about the task from the beginning, as John Fairlie says in his book *Remember Arnhem*:

'Gough's reasoning was that the function of any Reconnaissance unit, irrespective of how it was transported to battle, was the provision of information on whatever enemy dispositions and resources might lie in the way of the advancing division. He did not dispute the wisdom of a coup de main so much as the fact that it had been allocated to his force whose greatest military capability lay in the execution of a true reconnaissance role. They were respectable and logical arguments which he advanced, but they failed to convince Brigadier Lathbury. With the benefit of hindsight, it is now possible to say that if Gough had had his way, such forward-placed elements of his own unit as he suggested might precede each battalion of 1st Parachute Brigade could have provided information in such a way as to compensate in part for the disastrous communication breakdown which subsequently affected the entire division.'

Despite Brigadier Lathbury's insistence that the squadron perform the coup de main task, Gough attempted to obtain some armoured support. He investigated the possibility of obtaining a troop of 6th Airborne Armoured Reconnaissance Regiment which was equipped with the Tetrarch light tank that could be carried in the Hamilcar glider. He discovered that, of the thirty allotted to 1st Airborne Division, two Hamilcars were available. Despite his best efforts in this direction, nothing came of this idea.

Much of the blame for 1st Airborne Division's demise has been laid at the door of signals failures as well as the unsuitability of the radio equipment issued to the division and its failure to work satisfactorily under the conditions in which it was employed. Some accounts have been incorrect, over-emphasizing the extent of the failures. In his book *Echoes From Arnhem*, however, Lewis Golden, who was Adjutant of 1st Airborne Divisional Signals, provides a more technically accurate assessment of the problem, explaining the limitations of the equipment and why much of it was unable to perform satisfactorily during the operation.

There were four sets in service with the British airborne divisions at the time: the No. 68P manpack with a range of three miles; the No. 22, for static or vehicle-mounted use, for operation over ranges up to five miles; the No. 19 HP (High Power), again for either static or mobile operation, with a range of up to twenty-five miles; and the No. 76, a high frequency radio for carrier wave (Morse) only operation over ranges of up to 300 miles – mounted in a jeep, it could only be operated when the vehicle was stationary. Of these, the No. 19 set was very bulky and heavy and so only two were taken on the operation to provide communications with XXX Corps' artillery. No. 22 sets had been used by 1st Airborne Division in North Africa and in Sicily and Italy with 68P and 76 sets. All three types had been used by 6th Airborne Division in Normandy. Although the Nos. 22 and 68P sets were low-powered, they would provide satisfactory communications provided these were well within their established maximum ranges.

As Golden makes clear, the premise that the radios were 'inadequate for the purpose' is, generally speaking, correct. However, what is incorrect is any inference that the equipment had ever been considered adequate for use in 'Market Garden'. Since 1943, after returning from operations in Italy, 1st Airborne Divisional Signals, commanded by Lieutenant Colonel Tom Stephenson, had complained vociferously about the limitations of the radios issued to airborne forces. Despite assurances that suitable sets would be produced, none had been forthcoming by the time of 'Market Garden'. So it was common knowledge within 1st Airborne Divisional Signals, when considering the requirements for 'Market Garden' beforehand, that the sets possessed inadequate power to provide any degree of reliability under the conditions in which they would be operated. The unit's second in command, Major Tony Deane-Drummond, was particularly concerned about the whole question of signals for the operation, as he made clear in his book *Return Ticket*:

> 'Another result of spreading the Division over such a big area was the inadequacy of the wireless sets with which we were equipped. They were designed to communicate up to three miles and all our exercises and operations had been planned and had worked on this basis. At Arnhem the sets would have to work eight miles to the bridge and fifteen miles to Corps HQ at Nijmegen. My advice was that communications would be most unreliable, especially in view of the built-up nature of the ground north of the river, but again this risk was accepted.'

The degree of awareness of the problem is illustrated by the fact that, just prior to 'Market Garden', a signals exercise was held in Grimsby by the signals section of HQ 1st Parachute Brigade. The radios performed so badly under urban conditions that Captain Bill Marquand, the officer commanding the section, decided to take an increased number of field telephones and drums of cable as a precautionary measure.

The staff at divisional headquarters were therefore well aware of the problems concerning signals before the operation. But there was little that they could do to rectify the situation as strict limitations on size and weight of radios precluded the use of more powerful sets which were bulkier and heavier. Even if these had been introduced for 'Market Garden', none of the operators at divisional, brigade and battalion levels would have been familiar with them and the problem would have been far greater.

An illustration of this very point was the introduction at the last minute of the two American Air Support Signals Units. Lack of familiarity with the SCR 193 radios issued to them only a few hours before their departure for Holland meant that the signallers were incapable of operating them.

Throughout the duration of the fighting in Arnhem and Oosterbeek, signallers were working under extremely difficult conditions which reduced the effectiveness of their sets even further. Antennas were continually destroyed by shell and mortar fire and could only be replaced at night when there was less threat from snipers, battery charging engines broke down, and there was continual heavy interference from a powerful British radio transmitter which was operating on almost the same frequency as the command net of HQ 1st Airborne Division. This resulted in the net having to be switched to a new frequency, but the only way in which HQ 1st Parachute Brigade could be informed of this was by dispatch-rider because all radio contact with the brigade had been lost. This proved unsuccessful, so Major Tony Deane-Drummond set off on the same task on the early morning of 18 September, eventually reaching 1st Parachute

Battalion from where he passed the new frequency to brigade headquarters by radio.

However, Captain Bill Marquand, the brigade signals officer, later maintained that this information never reached him or his section and that it was only through searching the frequency band that contact was established with divisional headquarters during the morning of 20 September. This seems to indicate, therefore, that failure to establish communications was due to ignorance of the frequency change rather than equipment failure. It can only be assumed that in the confusion of the fighting around the northern end of the bridge, where brigade headquarters was located with 2nd Parachute Battalion, the message never got through to the signallers.

Radio communications were available, however, on 1st Airborne Division's artillery net which operated throughout the operation with periodic disruption. The commander of 3rd Airlanding Light Battery RA, Major Denis Munford, was located with HQ 1st Parachute Brigade alongside 2nd Parachute Battalion at the bridge. He was accompanied by two signallers equipped with a No. 22 set and a No. 68P set which were used to direct the battery's guns and to provide communications between brigade and divisional headquarters.

Elsewhere on the artillery net, communications were established on 21 September between a No. 22 set, located with a forward observation officer of 1st Airlanding Light Regiment RA, and 64th Medium Regiment RA at Nijmegen. Later that day, contact was established with the same regiment by HQ Royal Artillery 1st Airborne Division with its No. 19HP set. This link was subsequently used to pass requests for close air support to 1st Airborne Corps.

Close air support was not forthcoming from the RAF until the afternoon of 24 September. Requests transmitted by 1st Airborne Division from the 19th until the morning of 23 September were either turned down or went unanswered. Before communications were established between HQRA 1st Airborne Division and 64th Medium Regiment RA, requests for air support had been transmitted to any other formations with which contact could be established, subsequently being relayed to 1st Airborne Corps Rear in England which passed them on to 2nd Tactical Air Force. Apart from brief contact on the night of 17 September at 2145 hours, there were no communications between 1st Airborne Division and 1st Airborne Corps Main despite constant efforts to establish them. Contact with 1st Airborne Corps Rear was established at 0015 hours on 18 September but the signal was very weak to the point of being almost unworkable.

Much emphasis has previously been placed on the weather being a major factor in preventing the RAF from flying close support for 1st Airborne Division, but this was only partly the case. Before the start of the operation, it had been laid down by HQ First Allied Airborne Army that all close air support operations by 2nd Tactical Air Force would be suspended while transport aircraft were dropping troops or carrying out resupply sorties; for some reason there was no direct communications link between these two formations, nor were there liaison officers from either formation in the other's headquarters. When combined with the arrival of bad weather over airfields in England or target areas in Holland, the effect of the First Allied Airborne Army directive was such that there were many occasions when Typhoon fighter-bombers of 83 Group RAF could not take off to support the three airborne divisions.

When close air support did become available, it was hampered by the lack of forward controllers to guide aircraft on to the targets on the ground, but it brought welcome relief to the hard-pressed defenders of 1st Airborne Division's perimeter. Where fighting took place in close or wooded country, pilots experienced difficulties in pinpointing targets unless given a six-figure grid reference and so were unwilling to engage them. When supporting aircraft were overhead, the enemy artillery and mortars often held their fire for fear of giving away their positions and inviting attack. Rocket attacks by Typhoons proved particularly effective, the pilots taking their aircraft down to very low levels to ensure accuracy despite severe light anti-aircraft fire.

In spite of all the factors that militated against success, those who took part in 'Market Garden' so very nearly achieved it. Failure, however, later brought recriminations and the accusation that there had been a lack of urgency within XXX Corps and in particular in 43rd (Wessex) Infantry Division. In his memoirs, however, Lieutenant General Brian Horrocks refutes this allegation, making it quite clear that '... all the troops were imbued with a sense of desperate urgency'.

This was certainly the case in the Guards Armoured Division, the spearhead of XXX Corps. Within its leading element, 5th Guards Armoured Brigade, the Irish and Grenadier Groups were only too well aware of the importance of reaching Arnhem in two days. There was criticism of Brigadier Norman Gwatkins' decision to halt overnight at Valkenswaard on the first night, but this had been necessary because the Irish Group had been fighting hard all day and was in dire need of servicing its tanks as well as replenishing them and its infantry with ammunition and fuel of which there had been heavy consumption during the breakout from the bridgehead.

The terrain between the bridgehead over the Meuse–Escaut Canal and Arnhem was manifestly unsuitable for the use of armour, being flat, marshy and intersected by three major water obstacles. Furthermore, the advance was restricted to a single road along which there were stretches from which deployment by armour was not possible. The last stage, between Nijmegen and Arnhem, was the most difficult with the road running along the top of an embankment. This was terrain more suited to infantry, of which there was a lack because of the casualties suffered by the division before and during the operation. It was over sixty-four miles of such road and terrain that an armoured division was expected to advance to a schedule so tight that any delay would obviously cause major problems for the entire operation.

There was bewilderment and anger among the leading elements of 82nd US Airborne Division when the Guards Armoured Division halted at Nijmegen for the night of 20 September. This is understandable if one bears in mind that the 3rd Battalion 504th Parachute Infantry Regiment had just carried out an assault river crossing at great cost, in terms of casualties, to capture the road bridge. Indeed, it is likely that if 5th Guards Armoured Brigade had pressed on through the night, it would have succeeded in reaching Arnhem and 1st Airborne Division. According to Robert Kershaw in his book *It Never Snows in September*, the Nijmegen–Arnhem road was virtually undefended until between 1900 and 2359 hours when the enemy positioned a blocking force on the road just to the north of Nijmegen. But this fact was not known at the time and it was assumed from the previous pattern of enemy defence encountered that further stiff opposition would be met beyond the town. Also it must be remembered that the Guards Armoured Division was at that stage effectively operating with only one of its two brigades on the main route of advance: the Coldstream Group of 32nd Guards Brigade was still under command of 82nd US Airborne Division to protect the latter's right flank, and the Welsh Group was tied to defending the bridge at Grave.

Furthermore, by the time the Nijmegen bridges had been captured and secured in the late afternoon of 20 September, 5th Guards Armoured Brigade had suffered very heavy casualties in terms of tanks and infantry and was short of ammunition and fuel. The Irish Group had already sustained heavy casualties, as had the Grenadiers who had suffered to the extent that they had to be withdrawn into reserve. The Welsh Group, which had to be transferred from 32nd Guards Brigade, could only come forward to take over from the latter once it had been relieved from guarding the bridge at Grave. When it did arrive, it was immediately involved in heavy fighting.

The major problem facing 5th Guards Armoured Brigade, and the Guards Armoured Division as a whole, was the lack of infantry. When the Irish Group began the final stage of the advance on 21 September, the 3rd Battalion Irish Guards comprised merely five platoons. 69th Infantry Brigade was sent forward by 50th (Northumbrian) Infantry Division, providing welcome support for 5th Guards Armoured Brigade in subsequent fierce fighting around Bemmel. 129th, 130th and 214th Infantry Brigades, from 43rd Infantry Division, also moved up but their progress was impeded by the chaotic state of the single line of communication and the cutting of it by the enemy on more than one occasion. Having passed through Nijmegen, 129th and 214th Infantry Brigades soon encountered strong opposition on the main advance route and were eventually embroiled in very fierce fighting in the area of Elst, while 130th Infantry Brigade was halted by tough opposition at Oosterhout as it advanced through the north-western outskirts of Nijmegen.

Whatever the sense of urgency impressed by Horrocks on his senior commanders, the fact remains that a combination of adverse terrain, dogged defence by the enemy, heavy casualties and shortages of ammunition and fuel prevented XXX Corps from breaking through to 1st Airborne Division in time to relieve it. So the placing of blame on either the Guards Armoured Division or 43rd (Wessex) Infantry Division would appear to be unfair, given the heavy handicaps under which both were operating during the entire operation. Had VIII and XII Corps been able to advance more rapidly and so protect XXX Corps' flanks as planned, the story might have been very different, but they too were labouring under the same difficulties as XXX Corps, being short of transport and supplies, moving over difficult ground, encountering a resolute enemy and suffering heavy casualties. These four crucial factors became a sad litany for all three corps during 'Market Garden'.

Major General Roy Urquhart later voiced criticism of Horrocks and his divisional commanders when he summed-up the failure of XXX Corps to reach Arnhem:

'Even when one has taken into account every possible set-back, large and small, which occurred during our nine days north of the Neder Rhine, the fact remains that we were alone for much longer than any airborne division is designed to stay. I think it is possible that for once Horrocks' enthusiasm was not transmitted adequately to those who served under him, and it may be that some of his more junior officers and NCOs did not fully comprehend the problem and the importance of great speed. By and large, the impression is that they were "victory happy". They had advanced northwards very fast and had been well received by the liberated peoples, and they were now out of touch with the atmosphere of bullets and the battle. As is always the case, it took them a little time to attune themselves once more to the stern reality of tough fighting against the Germans. At first, the opposition seems to have caused them a certain amount of shock and surprise.'

Urquhart's implication that XXX Corps had had an easy time in Belgium prior to 'Market Garden' is unfair and incorrect. During the advance by the Guards Armoured Division from the Albert Canal up to the Meuse–Escaut Canal, the fighting had been fierce: for two days the Irish Group suffered heavy casualties from heavy and accurate shellfire during a tough fight in the Beeringen bridgehead against enemy armour and paratroops. At the same time, 50th (Northumbrian) Infantry Division was also meeting very stiff opposition short of the Albert Canal where it was attempting to establish a bridgehead at Gheel.

When the Guards Armoured Division did resume its advance from Beeringen on 8 September, the Coldstream Group encountered very fierce resistance and had to fight its way through factories, railway yards, and the villages of Beverloo and Heppen which were very strongly defended by infantry supported by self-propelled guns. During the night of 8 September, the enemy brought down very heavy shellfire on the area, which caused casualties. The Irish Group fought throughout the night in woods around the village of Helchteren, suffering many losses. Meanwhile, the enemy launched a counter-attack from the north-west on the Beeringen bridge, by then defended by the Princess Irene of The Netherlands Brigade, and succeeded in destroying some thirty vehicles of 8th Armoured Brigade, which was trying to push through to assist 50th (Northumbrian) Infantry Division, before they were repulsed.

Enemy reinforcements had arrived during the night, so when it resumed the advance on the morning of 10 September, the Guards Armoured Division found its way blocked by a strong force of paratroops, tanks and self-propelled guns at Bourg-Leopold and Hechtel. Fortunately, an alternative route was found by a troop of the 2nd Household Cavalry Regiment and the Grenadier and Irish Groups of 5th Guards Armoured Brigade were able to bypass Hechtel, fighting their way round to the west and rejoining the main road a mile short of the De Groot bridge spanning the Meuse–Escaut Canal. The bridge, which was strongly defended, was captured just before nightfall by the Irish Group after a very hard day's fighting and was subsequently christened 'Joe's Bridge' in honour of the Irish Group's commander, Lieutenant Colonel Joe Vandeleur. 32nd Guards Brigade, meanwhile, engaged the enemy in Hechtel and Bourg-Leopold which were attacked and taken after a battle lasting six hours on the morning of 11 September with the support of artillery from 11th Armoured Division.

Criticism has also been voiced in the past at the apparent lack of overall supervision by Lieutenant General Sir Miles Dempsey of what was after all a Second British Army operation. While delegation is one of the hallmarks of a good commander, in 'Market Garden' it does appear that the three corps commanders, Horrocks, O'Connor and Ritchie, were left very much to their own devices during the operation. Had Dempsey exercised closer supervision, it is possible that VIII and XII Corps would have made better progress and caught up sooner with XXX Corps than was the case. Indeed, it would appear that both O'Connor and Ritchie were largely excluded from any direct involvement with 'Market Garden'. In 1977, both were interviewed by John Fairlie, author of *Remember Arnhem*, who subsequently wrote:

> 'It was true that the original plan called for a degree of flank support to be supplied by 8 and 12 Corps but this planned strategy in no way resembled anything in the nature of a three-pronged advance. Generals O'Connor and Ritchie, the respective commanders of 8 and 12 Corps, have since confirmed that neither of their formations were involved, in a primary sense, in Market Garden. On the contrary, their function was one of broadening the base for 30 Corps whilst, at the same time, leaving Horrocks to provide the single main thrust towards the main objective.'

This apparent discrepancy in the perception of the roles of VIII and XII Corps during 'Market Garden' is puzzling. Montgomery was quite clear as to his when he stated later:

> '30 Corps (Horrocks) was to operate along the axis of the "carpet", link up with the 1st British Airborne Division in the Arnhem area, and establish a bridgehead over the Neder Rijn north of that place ... As 30 Corps moved northwards along the axis of the airborne "carpet", two other corps were to widen the axis of the advance 8 Corps (O'Connor) on the east and 12 Corps (Ritchie) on the west.'

This statement implies direct involvement by both corps in 'Market Garden' which was his much vaunted strong northward thrust. Certainly, the summary of Second British Army's plan, contained in the 21st Army Group post-operation report, is quite clear that the tasks of VIII and XII Corps were to advance in echelon on the right and left flanks of XXX Corps, progressively relieving the latter of responsibility for flank protection. So it seems strange that neither O'Connor nor Ritchie was apparently fully clear about their corps' tasks in relation to 'Market Garden'. If that were indeed the case, the responsibility for this shortcoming rests entirely with Dempsey, who was their immediate superior.

It has also been suggested that Montgomery did not keep as tight a grip on 'Market Garden' as he should have done, bearing in mind his strenuous efforts to obtain Eisenhower's approval for it. This was unusual because he was well known for taking too close an interest on occasions when, as an army or army group commander, he should have left matters to his divisional or corps commanders; he would frequently pay visits to their headquarters beside which he would locate his own. It is all the more surprising, therefore, that he did not visit Horrocks prior to 'Market Garden' or Dempsey until 23 September.

When later summing-up his reasons for 'why we did not gain complete success at Arnhem', Montgomery admitted that he should have stepped in during the planning of 'Market Garden':

First. The operation was not regarded at Supreme Headquarters as the spearhead of a major Allied movement on the northern flank designed to isolate, and finally to occupy, the Ruhr – the one objective in the west which the Germans could not afford to lose. There is no doubt in my mind that Eisenhower always wanted to give priority to the northern thrust and to scale down the southern one. He ordered this to be done, and he thought it was being done. It was not being done. We now know from Bradley's book [*A Soldier's Story*], page 412, that in the middle of September, there was parity of logistic resources between the First and Third American Armies in 12 Army Group.

'Eisenhower is a thoroughly genuine person; he is the very incarnation of sincerity and he trusts others to do as he asks. But in this instance his intentions were not carried out. The following quotation from page 531 of *The Struggle for Europe* by Chester Wilmot is of interest:

"If he [Eisenhower] had kept Patton halted on the Meuse, and had given full logistic support to Hodges and Dempsey after the capture of Brussels, the operations in Holland could have been an overwhelming triumph, for First US Army could have mounted a formidable diversion, if not a successful offensive, at Aachen, and Second British Army could have attacked sooner, on a wider front and in much greater strength."

Second. The airborne forces at Arnhem were dropped too far away from the vital objective – the bridge. It was some hours before they reached it. I take the blame for this mistake. I should have ordered Second Army and 1 Airborne Corps to arrange that at least one complete parachute brigade was dropped quite close to the bridge, so that it could have been captured in a matter of minutes and its defence soundly organized with time to spare. I did not do so.

Third. The weather. This turned against us after the first day and we could not carry out much of the later airborne programme. But weather is always an uncertain factor, in war and in peace. This uncertainty we all accepted. It could only have been offset, and the operation made a certainty, by allotting additional resources to the project, so that it became an Allied and not merely a British project.

Fourth. The 2nd SS Panzer Corps was refitting in the Arnhem area, having limped up there after its mauling in Normandy. We knew it was there. But we were wrong in supposing that it could not fight effectively; its battle state was far beyond our expectation. It was quickly brought into action against 1st Airborne Division.

As after Normandy, so after Arnhem, I was bitterly disappointed. It was my second attempt to try to capture the Ruhr quickly. Bill Williams used to tell me that the Germans could not carry on the war for more than three months after they lost the Ruhr. But we still hadn't got it.

And here I must admit a bad mistake on my part – I under-estimated the difficulties of opening up the approaches to Antwerp so that we could get the free use of that port. I reckoned that the Canadian army could do it while we were going for the Ruhr. I was wrong.'

In the final analysis, suffice it to say that Operation 'Market Garden' was launched too late for reasons already given and failed largely through errors, oversights and shortcomings at a heavy cost: the destruction of Arnhem and Oosterbeek, the virtual annihilation of 1st Airborne Division and a total of more than 16,000 casualties in the four corps that took part in the operation. It did achieve certain results in that it drove a wedge between 1st Parachute Army and von Zangen's Fifteenth Army, preventing the Germans from subsequently assembling forces for a counter-attack on Antwerp, and eventually provided a base for subsequent operations on the Rhine. It did not, however, open the back door into Germany and did not end the war before the end of 1944.

APPENDIXES

A. 1ST AIRBORNE DIVISION
ORDER OF BATTLE, SEPTEMBER 1944

HEADQUARTERS 1 AIRBORNE DIVISION

GOC	Maj Gen R. E. Urquhart, DSO
ADC	Capt G. C. Roberts
GSO 1 (Ops)	Lt Col C. B. Mackenzie
GSO 2 (Ops)	Maj O. F. Newton-Dunn
GSO 1 (Air)	Lt Col E. H. Steele-Baume
GSO 2 (Air)	Maj D. J. Madden
GSO 2 (Int)	Maj H. P. Maguire
AA & QMG	Lt Col P. H. H. H. Preston
DAAG	Maj L. K. Hardman
DAQMG	Maj E. R. Hodges

1 PARA BRIGADE

Comd	Brig G. W. Lathbury DSO MBE
BM	Maj J. A. Hibbert
DAA & QMG	Maj C. D. Byng-Maddick
1 Para Bn	Lt Col D. Dobie DSO
2 Para Bn	Lt Col J. D. Frost, DSO, MC
3 Para Bn	Lt Col J. A. C. Fitch

4 PARA BRIGADE

Comd	Brig J. W. Hackett, DSO, MBE, MC
BM	Maj C. W. B. Dawson
156 Para Bn	Lt Col Sir W. R. de B. des Voeux
10 Para Bn	Lt Col K. B. I. Smyth, OBE
11 Para Bn	Lt Col G. H. Lea

1 A/L BRIGADE

Comd	Brig P. H. W. Hicks, DSO, MC
Dep Comd	Col H. N. Barlow
BM	Maj C. A. H. B. Blake
1 Border	Lt Col T. Hadden
7 KOSB	Lt Col R. Payton-Reid
2 South Staffs	Lt Col W. D. H. McCardie

DIVISIONAL TROOPS
RA

CRA	Lt Col R. G. Loder-Symonds, DSO
BMRA	Maj P. T. Tower, MBE
1st A/L Lt Regt RA	Lt Col W. F.K. Thompson
1 A/L Lt Bty RA	Maj A. F. Norman-Walker
2 A/L Lt Bty RA	Maj J. E .F. Linton
3 A/L Lt Bty RA	Maj D. S. Munford
No. 1 FOU RA	Maj R. Wight-Boycott
1 A/L A/Tk Bty RA	Maj W. F. Arnold
2 A/L A/Tk Bty RA	Maj A. F. Haynes

RE
CRE	Lt Col E. C. W. Myers, CBE, DSO
Adjt RE	Capt M. D. Green
1 Para Sqn RE	Maj D. C. Murray, MC
4 Para Sqn RE	Maj A.E. J. M. Perkins
9 Fd Coy RE	Maj J. C. Winchester
261 Fd Pk Coy RE	Maj J. N. Chivers

Div Sigs
OC Div Sigs	Lt Col T. C. V. Stephenson
2 i/c	Maj A. J. Deane-Drummond, MC
Adjt	Capt L. Golden

Recce
1st Abn Recce Sqn	Maj C. F. H. Gough, MC
Pathfinders	
21 Indep Para Coy	Maj B. A. Wilson

RASC
CRASC	Lt Col M. St J. Packe
2 i/c	Maj D. G. Clark
93 Comp Coy	Maj F. Tompkins
250 Lt Comp Coy	Maj J. L. Gifford
253 Comp Coy	Maj R. K. Gordon

RAMC
ADMS	Col G. M. Warrack
DADMS	Maj J. E. Miller, MC
16 Para Fd Amb	Lt Col E. Townsend, MC
133 Para Fd Amb	Lt Col W. C. Alford
181 A/L Fd Amb	Lt Col A. T. Marrable

RAOC
ADOS	Lt Col G. A. Mobbs
Ord Fd Pk	Maj C. C. Chidgey

REME
CREME	Lt Col E. J. Kinvig
Adjt REME	Capt F. W. Ewens
Div Wksps	Maj W. S. Carrick

Provost
APM	Maj O. P. Haig
Div Pro Coy	Capt W. R. Gray

Security
89 Fd Sy Sect	Capt J. E. Killick

Glider Pilot Regt
No. 1 Wing GPR	Lt Col I. A. Murray, DSO
No. 2 Wing GPR	Lt Col J. W. Place

B. GUARDS ARMOURED DIVISION
ORDER OF BATTLE, SEPTEMBER 1944

DIVISION HEADQUARTERS
GOC	Maj Gen A. H. S. Adair, DSO, MC
GSO 1	Lt Col J. D. Hornung, MC, IG
AA & QMG	Lt Col W. M. Sale, RHG

DIVISION RECCONNAISSANCE REGIMENT
2nd Household Cavalry Regt	Lt Col H. Abel Smith, RHG

5 GUARDS ARMURED BRIGADE

Comd	Brig N. W. Gwatkin, MVO
BM	Maj The Hon M. F. Fitzalan Howard, MC, GG
DAA & QMG	Maj T. F. Winnington, GG
1st (Motor) Bn Gren Gds	Lt Col E. H. Goulburn
2nd (Armd) Bn Gren Gds	Lt Col J. N. R. Moore
2nd (Armd) Bn Irish Gds	Lt Col G. A. M. Vandeleur
3rd (Motor) Bn Irish Gds	Lt Col J. O. E. Vandeleur

32 GUARDS BRIGADE

Comd	Brig G. F. Johnston
BM	Maj The Hon M. Fitzalan Howard, MC, SG
DAA & AQMG	Maj T. C. Dundas, SG
1st (Armd) Bn Coldm Gds	Lt Col R.F.S. Gooch, MC
5th (Motor) Bn Coldm Gds	Lt Col E. R. Hill
1st (Motor) Bn Welsh Gds	Lt Col J. F. Gresham
2nd (Armd) Bn Welsh Gds	Lt Col J. C. Windsor-Lewis, DSO, MC No. 1
Indep MG Coy RNF	Maj R. M. Pratt

DIVISIONAL TROOPS
RA

CRA	Brig H. C. Phipps
BMRA	Maj G. E. Maitland
55 Fd Regt RA	Lt Col B. Wilson
153 Fd Regt RA	Lt Col J. S. Atkins, TD
21 A/Tk Regt RA	Lt Col R. C. Hulbert
94 LAA Regt RA	Lt Col E. I. E. Strong

RE

CRE	Lt Col C. P. Jones, MC
Adjt	Capt M. I. Fletcher
14 Fd Sqn RE	
615 Fd Sqn RE	
11 Bridging Tp RE	
148 Fd Pk Sqn RE	

DIV SIGS

C Sigs	Lt Col W. D. Tucker, OBE
Adjt	Capt J. C. Clinch

RASC

CRASC	Lt Col A. K. Woods, OBE
Adjt	Capt R. O. Barker
224 Coy RASC	
310 Coy RASC	
535 Coy RASC	

RAMC

ADMS	Col B. J. Daunt
19 Lt Fd Amb	Lt Col B. M. Nicol
128 Fd Amb	Lt Col J. M. Scott
8 FDS	
60 Fd Hy Sect	
RAOC	
ADOS	Lt Col F. B. H. Villiers
Ord Fd Pk	

REME

CREME	Lt Col L. H. Atkinson, OBE
5 Gds Armd Bde Wksps	Maj H. G. Good

32 Gds Bde Wksps	Maj A. W. Page
Provost	
DAPM	Maj H. D. Bailey, WG
Pro Coy	Maj D. A. C. Rasch, GG

Note: The order of battle given in this appendix is that in which the division fought during Operation 'Market Garden'. During the operation, regimental battle groups were transferred between the two brigades.

C. 43RD (WESSEX) INFANTRY DIVISION ORDER OF BATTLE, JUNE 1944 TO MAY 1945

HEADQUARTERS 43RD INFANTRY DIVISION

GOC	Maj Gen G. I. Thomas
GSO 1	Lt Col D. Meynell
	Lt Col J. A. Grant-Peterkin
	Lt Col R. W. Urquhart
AA & QMG	Lt Col J. B. McCance
	Lt Col D. A. B. Clarke

Divisional Recce Regt

43rd Reconnaissance Regt	Lt Col F. Lane Fox
(The Gloucestershire Regt)	Lt Col C. H. Kinnersley

129th Inf Bde

Comd	Brig G. H. L. Mole
BM	Maj R. G. Levett
	Maj B. G. D. Garside
DAA & QMG	Maj O. S. Masefield
4th Bn Somerset Light Infantry	Lt Col W. S. C. Curtis
	Lt Col C. G. Lipscomb
4th Bn The Wiltshire Regt	Lt Col E. L. Luce
	Lt Col J. E. L. Corbyn
5th Bn The Wiltshire Regt	Lt Col N. C. E. Kenrick
	Lt Col J. H. C. Pearson
	Lt Col W. G. Roberts
	Lt Col J. L. Brind

130TH INFANTRY BRIGADE

Comd	Brig B. B. Walton
BM	Maj G. G. Reinhold
	Maj A. N. Buchanan
DAA & AQMG	Maj D.G . Pascall
7th Bn Royal Hampshire Regt	Lt Col D. W. G. Ray
	Lt Col J. R. C. Mallock
	Lt Col D. E. B. Talbot
4th Bn The Dorsetshire Regt	Lt Col G. Tilly
5th Bn The Dorsetshire Regt	Lt Col B. A. Coad

214TH INFANTRY BRIGADE

Comd	Brig H. Essame
BM	Maj J. E. L. Corbyn
	Maj W. J. Chalmers
DAA & AQMG	Maj J.L . Denison
7th Bn Somerset Light Infantry	Lt Col R. G. P. Besley
	Lt Col G. C. P. Lance

	Lt Col E.J . Bruford
	Lt Col J. W. Nichol
	Lt Col H. A. Borradaile
	Maj T. B. Elliott
	Lt Col I. L. Reeves
	Lt Col C. Brooke Smith
1st Bn The Worcestershire Regt	Lt Col A. R. Harrison
	Lt Col R. E. Osborne-Smith
	Lt Col A. W. N. L. Vickers
	Lt Col M. R. J. Hope Thomson
5th Bn Duke of Cornwall's Light Infantry	Lt Col G. Taylor

8TH ARMOURED BRIGADE

Comd	Brig G. E. Prior Palmer
BM	Maj R. Dayer Smith
DAA & QMG	Maj W. Spanton
4th/7th Royal Dragoon Guards	Lt Col R. G. G. Byron
	Lt Col G. K. Barker
13th/18th Royal Hussars	Lt Col R. T. G. Harrap
	Lt Col V. A. B. Dunkerley
	Lt Col The Earl of Feversham
The Nottinghamshire Yeomanry	Lt Col J. Anderson
(Sherwood Rangers)	Lt Col S. Christopherson
12th Bn 60th Rifles	Lt Col R. G. R. Oxley
(King's Royal Rifle Corps)	Lt Col The Hon M. Edwards

DIVISIONAL TROOPS
RA

CRA	Brig G. W. E. Heath
	Brig E. T. A C. Boylan
	Brig K. F. Mackay Lewis
BMRA	Maj G. S. Heathcote
	Maj P.G . E. Davies
	Maj H. G. Loosely
94th Field Regt RA	Lt Col T. I. Bishell
	Lt Col M. P. Concannon
112th Field Regt RA	Lt Col G. E. G. Gadsden
179th Field Regt RA	Lt Col G. L. Pethick
	Lt Col W. D. Blacker
	Lt Col Sir John E. Backhouse
	Lt Col F. B. Wyldbore-Smith
59th Anti-Tank Regt RA	Lt Col H. S. Barker
	Lt Col A. F. Johnson
110th Light Anti-Aircraft Regt RA	Lt Col O. W. R. Dent
	Lt Col F. S. Cowan

R.Sigs

CR.Sigs	Lt Col M. Trethowan

RE

CRE	Lt Col M. C. A. Henniker
204th Field Coy RE	
260th Field Coy RE	
553rd Field Coy RE	
207th Field Park Coy RE	

RASC
CRASC | Lt Col F. J. Leland
| Lt Col E. H. Reeder

54th Coy
504th Coy
505th Coy
506th Coy
RAMC
ADMS
129th Field Ambulance | Lt Col A. D. Bourne
| Lt Col W. Stewart
130th Field Ambulance | Lt Col F. L. Ker
| Lt Col R. A. Smart
213th Field Ambulance | Lt Col E. A. L. Murphy
| Lt Col J. Clay
14th Forward Dressing Stn | Maj J. A. Manifold
| Maj N. L. Crawford

RAOC
CRAOC | Lt Col V.A. Lines
43rd Ord Field Park | Maj R. L. Streather
REME
CREME | Lt Col J. M. Neilson
129th Inf Bde Wksp | Maj N.W. Knowles
130th Inf Bde Wksp | Maj Bailey
214th Inf Bde Wksp | Maj S. Yeol
Provost
APM | Maj M. Ingram
Div Pro Coy | Capt Winwood
Security
57th Field Sy Sect | Capt R.S. Hallmark

Note:
Where identities of officers holding certain appointments at the time of Operation Market Garden are not precisely known, names are listed of those who held the posts during the period between June 1944 and May 1945.

D. **ALLIED / GERMAN COMMISSIONED RANK EQUIVALENTS**

Allied	Wehrmacht	SS
Second Lieutenant	Leutnant	SS-Untersturmführer
Lieutenant	Oberleutnant	SS-Obersturmführer
Captain	Hauptmann	SS-Hauptsturmführer
Major	Major	SS-Sturmbannführer
Lieutenant Colonel	Oberstleutnant	SS-Obersturmbannführer
Colonel	Oberst	SS-Standartenführer
Brigadier / Brigadier General	Oberstgeneral	SS-Brigadeführer
Major General	Generalmajor	SS-Gruppenführer
Lieutenant General	Generalleutnant	SS-Obergruppenführer
General	General	SS-Oberstgruppenführer
Field Marshal	Generalfeldmarschall	Reichsführer-SS

BIBLIOGRAPHY

Adair, Maj Gen Sir Allan. *A Guards General*. Hamish Hamilton, 1986.

Bauer, Cornelis. *The Battle of Arnhem*. Hodder & Stoughton, 1966.

Baynes, John. *Urquhart of Arnhem*. Brassey's, 1993.

Bradley, Omar N. *A Soldier's Story*. Eyre & Spottiswood, 1951.

Bryant, Arthur. *Triumph in the West*. Collins, 1959.

Chatterton, George S. *The Wings of Pegasus*. Macdonald & Co., 1962.

Deane-Drummond, Maj Gen A. *Return Ticket*. Collins, 1967.

Essame, Maj Gen H. *The 43rd Wessex Division At War: 1944-1945.*, William Clowes, 1952.

Fairley, John. 'Remember Arnhem' in *Pegasus Journal*, 1978.

Frost, Maj Gen John. *A Drop Too Many*. Cassell, 1980.

Giskes, Hermann. *London Calling North Pole*. William Kimber, 1953.

Golden, Lewis. *Echoes From Arnhem*. William Kimber, 1984.

Gregory, Barry. *British Airborne Troops*. Purnell Book Services, 1974.

Hackett, Gen Sir John. *I Was a Stranger*. Chatto & Windus, 1977.

Hamilton, Nigel. *Monty: The Field Marshal 1944-1976*. Hamish Hamilton, 1986

Harclerode, Peter. *PARA! Fifty Years of The Parachute Regiment*. Arms & Armour Press, 1992.

Hibbert, Christopher. *The Battle of Arnhem*. Batsford, 1962.

Horrocks, Lt Gen Sir Brian. *A Full Life*. Collins, 1960.

— , Eversley Belfield and Maj Gen H. Essame, *Corps Commander*. Sidgwick & Jackson, 1977.

Irving, David. *The War Between the Generals*, Allen Lane, 1981.

Kershaw, Robert J. *It Never Snows in September*. The Crowood Press, 1990.

Lewin, Ronald. *ULTRA Goes to War*. Hutchinson, 1978.

Montgomery, FM The Viscount. *From Normandy to the Baltic*, Hutchinson, 1946.

— *The Memoirs of Field Marshal Montgomery*. Collins, 1958.

Otway, Lt Col T. B. H. *The Second World War 1939-1945: Airborne Forces*. Imperial War Museum, 1990.

Powell, Geoffrey. *The Devil's Birthday*. Buchan & Enright, 1984.

Rosse, Capt The Earl of, and Col E. R. Hill. *The Story of The Guards Armoured Division*. Geoffrey Bles, 1956.

Ryan, Cornelius. *A Bridge Too Far*. Book Club Associates, 1974.

St. George Saunders, Hilary. *The Red Beret*, Michael Joseph, 1950.

Shulman, Milton. *Defeat in the West*. Martin Secker & Warburg, 1947.

Strong, Maj Gen Sir Kenneth. *Intelligence at the Top*. Cassell, 1968.

Tugwell, Maurice. *Airborne to Battle*. William Kimber, 1971.

— *Arnhem – A Case Study*. Thornton Cox, 1975.

Urquhart, Maj Gen R. E. *Arnhem*. Cassell, 1958.

Vandeleur, Brig J. O. E. *A Soldier's Story*. Gale & Polden, 1967.

Verney, Maj Gen G. L. *The Guards Armoured Division*. Hutchinson, 1955.

Verney, Peter. *The Micks – The Story of The Irish Guards*. Peter Davies, 1970.

Wilmot, Chester. *The Struggle for Europe*. Collins, 1952.

By Air to Battle. HMSO, 1945.

PUBLIC RECORD OFFICE FILES

AIR 16/1026 US 18th Airborne Corps – Operation Market.

AIR 16/1026 US 82nd Airborne Division – Lessons & Operational Report on Operation Market.

AIR 16/1026 US 101st Airborne Division – Participation in Operation Market for Period D–D+10.

AIR 20/2333 16th SS Panzer Grenadier & Reserve Battalion Report.

AIR 24/43 Allied Expeditionary Air Force Report –Operation Market Garden.

AIR 37/418 38 & 46 Groups RAF – Report on The British Airborne Effort In Operation Market Garden.

AIR 37/693 1st Allied Airborne Army – Report on German Air Force Reaction To Airborne Landings In Holland.

AIR 37/981 38 Group RAF – Operation Order Market

AIR 37/1214 1st British Airborne Corps – Allied Airborne Operations in Holland Sept – Oct 1944.

AIR 37/1249 21st Army Group – Operation Market Garden.

WO 171/1341 HQ XXX Corps War Diary – Sept 1944.

WO 171 366 HQ 1st Airborne Corps Main War Diary – Sept 1944.

WO 171 367 HQ 1st Airborne Corps Rear War Diary – Sept 1944.

WO 171 376 HQ Guards Armoured Division War Diary – Jan to Sept 1944.

WO 171 393 HQ 1st Airborne Division War Diary – Sept to Dec 1944.

WO 171 480 HQ 43rd (Wessex) Division War Diary – Aug to Sept 1944.

WO 171 514 HQ 50th (Northumbrian) Infantry Division War Diary – Aug to Sept 1944.

WO 171 589 HQ 1st Airlanding Brigade War Diary – Jan to Dec 1944.

WO 171 592 HQ 1st Parachute Brigade War Diary – Jan to Dec 1944.

WO 171 594 HQ 4th Parachute Brigade War Diary – Jan to Sept 1944.

WO 171 605 HQ 5th Guards Armoured Brigade War Diary – Jan to Dec 1944.

WO 171 638 HQ 32nd Guards Brigade War Diary – Jan to Dec 1944.

WO 171 651 HQ 69th Infantry Brigade War Diary – Jan to Dec 1944.

WO 171 658 HQ 129th Infantry Brigade War Diary – Jan to Dec 1944.

WO 171 660 HQ 130th Infantry Brigade War Diary – Jan to Dec 1944.

WO 171 708, 709 HQ 214th Infantry Brigade War Diary – Jan to Dec 1944.

WO 171 1341 XXX Corps Operation Order for 'Garden.'

WO 205 1126 Operation 'Market Garden' 17-26 Sept 1944.

WO 205 313, 314 21st Army Group – Operation 'Market Garden' Outline Plans.

WO 205 850 HQ Airborne Troops Instruction No. 1 'Comet'.

WO 285 3 Second Army Intelligence Summaries May to 12 Sept 1944.

WO 285 4 Second Army Intelligence Summaries Sept to Dec 1944.

PRO 31/20 13 1st Allied Airborne Army.

DEFE 3 220 Ultra Decrypts 31 Aug – 3 Sept 1944.

DEFE 3 221 Ultra Decrypts 3 – 6 Sept 1944.

DEFE 3 222 Ultra Decrypts 6 – 8 Sept 1944.

DEFE 3 223 Ultra Decrypts 8 – 11 Sept 1944.

DEFE 3 224 Ultra Decrypts 11– 13 Sept 1944.

DEFE 3 225 Ultra Decrypts 13 – 15 Sept 1944.

DEFE 3 226 Ultra Decrypts 15 – 18 Sept 1944.

INDEX